The Rule of Law:

Perspectives on Legal and Judicial Reform in West Virginia

Edited by:
Russell S. Sobel, Ph.D.
WEST VIRGINIA UNIVERSITY

Associate Editor:
Joshua C. Hall
BELOIT COLLEGE

Published by The Public Policy Foundation of West Virginia, through its Center for Economic Growth. This research made possible by support from the West Virginia University College of Business & Economics Kendrick Fund for Free Market Research.

The Rule of Law: Perspectives on Legal and Judicial Reform in
West Virginia / Russell S. Sobel, editor.
    p.   cm.
Includes bibliographic references.
 ISBN: 978-0-578-01450-0
1.   United States – Economic Policy
2.   West Virginia – Economic Policy
3.   Judges – United States – States – Election
I. Sobel, Russell S., 1968-

Cover design by Finney Creative © 2009

Printed and bound in the United States by Lulu.com

TABLE OF CONTENTS

PREFACE

My first edited book, *Unleashing Capitalism: Why Prosperity Stops at the West Virginia Border and How to Fix It*, examined how West Virginia's policies could be reformed to better embrace the principles of free-market capitalism—creating a better business climate and a more prosperous future for West Virginia. The success of that book, which has sold over 5,000 copies and won the 2008 Sir Antony Fisher International Memorial Award, provides the foundation on which we launch this effort.

Like a three-legged stool, West Virginia's tax policy, regulatory climate, and legal system, must all be properly structured to create the right balance for economic growth. While all three of these areas were addressed in *Unleashing Capitalism*, only two of the book's 14 chapters were devoted to judicial and legal reform. With this now becoming a pressing political issue, *The Rule of Law* devotes itself entirely to that subject. The 'rule of law' is a broad concept that describes a society that is governed not by *people*, but instead by established, fair, and predictable *rules* of interaction.

Again, a team of scholars has contributed their expertise to this effort, and each chapter represents the viewpoint of the chapter's authors. We have made every effort possible to make this book readable by the average citizen, although some of the policy reforms are more complex by their very nature.

The first six chapters examine reform of West Virginia's method of selecting judges. As one of the few remaining states employing partisan political elections to select judges, there are calls for switching to either nonpartisan elections or some form of gubernatorial appointment. With the exception of Chapter 4, these chapters were based on a panel discussion held on September 7, 2008 for Judiciary Subcommittee C at the Legislative Interim Meetings in Bridgeport, West Virginia. Each of the panelists prepared written comments based on their presentation at that event for inclusion in this book. While retired U.S. Supreme Court Justice Sandra Day O'Connor could not attend the event, she was willing to write a letter specifically addressing her thoughts on West Virginia's judicial selection reform for the panel. That letter is included in this book along with the contributions from the other panelists. These chapters provide competing viewpoints, with some authors (O'Connor, Bryant, Tabarrok, and Hall/Sobel) being in favor of judicial selection reform and others (Bonneau and McLeod) not, and this is why we title this section a symposium.

The six chapters that make up part two of this book explore a host of other pressing issues in legal reform. Edward Lopez (Chapter 7) provides a discussion of why the rule of law is important for economic growth, and an overview of some of the major conclusions reached in the vast academic literature in the field of 'law and economics' regarding property and contract law. Among other conclusions, his chapter calls for restrictions on punitive damage awards in breach of contract actions, and restrictions on eminent domain to prohibit private to private transfers of property. Kristen Leddy and Matthew Yanni have updated their chapter on assorted legal reforms from *Unleashing Capitalism* for inclusion here (Chapter 9). This chapter calls for the elimination of the doctrine of joint and several liability in all civil tort claims, imposing meaningful venue requirements, imposing limits on (or changing the standard for awarding) punitive damages, and changes to medical monitoring to either eliminate lump sum awards or require the money actually be spent on medical monitoring. I also join them in authoring a chapter that examines the economic impact of the recent decisions of the West Virginia Supreme Court of Appeals (Chapter 8), which is an updated version of a study originally done for The Federalist Society.

The chapter by Matthew Bowles and Mark Sadd (Chapter 10) argues that West Virginia should join the vast majority of other states that guarantee their citizens an appeal of right, and handle these cases through an intermediate court system. Ronda Harvey's chapter (Chapter 11) calls for changes to the standard used to decide deliberate intent in workers' compensation cases. Finally, for those skeptics who question whether judicial and legal reforms can have significant impacts on economic outcomes, the concluding chapter by Evan Jenkins and Juliet Terry (Chapter 12) shows the considerable evidence on the effectiveness of recent reforms to our state's medical malpractice laws. As you will see, the Medical Professional Liability Act has been highly effective and provides clear evidence that good legal reforms can, and do, have significant positive impacts on West Virginia's health and prosperity. They also express concern that future court decisions could strike down major provisions of this highly successful reform.

We hope that readers will come away with a better understanding of the need for, and issues involved with, changes to West Virginia's judicial and legal systems. Once again, our main goal is to provide the research that can inform state policy decisions, and to open a much needed dialogue on growth-oriented policy reform in West Virginia.

We owe thanks to more people than we could possibly list. We are indebted to the dozens of West Virginia citizens, business owners, and policy makers who have leant their comments and encouragement on our efforts. We thank our friends and family for their support. Most importantly, we would like to thank Ken and Randy Kendrick for providing the financial support necessary to fund such a major research project. Without their support this book would not have been possible.

RUSSELL S. SOBEL, PH.D.
Professor of Economics
James Clark Coffman Distinguished Chair
WEST VIRGINIA UNIVERSITY

PART I:

SYMPOSIUM ON JUDICIAL SELECTION REFORM

CHAPTER 1

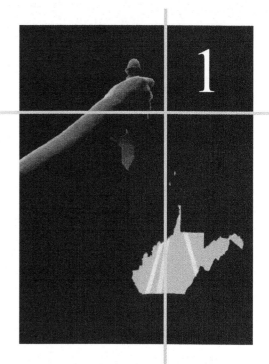

A LETTER FROM JUSTICE O'CONNOR
by The Honorable Sandra Day O'Connor

The Rule of Law

1

A LETTER FROM JUSTICE O'CONNOR

Supreme Court of the United States
Washington, D. C. 20543

CHAMBERS OF
JUSTICE SANDRA DAY O'CONNOR (RET.)

September 7, 2008

The Honorable Daniel Foster
Chairman, Joint Judiciary Subcommittee C
West Virginia Senate
Room 223W, Building 1
State Capitol Complex
Charleston, WV 25305

The Honorable Clif Moore
Chairman, Joint Judiciary Subcommittee C
West Virginia House of Delegates
P.O. Box 67
Thorpe, WV 24888

Dear Chairman Moore, Chairman Foster, and members of the
Joint Judiciary Subcommittee C:

I have been asked to share my thoughts on the issue of judicial
selection reform. I understand that you are contemplating changes to West
Virginia's judicial selection system, and I applaud your thoughtful consideration
of that subject.

The framers of our United States Constitution wisely chose to have
an appointment process for all federal judges. That system has worked well for
over two centuries. A majority of our 50 states have opted to have contested
elections for state court judges. Problems have emerged with the election
process. They frequently produce judicial candidates who raise money for their
campaigns from the very lawyers who will appear before them and from special
interest groups that have or will have legal issues to be resolved in the courts.
Such fundraising leads to the perception, and sometimes the reality, that justice
is not blind but bias. It has been shown that voters in states that elect judges
through partisan elections are more cynical about the courts, more likely to
believe that judges are legislating from the bench, and less likely to believe that
judges are fair and impartial. The influence of money in judicial races across the
country is getting worse, with some candidates in contested judicial elections

currently raising more money than candidates running for United States Senate. West Virginians already know how ugly partisan judicial elections can get. In a 2004 supreme court race in West Virginia, four out of five of ads run by either candidate were attack ads. And many more attack ads were run by special interest groups with particular biases.

An appointment process for judges followed by periodic retention elections offers clear advantages over partisan judicial elections. Citizens can be confident that appointed judges are insulated from special interests who would seek to buy justice through campaign donations. Judges who don't need to raise money for partisan campaigns can focus on applying the law fairly and impartially to each litigant. As a member of the Arizona Senate in 1974, I helped to change Arizona's judicial selection process from one of partisan judicial elections to one of appointment and retention. It remains one of my proudest achievements, and it has led to a well-functioning and well-respected judicial system in Arizona.

If contested judicial elections are to continue, they should be made non-partisan. Judges should be fair and impartial, with allegiance to the law rather than to a particular political party. In addition, campaign conduct committees should be set up to educate voters and the media about the criteria people should use to select judges, and to publicize accurate information about the source of campaign donations. Finally, states with contested elections should distribute voter education guides to provide information about the qualifications of judicial candidates that is often left out of campaign ads and meager media coverage.

A fair and impartial judiciary is one of the essential elements of good government. I wish you success as you consider reforms to the judicial selection methods used in West Virginia that will safeguard judicial independence and the rule of law in the years to come.

Sincerely,

Sandra Day O'Connor

CHAPTER 2

STATEMENT ON JUDICIAL CAMPAIGN FINANCE REFORM
by The Honorable Wanda G. Bryant

The Rule of Law

2

STATEMENT ON JUDICIAL CAMPAIGN FINANCE REFORM

The Honorable Wanda G. Bryant

I was appointed to the North Carolina Court of Appeals in 2001 by Gov. Mike Easley. Since then I have run for election under the old partisan system which allowed private financing of judicial campaigns as well as the new public financing system. The 2002 judicial election was partisan and I ran on the Democratic ticket along with several other incumbent judges on my Court. Despite our experience as Court of Appeals judges, we all lost our elections. However, a vacancy occurred in December 2002 and I was reappointed to the Court.

In order to keep my seat I had to again run a statewide election in 2004. Meanwhile, our legislature had enacted a Judicial Campaign Finance Reform Act (JCFRA) which changed the way in which appellate judicial races are conducted. The JCFRA made judicial races nonpartisan and gave appellate judicial candidates (for the North Carolina Supreme Court and Court of Appeals) the option to voluntarily participate and receive public funding upon agreeing to certain fund raising and spending limits. As a sitting judge and statewide judicial candidate, I was one of the first candidates to opt-in and participate and win election under this new system. I was strongly in favor of a reform that would limit the influence of big money contributions and reduce partisan politics in judicial campaigns. I am very pleased to say that North Carolina's first-ever publicly funded appellate judicial elections were successful, just as subsequent ones have been.

This system of electing appellate judges provides a very important step toward an independent and impartial judiciary. By voluntarily agreeing to opt-in and abide by fund raising and spending limits as required, candidates receive public financing. Candidates are required to show a broad base of public support by collecting a select number of small donations ($10 to $500) from a large number of people (at least 350 registered North Carolina voters) prior to the primary elections. After qualifying to participate in the funding program and upon certification by the North Carolina Board of Elections, candidates agree to take no private money and to adhere to strict spending limits. If a publicly financed candidate faces a privately financed opponent, matching rescue funds are available under certain circumstances to ensure a level playing field.

These requirements not only help to dispel the perception of large money influence on judicial campaigns in North Carolina, but help judicial candidates obtain a larger base of committed voters (and campaign volunteers) at an early point in the campaign season. Once the qualifications are met, candidates are certified and public funding received pursuant to the Act, judicial campaigns know exactly how much money is available for a campaign budget. This allows candidates to make informed decisions on early media buys and other important campaign expenditures, one of the many positive aspects of the financial portion of the JCFRA.

Funds to support this program come from several sources, most notably a check off option for taxpayers on the state income tax form. The check off is a designation, not an additional tax. All North Carolina lawyers are assessed a fee, currently $50 per year, that is also deposited into the public fund. Because of public financing, appellate judicial campaigns in 2004 relied on attorneys and special-interest groups for less than 14 percent of their non-family qualifying funds, compared to 73 percent for candidates in 2002, before judicial campaign reform was implemented. The level of public funding of judicial races might seem to some to be insufficient to adequately reach the attention of the voting public in an increasingly expensive media environment; however, the fact is the amount of money available to candidates in appellate judicial races (particularly Court of Appeals) in the 2004, 2006 and likely 2008 elections under the public financing program was greater than the amount candidates raised in previous election cycles.

The nonpartisan aspect of campaign reform is also a welcome change. Trial judges in North Carolina, District and Superior Court judges, have been elected on nonpartisan ballots at the local level for several years now. Only appellate judicial races recently became nonpartisan. While statewide judicial campaigns require more time —more grassroots efforts and more direct contact with voters — it helps to ensure that the voting public cast their ballots for judicial candidates based on something other than party affiliation. Voters are no longer able to vote for judges along party lines by simply voting a straight ticket. Voters now have to go to a separate, nonpartisan portion of the ballot and make a decision about which judicial candidates will receive their vote.

The Judicial Voter Guide, an integral part of the JCFRA, is another one of the most positive aspects of the Act. The voter guide is a great educational piece which sets out the qualifications and experience of the appellate judicial candidates and also contains a statement (approximately 300 words) from each candidate. The voter guide is distributed by mail to the households of all registered voters in North Carolina. It is also available on line.

As a candidate, I found the voter guide to be extremely helpful in disseminating information to registered voters in a timely manner to enable them to make "informed" decisions about the candidates for the two highest courts in our state. Notwithstanding statistics which show that after enactment of campaign finance reform and the shift to nonpartisan judicial elections significantly fewer votes were cast for judicial candidates than for candidates in other statewide races, I prefer the nonpartisan system with all its frailties, to the former partisan judicial election system. And I prefer "informed voters" voting the separate nonpartisan ballot rather than "uniformed voters" pulling a straight-party ticket.

We have had public financing of judicial races in place for three election cycles in North Carolina. During those three cycles in which a total of forty-one (41) appellate court candidates were on the ballot, thirty-one (31) candidates qualified for and accepted public financing. Of the eighteen (18) seats up for election in those three cycles — 2004, 2006, and 2008 — fifteen (15) have been won by publicly financed candidates. To date, fourteen (14) justices and judges on the North Carolina Supreme Court and Court of Appeals have been elected using the system, including our Chief Justice, Sarah Parker (who has won twice as a publicly financed candidate).

Because of public financing, appellate judicial campaigns in 2004 relied on attorneys and special-interest groups for less than 14 percent of their non-family qualifying funds, compared to 73 percent for candidates in 2002, before judicial campaign reform was implemented.

In 2007 the North Carolina General Assembly took the extraordinary step of expanding public financing to three Council of State elections: State Auditor, Insurance Commissioner and Superintendent of Public Instruction. The legislation known as the "Voter-Owned Elections Act," ratified on August 2, 2007 and signed by Governor Easley, is a pilot program designed to work much like the judicial campaign financing program, absent the nonpartisan requirement. Five of the six candidates opted to use the program in the 2008 election. Four candidates were certified and two won office as publicly financed candidates. The new "Voter-Owned Elections Act" appears to have had a successful debut. It remains to be seen whether it will be as popular as Judicial Campaign Finance Reform.

I fully support judicial public financing. I think it is a strong means of ensuring an independent judiciary. Public financing reduces the concern of undue influence perceived in large-money contributions, and protects the integrity of the individual judicial candidate. Further, public financing under North Carolina's JCFRA benefits the voters, allowing them direct participation through funding of candidates prior to primary elections as well as casting informed ballots. Voters who are donors who contribute small amounts of money can feel like they make a difference; because they do.

Public financing may not be a perfect solution. However, if the ultimate goal is, as I believe, to have an independent judiciary immune to outside influences, this system of public financing is far superior to judicial races run on strictly privately financed campaigns.

Not only does public financing prevent the appearance of undue influence, it also curbs the escalating costs of campaign spending. As a recent (and future) participant in the judicial public financing system and with over 25 years of legal experience, I fully support a system which: 1) allows for fewer concerns about the influence of big money campaign contributions; 2) promotes a better educated electorate; and 3) promotes less blatant partisanship.

Isn't that a better way to run our judicial elections?

Isn't that a better way to ensure judicial independence? I think so.

CHAPTER 3

JUDICIAL ELECTIONS, ELECTORAL INCENTIVES, AND CHECKS AND BALANCES
by Alexander Tabarrok

The Rule of Law

3

JUDICIAL ELECTIONS, ELECTORAL INCENTIVES, AND CHECKS AND BALANCES

Alexander Tabarrok

Politicians serve the people who elect them. But in serving the people who elect them do politicians serve the common interest? Not necessarily. A Senator from Alaska serves the people of Alaska, a Senator from West Virginia serves the people of West Virginia, and a Senator from California serves the people of California. We hope that with debate, compromise, and trade these divergent interests will converge to produce something approximating the common interest. But we also recognize that politicians are rewarded for bringing home the bacon. Or in more scholarly terms, politicians pursue policies that concentrate benefits on their own constituents while diffusing costs over everyone else's constituents—even when the concentrated benefits are considerably less than the sum of the diffused costs. All of this is familiar to students of political science. What is less well recognized by legal scholars is that judges, especially elected judges, are also politicians.

Just like other politicians, elected judges have an incentive to serve their constituents. Since plaintiffs typically sue in the state in which they live, elected judges have an incentive to transfer wealth from out-of-state defendants to in-state plaintiffs. In particular, an elected judge has an incentive to transfer wealth from out-of-state corporations with deep pockets to in-state plaintiffs. Some evidence that judges might act in this way is provided by Richard Neely, a retired West Virginia Supreme Court judge, who was unusually frank about the incentives he thought were faced by elected judges. Neely wrote:

> As long as I am allowed to redistribute wealth from out-of-state companies to injured in-state plaintiffs, I shall continue to do so. Not only is my sleep enhanced when I give someone's else money away, but so is my job security, because the in-state plaintiffs, their families, and their friends will reelect me ((Neely 1988), 4).

And, he continued, "it should be obvious that the in-state local plaintiff, his witnesses, and his friends, can all vote for the judge, while the out-of-state defendant can't even be relied upon to send a campaign donation ((Neely 1988), 62)."

WHAT ABOUT JURIES?

Judges decide only a minority of tort cases directly (i.e. in non-jury trials) and occasionally they decide cases by overruling juries. But judges are always influential in the courtroom. Judges must interpret the law for juries, instruct the juries, allow or disallow objections, rule on motions and counter-motions, limit or not limit the lawyers to certain theories of liability and damages, etc. In order to transfer wealth to in-state plaintiffs, elected judges need not make blatantly biased rulings or often interfere in jury decisions. Judges have significant control over the trial outcome even without making use of their highest powers.

BACKGROUND ON ELECTORAL SYSTEMS

The dominant methods of judicial selection are partisan elections, non-partisan elections, gubernatorial appointment, legislative election, and merit plans. The "merit plan," however, is gubernatorial appointment from a slate of candidates put forward by a nominating commission. Furthermore, the governor typically appoints at least some members of the nominating commission. The governor also plays an important role when the legislature elects judges, a process used in only three states. The main categories are thus partisan elections, non-partisan elections, and appointment systems.

Elected judges must cater to the demands of the voters, and they must seek campaign funds from interested parties. Appointed judges, by contrast, do not answer to the voters in competitive elections nor do they need to raise significant campaign funds. Furthermore, appointed judges tend to have longer terms than elected judges, on average 21 percent to 27 percent longer for general and supreme courts, respectively (Hanssen 1999). Appointed judges are also more secure than elected judges; they are returned to the bench—through reappointment or a retention election—more often than are elected judges.[1] Appointed judges are thus more insulated from direct political pressure than are elected judges and will tend to be more independent ((Hanssen 1999), (Posner 1993), (Dubois 1990)).

In a partisan election state, judges run under a party banner, just as do other politicians. In a non-partisan election state, judges do not run under banners and are required by law to be independent of party. Elections tend to be more competitive in partisan than in non-partisan states. Although judicial elections in non-partisan states are more competitive than retention elections, they are still not very competitive. Many judges run unopposed, and when they are opposed, few incumbents are defeated. Partisan elections tend to be contested more often and as a result voter turnout is higher and incumbents are defeated more regularly than in non-partisan elections ((Dubois 1979), (Glick 1983)). Of elected states, ten use partisan elections.[2]

---

[1] Many judges in appointed states maintain their office by running in a retention election. These elections are *unopposed* elections in which the judge is either voted up or down. Hall and Aspin (1987) find that retention elections return the incumbent to office 98.8 percent of the time. Carbon (1980) points out that retention elections were designed to create lengthy judicial tenures and to insulate judges from the public. Retention elections also insulate appointed judges from pressures from the governor. Since retention elections are essentially perfunctory we define states using initial appointment followed by retention elections as appointed states.

[2] There are a few states with mixed systems that are sometimes classified differently across studies (e.g., New York has a mixed system). For more details on our classification of electoral systems see *The Book of the States*

Tabarrok and Helland (1999) find that the primary difference between electoral systems with regards to tort awards is between partisan systems and all other systems. Thus, the focus here will be on the effect of partisan electoral systems on awards.

Although awards vary by electoral system, electoral systems appear to have very little effect on the demographic characteristics of judges. A large literature has tested whether judicial elections or appointments bring more minorities, women, conservatives, and so on to the bench or whether the American Bar Association ratings of appointed judges are higher or lower than those of elected judges. Almost unanimously, this literature concludes that selection mechanisms have no significant effects on any judicial characteristics (see, for example, (Flango and Ducat 1979); (Glick and Emmert 1987); (Alozie 1990); and the reviews of the literature in (Baum 1983); and (Stumpf and Culver 1992)). Notice that the hypothesis here, however, is that selection mechanisms affect outcomes through incentives even if they have little or no effect on measurable judicial characteristics.[3]

EVIDENCE

Helland and Tabarrok (2002) use data on over 52,000 tort trials to examine how awards vary with judicial electoral systems. Figure 3.1 looks at the average award in five types of cases, non-business cases and the four types of cases we have a special interest in. We have labeled the types of cases Partisan Out, Partisan In, Non Partisan Out, and Non Partisan In. Partisan Out denotes cases in states that use partisan elections to select their judges when the defendant was an out-of-state business. The other variables are defined similarly. The primary idea is to compare Partisan Out with Non Partisan Out. In other words is the bias against out of state businesses bigger in states that use partisan elections to select their judges than in other states?

Figure 3.1 indicates that in partisan states, the average award against an out-of-state business defendant is \$936,190 but in non-partisan states the average award against an out-of-state business is only \$272,780. The difference (Partisan Out – NonPartisan Out) measures the total "partisan effect." Awards against out-of-state businesses are on average \$663,410 higher in partisan than in non-partisan states. The difference is statistically significant at the (far) greater than 1 percent level, (F[1,52540] = 16.31 with p = 0.0001). This evidence supports the hypothesis that awards against out-of-state businesses are significantly higher in states with partisan elections than in states that use other selection mechanisms.

Awards against out-of-state companies in partisan elected states may be higher than similar cases in non-partisan states because awards are higher against out-of-state companies in partisan states (the partisan out-of-state effect) or because awards against businesses in general are higher in partisan states (the partisan business effect). The two effects can be decomposed. The partisan out-of-state effect is measured by (Partisan Out – Partisan In) – (NonPartisan Out – NonPartisan In). By subtracting out awards against in-state businesses, we control for any increase in awards against businesses in general in partisan elected states, thus isolating the partisan out-of-state effect. The partisan out-of-state effect has value

---

and the discussion in Tabarrok and Helland (1999). Our conclusions are robust to reclassification of any states with significant mixing of elected and non-elected elements.

[3] The discovery that sociological characteristics do not differ across selection mechanisms strengthens our conclusion that the primary independent variable is the incentive structure. Ashenfelter et al. (1995) find that sociological characteristics of judges are of no help in predicting outcomes.

$393,690 (F[1,52540] = 4.84 and p = 0.027). The partisan business effect is measured by (Partisan In – Non Partisan In) and has a value of $269,720 (F[1, 52540] = 15.7801, p = .0001). Awards against businesses in general are larger in partisan states than in non-partisan states, but the majority of the partisan effect is due to a particular bias against *out-of-state* business defendants.

Figure 3.1 Differences in Mean Award

Variable	Total Award (all awards)	
Constant (Non-Business Cases)	$252,540	***
	(19,524)	
Partisan Out	$936,190	***
	(143,800)	
Partisan In	$408,450	***
	(60,090)	
Non Partisan Out	$272,780	***
	(84,070)	
Non Partisan In	$138,730	***
	(43,003)	
Number of Cases	53,545	
Partisan Out - Non Partisan Out	936,190 - 272,780 = 663,410	***

*** denotes statistical significance at the 1 percent level.

Although suggestive, these differences in means awards raise the question of whether the larger awards in partisan states are caused by differences in the electoral system or by some other differences which are merely correlated with differences in the electoral system. Helland and Tabarrok (2002) refine the above analysis to control for a large variety of factors other than the electoral system that could influence awards. Helland and Tabarrok include controls for the type of injury (e.g. death, major injury, minor injury, emotional distress, rape, sexual assault and other types of injuries), the type of case (e.g., product liability, medical malpractice), and the major tort laws in a state (e.g., weakened joint and several rule, collateral source rule, punitive cap rule). In addition, they control for case selection via settlement and winning.

The inclusion of a large number of control variables and procedures does not eliminate the partisan effect although it reduces it in size. The best evidence is that moving a case with an out-of-state defendant from a non-partisan to a partisan state raises the expected award by 40 percent or about $362,988 evaluated at the mean award. The large size of the partisan effect indicates the potential profitability of forum shopping.

As a further test of the partisan electoral hypothesis, Helland and Tabarrok (2002) look at awards when federal judges, who are appointed not elected, use state law to decide cases. The U.S. Constitution (Article III, Section 2(1)) gives the federal courts the power to decide controversies between citizens of different states. Historically, federal diversity jurisdiction was supported by out-of-state businesses that feared they would be disadvantaged in pro-plaintiff/pro-debtor state courts (Friendly 1928). Today lawyers continue to cite out-of-state and anti-business bias as one reason for removing cases to federal court (Miller 1992). For more than a century, federal judges decided diversity-of-citizenship cases based on federal common law. The Supreme Court, however, overturned this rule in the 1938 case *Erie Railroad v. Tompkins* (304 U.S. p. 64). Since the 1938 Supreme Court decision, diversity-of-citizenship cases have been decided on the basis of state law.[4]

Helland and Tabarrok (2002) find that when federal judges decide tort cases there is little or no bias against out-of-state firms even when these judges are using the law of partisan states to decide the cases. This is further evidence that the partisan electoral effect is caused by judicial incentives and not by any differences in state law that happen to be correlated with electoral systems.

DISCUSSION

Electoral incentives encourage judges to redistribute wealth from out-of-state business defendants to in-state plaintiffs. It's difficult to see how these incentives cohere with justice. If all tort cases were local, the incentive to redistribute wealth from out-of-state firms would be moot. But in today's economy state judges and juries are often called upon to decide cases involving out-of-state firms.

Consider, for example, *Garvey v. Roto-Rooter Services Co.* a class-action case filed in Madison County, Illinois.[5] The single Madison County resident named in the suit is suing "on behalf" of customers of Roto-Rooter in thirty other states. The complaint does not allege a defect in service, but instead that the individuals performing the service were not licensed plumbers. Put aside the concern that many economists, not to mention consumers, would consider the resulting lower prices a blessing, and consider the absurdity that a judge and jury from Madison County, Illinois, will in effect be deciding plumbing laws and regulation for thirty other states. Not surprisingly, judges in Madison County are elected.

Class-action cases like this can be decided in state courts only because of an anomaly in federal law. The Constitution provides that cases between citizens of different states be decided by federal judges, but in implementing this constitutional requirement, Congress and the courts decided that a case would be subject to federal diversity jurisdiction only if there

---

[4] The definitive source for diversity of citizenship law is Wright (1994), Posner (1996) and Lieberman (1992) give short overviews.
[5] No. 00-L-525 (Ill. Cir. Ct. Madison County filed June 13, 2000). See Beisner and Miller (2001) for this case and others.

was "complete diversity"—every defendant had to be an out-of-state defendant.[6] As a result, it becomes quite easy to "defeat diversity" by suing a local defendant. In Jefferson County, Mississippi, for example, the Bankston Drug Store has been sued hundreds of times—not because the pharmacy did anything wrong, but simply as a way to defeat diversity in lawsuits against out-of-state pharmaceutical manufacturers.

Keeping the amount in controversy below $75,000 can also defeat diversity. Unfortunately, this common-sense provision has been interpreted to mean that so long as none of the plaintiffs, numbering possibly in the millions, asks for more than $75,000, the case can be kept in state court even if it involves millions of dollars in total (Beisner and Miller 2001).

Some of the defects in 28 USC S. 1332 have been remedied by the Class Action Fairness Act (CAFA), first introduced into Congress in 1999. CAFA requires federal diversity jurisdiction if the class has at least one hundred plaintiffs and damages exceed an aggregate of $5 million. CAFA is a modest step in the right direction toward tort reform. It is especially appropriate because as compared with other, cruder reforms, it is consistent with American legal tradition. The framers of the U.S. Constitution gave federal judges control over cases between citizens of different states precisely because they feared that local courts would use their powers unfairly against out-of-state defendants (Friendly 1928). In 2000, a Senate Report on the CAFA emphasized this point:

> Clearly, a system that allows State court judges to dictate national policy from
> the local courthouse steps is contrary to the intent of the Framers, when they
> crafted our system of federalism.[7]

The defects of elected judges are being remedied in part at the federal level. But should more be done at the state level?

First, it's important to understand that the out-of-state bias problem is not caused by elections that work poorly. Indeed, the better that elections work the worse we can expect the out-of-state bias problem to get—which is one reason we see the effect most strongly in states which use partisan elections to select their judges. Thus a defense of judicial elections based upon their similarity to other elections (e.g. (Bonneau and Hall 2009)) does not counter the problems raised here. Moreover, the out-of-state bias problem will not be solved by better informed voters or more transparency in campaign contributions.

There is a fundamental difference between electing judges and electing other politicians. As noted in the introduction, we hope that the divergent interests of politicians from different states or regions will—with debate, compromise, and trade—converge to produce something approximating the common interest. But we cannot rely on this hope for judicial elections. Judges from West Virginia and judges from Alabama do not meet to debate, compromise and trade. Nor, even if this were to occur, does it seem likely that two wrongs (biases) would make a right. Plaintiffs and defendants in West Virginia and Alabama have more than a right to be heard and their interests weighed. Plaintiffs and defendants throughout the United States have a right to justice.

---

[6] The key statute is 28 U.S.C. Section 1332. For court interpretation see *Strawbridge vs. Curtiss*, 7 U.S. (3 Cranch) 267 (1806). Note that the legislation and its interpretation long predate modern class action law.
[7] Class Action Fairness Act of 2000, S. Rep. No. 106-420, 106th Congress (2000) at 20. Quoted in Beisner and Miller (2001).

Judicial elections do not necessarily promote justice. On the positive side, electing judges may be thought of as part of the U.S. checks and balances system—a way of keeping judges "closer to the people." One problem with this interpretation, however, is that in most tort cases the people are on both sides. Most tort cases are disputes between private parties and it's not obvious why we would want to make judges more responsive to one party, the voting party, typically the plaintiff.

In criminal cases the case for elected judges may have more merit and is similar to the case for juries. Elected judges and juries provide a check on the government. The founders thought the jury trial was important enough to be guaranteed in the Bill of Rights because they were impressed with the jury as a form of check and balance against oppressive government. One person's check on the government, however, is another person's "nullification."

From a larger perspective, however, it's not obvious that checks and balances require that all political actors be elected. Consider the complicated issue of political representation. Does a politician best represent the people when she does what the people want? Or does she best represent the people when she does what the people would have wanted had they been as informed as the politician? If the former is the right notion of representation then why not submit all decisions to referenda? If the latter is the right notion then at some times and places citizens can be better off if they *do not* have the right to decide an issue.

How can citizens be better off without the right to decide an issue? We all face dilemmas between our short-term and our long-term selves. The short-term self makes decisions that our long-term self may regret. Our long-term self fights back with commitment devices that take away our opportunities to make short-term choices that we may regret. In the public arena, it seems wise to also have such commitment devices. The Founders gave federal Senators longer terms than Representatives and they staggered the terms so that our short-term political selves would not control all decisions. In a sense, the Supreme Court is the ultimate commitment device in that it gives power to a part of the polity who are long departed. Nevertheless, the long departed may better represent our long-term interests than will our short-term selves. Perhaps instead of insulating judges from "the people" we should think of appointed judges with long terms as a commitment device to better represent the people's long-term interests.

REFERENCES

Alozie, Nicholas O. 1990. Distribution of Women and Minority Judges: The Effects of Judicial Selection Methods. *Social Science Quarterly* 71(2): 315-326.

Ashenfelter, Orley, Theodore Eisenberg, and Stuart Schwab. 1995. Politics and the Judiciary: The Influence of Judicial Background on Case Outcomes. *Journal of Legal Studies* 23(1): 257-281.

Baum, Lawrence. 1983. The Electoral Fate of Incumbent Judges in the Ohio Court of Common Pleas. *Judicature* 66: 420-430.

Beisner, John H., and Jessica D. Miller. 2001. They're Making a Federal Case out of It . . . In State Court. *Harvard Journal of Law and Public* Policy 25(1): 143-207.

Bonneau, Chris W. and Melinda G. Hall. 2009. *In Defense of Judicial Elections*. New York: Routledge.

Carbon, Susan B. 1980. Judicial Retention Elections: Are They Serving Their Intended Purpose? *Judicature* 64(5): 211-233.

Dubois, Philip. 1979. Voter Turnout in State Judicial Elections: An Analysis of the Tail on the Electoral Kite. *Journal of Politics* 41: 865-885.

Dubois, Philip. 1990. The Politics of Innovation in State Courts: The Merit Plan of Judicial Selection. *Publius* 20(1): 23-42.

Flango, Victor E., and Craig Ducat. 1979. What Difference Does Method of Judicial Selection Make? *The Justice System Journal* 5(1): 25-44.

Friendly, Henry J. 1928. The Historic Basis of Diversity Jurisdiction. *Harvard Law Review* 41(483): 483-510.

Glick, Henry R. 1983. *Courts, Politics, and Justice*. New York: McGraw-Hill.

Glick, Henry R., and Craig F. Emmert. 1987. Selection Systems and Judicial Characteristics. *Judicature* 70: 228-235.

Hall, William K., and Larry T. Aspin. 1987. What Twenty Years of Judicial Retention Elections Have Told Us. *Judicature* 70(6): 340-347.

Hanssen, Andrew. 1999. The Effect of Judicial Institutions on Uncertainty and the Rate of Litigation: The Election versus the Appointment of State Judges. *Journal of Legal Studies* 28(1): 205-232.

Helland, Eric, and Alexander Tabarrok. 2002. The Effect of Electoral Institutions on Tort Awards. *American Law and Economics Review* 4(2): 341-370.

Lieberman, J. K. 1992. *The Evolving Constitution*. New York: Random House.

Miller, Neil. 1992. An Empirical Study of Forum Choices in Removal Cases under Diversity and Federal Question Jurisdiction. *American University Law Review* 41(369): 369-452.

Neely, Richard. 1988. *The Product Liability Mess*. New York: The Free Press.

Posner, Richard. 1993. What Do Judges Maximize? (The Same Thing Everybody Else Does). *Supreme Court Economic Review* 3: 1-41.

Posner, R. A. 1996. *The Federal Courts: Challenge and Reform*. Cambridge, MA.: Harvard University Press.

Stumpf, Harry P., and John H. Culver. 1992. *The Politics of State Courts*. New York: Longman.

Tabarrok, Alexander, and Eric Helland. 1999. Court Politics: The Political Economy of Tort Awards. *Journal of Law and Economics* 42(1): 157-188.

Wright, C. A. 1994. *Law of Federal Courts.* Fifth ed. St. Paul, Minn.: West Publishing Co.

CHAPTER 4

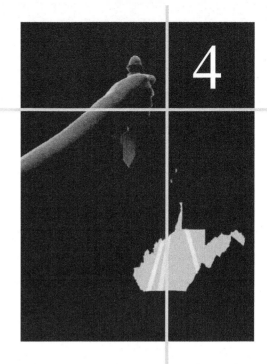

JUDICIAL SELECTION METHODS AND LEGAL SYSTEM QUALITY

by Joshua C. Hall and Russell S. Sobel

The Rule of Law

4

JUDICIAL SELECTION METHODS AND LEGAL SYSTEM QUALITY[1]

Joshua C. Hall and Russell S. Sobel

Since West Virginia achieved statehood in 1846, partisan elections have been used to select nearly all its judges.[2] In choosing partisan judicial elections, West Virginia was squarely in line with the trends regarding judicial selection at the time. Many states were abandoning their previous method of judicial selection – appointment by the governor or legislature – for direct elections, both partisan and nonpartisan. One reason for this change was it was thought at the time that elected judges would be more accountable to voters.

In 1940, the state of Missouri amended its constitution to allow for the merit selection of judges and in doing so became the first state to attempt to minimize the impact of electoral politics on judicial selection. The reasons for the change were many, but public concern about the involvement of political parties in the election of judges played a large role.[3] Many felt that elected judges were too partisan and too influenced by political pressures to apply the law in a fair and even-handed manner. By switching from an elected to an appointed system of choosing judges — to increase "judicial independence" — Missouri began a nationwide trend. So many states followed in its footsteps that the merit system of judicial appointment is frequently referred to as the "Missouri Plan." Today, 26 states use some form of merit system to appoint judges to their highest courts.[4]

Many of these states use slight variations of the original Missouri Plan. Most have a nominating commission comprising several citizens and lawyers, with the citizens typically appointed by the governor and the lawyers appointed by the state bar association. The nominating commission submits several candidates to the governor, who then selects one to

---

[1] This is a revised version of Hall and Sobel (2008). We thank Joe Haslag and the Show-Me Institute staff for their insightful comments and permission to incorporate material from that study into this essay.

[2] The one exception would be municipal judges, whose method of selection varies by jurisdiction. For more, see American Judicature Society (2008b).

[3] For a nice discussion of the history of state changes in judicial selection procedures, see Hall (2001) and Hanssen (2004). On this point, Hall states, on page 316, "Reformers assert that the Missouri Plan, of which retention races are a part, and to a lesser extent nonpartisan elections remove judges from the vicissitudes of interpartisan competition...."

[4] See Figure 4.1 for a list of the 26 states.

be appointed to the court. Some states require an additional step, like ratification by the state senate. After the judge has served on the court for a certain period of time, many states require a retention election in which voters may cast a ballot for or against a justice in an up-or-down vote. This merit method of appointive system is in contrast, however, to the other forms of judicial selection used in many states, such as direct appointment by the legislature, or partisan or nonpartisan statewide judicial elections.

In West Virginia, election to the West Virginia Supreme Court of Appeals has become quite contentious in recent years. In 2004, special interests lined up behind both candidates in the election between incumbent Warren McGraw and challenger Brent Benjamin. A group called "And for the Sake of the Kids," primarily representing business interests, spent over two million dollars trying to get Benjamin elected. In addition, other special interests such as West Virginians Against Lawsuit Abuse and the West Virginia Chamber of Commerce were involved in the election. On the other side, a group financed primarily by trial lawyers and labor unions called West Virginia Consumers for Justice spent over a million in television ads during the race. While the rhetoric has been toned down some in more recent elections, special interests and partisanship continue to play a large role in West Virginia's judicial selection process.

While these races can seem like mere partisan bickering, the issue of judicial selection and its effect on the quality of courts is important. Judicial independence is critical to a well-functioning legal system, and the quality of a state's judicial system is an important determinant of economic growth.[5] States with highly regarded legal systems better protect and define property and contract rights, providing the proper foundation for entrepreneurial activity and economic growth.[6] Bad court systems, on the other hand, can impede economic development by creating uncertainty, driving up the costs of doing business (such as liability insurance or worker compensation), and infringing on the liberties that underpin a free and prosperous market economy.

A growing literature in economics has found that judicial independence and quality matter for economic growth across countries and states. Economist Abdiweli Ali (2003) found that the quality of a country's judicial system is a significant determinant of the country's economic growth.[7] Using a different data sample and a different measure of judicial

---

[5] The economic literature typically defines judicial independence as freedom from the other branches of government. Judicial independence can manifest itself in many ways, such as a judge's permanence in office. As Alexander Hamilton ([1788] 1996) pointed out in Federalist Paper no. 78 (p. 491), "nothing can contribute so much to [the judiciary's] firmness and independence as permanency in office." When formally measuring independence, scholars tend to focus on how judges are insulated from political pressures through appointment procedures and tenure length (see La Porta et al. (2004) for an example).

[6] According to Gray (1997), a well-functioning legal system is one that has: 1) market-friendly laws; 2) adequate institutions (such as independent courts) to implement and enforce them; and, 3) a demand for those laws from citizens. Market-friendly laws clearly delineate the rights *and responsibilities* of market participants so they can go about the business of economic life without uncertainty about the legality of their actions.

[7] Ali measures the quality of a country's legal system in using data from the International Country Risk Guide and Business Environmental Risk Intelligence. These variables try to measure the rule of law (the extent to which citizens are equal under the law), the likelihood that private property will be confiscated by the government, the effectiveness of the judiciary, and the risk of contract repudiation without recourse. Ali finds a positive relationship between both of these measures of legal quality and a country's economic growth as measured by the average annual growth rate of GDP from 1974–1989.

independence, economists Lars Feld and Stefan Voigt reached a similar conclusion.[8] At the U.S. state level, Berkowitz and Clay (2004) found a positive relationship between the quality of a state's legal system and median household income in the state. They estimated that a one-and-one-third standard deviation increase in state legal quality would increase median income by 11.3 percentage points. Thus, this literature clearly shows that an independent and well-regarded judicial system is an important determinant of economic growth.

Further evidence is presented in Figure 4.1 and Figure 4.2. As discussed in further detail later in the report, there exists one survey-based measure of state-legal system quality—the Institute for Legal Reform's *State Liability Systems Ranking Study*. The study is produced annually for the U.S. Chamber of Commerce by the Harris Poll and tries to derive a measure of "how reasonable, fair and balanced" the tort liability system in each state is perceived to be by American business. Based on a survey of over 1,000 corporate attorneys, each state's legal system is given a score (from zero to 100 with higher scores meaning higher quality) and ranked from one to fifty.

Figure 4.1:
State Legal System Scores and State Income Growth

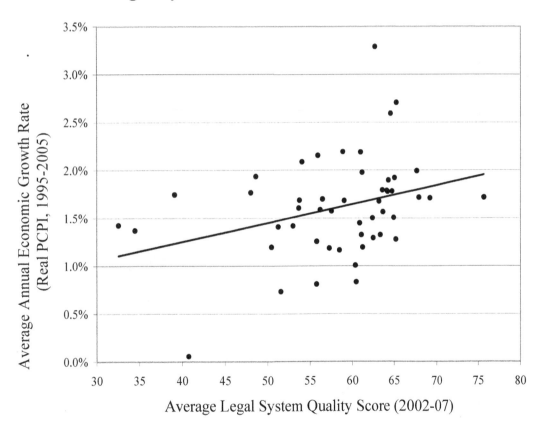

Average Legal System Quality Score (2002-07)

---

[8] Feld and Voigt (2003). They are primarily interested in the difference between *de jure* and *de facto* judicial independence. They calculate their *de jure* measure according to the independence given judges in that country's legal documents concerning the judiciary (usually their constitutions). An example of a *de jure* measure of independence would be whether judges have life terms. They find a strongly positive relationship between *de facto* judicial independence and growth of GDP per capita from 1980 to 1998.

Figure 4.1 shows the positive relationship between the average legal system quality score of a state between 2002 and 2007 and its average annual growth rate in per capita income during the past decade. Figure 4.2 provides this information from a different perspective, showing the positive relationship between a state's average score from 2002 to 2007 and its level of per capita income in 2005.[9] Thus states with higher scores in this legal index have higher incomes *and* grow faster. It is clear that the quality of a state's legal system is important for growth. The question of interest is how the method of judicial selection influences the quality of a state's legal system.

Figure 4.2:
State Legal System Ranking and State Income Level

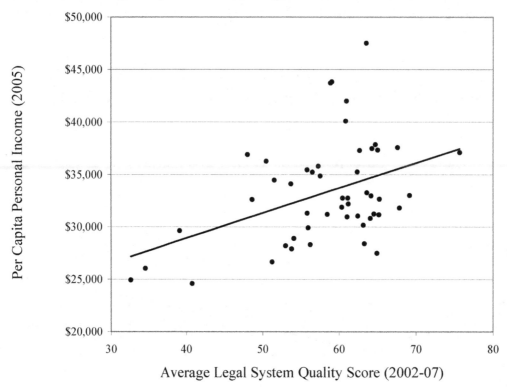

Average Legal System Quality Score (2002-07)

Many studies show that the method of judicial selection does influence judicial independence, which should impact the overall quality of a state's legal system. Most of this work, however, focuses primarily on the difference between elected and appointed systems, with some recent work focusing on the difference between partisan and nonpartisan elections.[10] Almost no empirical research looks at whether there are any differences among *all* types of judicial selection mechanisms, from partisan elections to different versions of the

---

[9] We also find a positive and statistically significant relationship between a state's legal quality and its average annual per-capita income growth. The following statistically significant result was found using ordinary least squares (t-statistics in parentheses): Average annual growth in per capita income 1995–2005 = 0.01957 State Legal Quality Score 2002–07 (2.339). Similar results were found using state rankings instead of scores, and for different time periods.

[10] Sobel and Hall (2007a).

Missouri Plan of appointment. The intense public debate surrounding judicial reform in West Virginia makes it imperative that policymakers and voters have accurate evidence about the relationship between different mechanisms of judicial selection and the quality of a state's legal system. To this end, we provide a closer look at how different features of judicial selection mechanisms, especially the difference between partisan elections and versions of the "Missouri Plan," affect the quality of legal systems across the states.

METHODS OF JUDICIAL SELECTION: A HISTORY AND OVERVIEW

At the federal level, judicial selection is fairly straightforward. The U.S. Constitution lays out the selection procedure for federal judges, which involves the president nominating a candidate by submitting his or her name to the U.S. Senate for confirmation.[11] At the state level, however, there are numerous differences in the method of selecting judges. Even within states, there are differences in how judges are selected at different levels of the state judiciary. In West Virginia, for example, judges on all courts above the municipal level are chosen using partisan elections.[12] At the municipal level, however, judicial selection methods vary from municipality to municipality.

In general, there are two ways of choosing judges: appointment and election. In addition to being the method chosen for the federal government in the U.S. Constitution, appointment was also the method chosen by each of the original 13 states. In fact, until 1832, all states delegated the responsibility of judicial appointment to the governor or legislature (with perhaps a requirement that the other confirm).[13] Virginia, for example, chose judicial appointment by the state legislature as its method of judicial selection for its highest court shortly after ratification of the U.S. Constitution, and has used that method ever since.[14]

Some have argued that judicial appointment was popular during this period because the Founding Fathers recognized the importance of judicial independence.[15] More likely, the opposite is true. Americans had developed a suspicion of both the executive branch and the judicial branch during the colonial period because they tended to be faithful agents of the British Crown, in stark contrast to the colonial legislatures. When one observes that the federal and state constitutions afford tremendous powers to the legislature, this perspective becomes clear. In fact, as Alexander Hamilton points out in Federalist No. 81, the judiciary was considered to be the weakest of the three branches of the government.[16] Instead of cultivating independence, judicial appointments would keep the courts subordinate to the

---

[11] See Stratmann and Garner (2004) for an excellent overview of the federal judicial selection process.

[12] See American Judicature Society (2008a) for more information on how other states select their justices at each level and American Judicature Society (2008b) for more information on West Virginia.

[13] Of the 13 original states, seven used legislative appointment and six used gubernatorial appointment (Streb 2007). For a discussion of the evolution of state judicial selection procedures, see Hanssen (2004).

[14] Streb (2007), p. 6.

[15] See, for example, Streb's invocation of Alexander Hamilton (2007), p. 8: "After all, Alexander Hamilton was quite clear that if a judge were forced to run for re-election, judicial independence — and hence the judiciary itself — would be threatened."

[16] Hamilton argues that this is a good thing, because it means that the judiciary will not be able to usurp the policymaking role of the legislature (Owsiany 2001).

legislature.[17] Legislatures were seen as faithful agents of voters because they were directly elected by voters, and thus directly accountable to them.

Beginning with Mississippi in 1832, however, most states amended their state constitutions to mandate judicial election instead of appointment.[18] In 1850 alone, seven states made the switch.[19] The preference for partisan elections over appointive systems was nearly universal during this time; 20 of the 29 states already in the Union in 1847 switched to partisan judicial elections at some point during the next half century, and every state that joined between 1847 and 1910 adopted partisan judicial elections.[20] Thus, by 1910, 80 percent (37 of 46) of the states were using elections to select judges.

The conversion to partisan judicial elections was part of a larger movement toward direct elections. In the 1830s and 40s, legislatures were seen as being too powerful and beholden to special interests. Bad state investments in railroads, highways, and canals had resulted in growing state debts, which led to dissatisfaction with legislative performance and recognition that additional checks were needed on state power.[21] According to law historian Kermit Hall, "The populist and antigovernmental stirrings of the late 1840s and 1850s climaxed in an outburst of constitutional reform that diminished legislative power."[22] These constitutional reforms needed to be enforced, however, and that enforcement could only come from a more independent judiciary.[23] While it is true that partisan elections made judges directly accountable to voters, reformers at the time were more interested in making judges more independent of legislative influence.[24] Reformers thought that partisan elections would give judges the political power necessary to act as faithful agents of voters in checking legislative power.[25]

The notion that elected judges would act as an independent check on the legislature because they were beholden directly to voters was soon found to be incorrect. Just as the legislature was captured by special interests, the judiciary was now viewed as having been captured by political parties.[26] Judicial reformers, believing that it was the partisan nature of the elections that were causing much of the problem, now advocated nonpartisan elections in which candidates would run without any party affiliation. From 1910 to 1958, 17 states switched to nonpartisan elections, so that by the end of the period more states (17 of 47) were using nonpartisan elections to select judges than any other method.[27]

During the nonpartisan period, however, the groundwork was being laid for yet another transformation of judicial selection procedures. In 1913, the American Judicature Society was founded to help improve the justice system in the United States by promoting an

---

[17] Hanssen (2004) p. 444.

[18] Streb (2007) p. 9.

[19] Haynes (1944).

[20] Hanssen (2004) p. 436.

[21] Hanssen (2004) pp. 445-446.

[22] Hall (1989, p. 89), quoted in Hanssen (2004).

[23] The ideal of judicial independence from the will of the other two branches is at the heart of the principle of "checks and balances" (La Porta et al., 2004). Constitutions are written to guarantee citizen freedoms against encroachment by government. Historically, the courts have been thought of as the bulwark against overreaching executive and legislative branches (Hayek, 1960; Buchanan, 1975). For an alternate perspective on judicial independence, see Anderson, Shughart, and Tollison (1989).

[24] Hall (1983).

[25] Hanssen (2004) p. 448.

[26] Hanssen (2004), p. 450.

[27] Hanssen (2004), p. 437.

independent judiciary free of political influence. The society's co-founder, Albert Kales, drafted a procedure for merit-based selection of judges that would give them greater independence from political pressures, but would also retain enough political control to be palatable to populists.[28] His plan was first enacted in Missouri in 1940, and from there it spread to more than two dozen states.[29] Today, it is the most popular method of electing justices at the state supreme court level.

DOES JUDICIAL SELECTION MATTER?

While history can tell us what individuals were saying when judicial selection policies were changed, it tells us very little about the effects of different selection methods. During the 19th century, judicial reformers thought that switching to partisan elections would make judges more independent by giving them a power base apart from the legislative and executive branches. When in the 20th century partisan elections were dropped in many states, in favor of nonpartisan elections, the rationales amounted to little more than normative appeals or responses to a crisis, such as judicial corruption or failure to check an out-of-control legislature overstepping its constitutional boundaries. That is, the change was not informed by evidence that partisanship per se was impairing voters' ability to elect judges who would serve more virtuously or effectively. Nor did the actual experience with nonpartisan elections provide such evidence.

In many states, including West Virginia, state supreme courts have come under fire as being too "politicized." For example, business interests have suggested that West Virginia court decisions have made the state a "judicial hellhole."[30] Regardless of whether this pejorative description is correct, the bottom line is that West Virginia's court system – and consequently, the method of judicial selection used in the state – has come under intense scrutiny.[31]

West Virginia is not alone in this regard. Intense debate has surrounded the election of judges in both Wisconsin and Ohio. Appointive systems are not immune from controversy either. Consider the fact that Missouri — the home of the non-partisan, appointive system known as the Missouri Plan — has recently seen considerable debate over whether the system is in need of modification.

At issue in all of these debates is the relationship between judicial selection, jurisprudence, and economic outcomes. In Missouri, for example, a recent report argues that the court's composition has changed considerably over the past two decades and that the court's jurisprudence changed (for the worst).[32] The authors suggest that the first change explains the second:

> It is clear ... that the court has taken a new direction in recent years, and this shift followed changes in the court's composition. The seeds of some of today's majority opinions can be found in earlier dissenting opinions.

---

[28] Hanssen (2002), p. 81.
[29] Here, we will use the terms "merit plan" and "Missouri Plan" interchangeably.
[30] American Tort Reform Association (2008).
[31] For a detailed analysis of the labeling of West Virginia as a judicial hellhole, see Thornburg (2008).
[32] Eckhardt and Hilton (2007).

Partisanship and personal preferences aside, the obvious lesson is that judicial selection has consequences.[33]

Similar reasoning appears to have motivated West Virginia Governor Joe Manchin to suggest a switch to nonpartisan elections.

While "thick" legal analysis can shed much light on what is going on in a particular case or series of cases, it is difficult to draw broader conclusions from such a case-by-case analysis.[34] The Missouri report implies that it is the current method of judicial selection in that state which led to the change in court composition and hence the change in jurisprudence.[35] But we do not know whether this is true, because we cannot examine or be certain of the counterfactual. We do not know who would have been selected if Missouri had used a different judicial selection system. It's therefore unclear whether the result can be attributed to the method of judicial selection or to some other trend. Consider Ohio, which has also seen considerable change in jurisprudence during the last decade.[36] As in Missouri, concern over changing jurisprudence has spawned intense public battles over judicial selection. In Ohio, though, the debate has inspired calls to switch from a mixed election system to a merit system — the very system now found wanting in Missouri.[37] So, the undesirable changes in jurisprudence might be a function of judicial selection or they might be the product of some underlying trend.

Judicial selection can influence judicial outcomes mainly by: (a) changing which people are chosen as judges; and/or, (b) changing the incentives judges face. That is, different processes may result in the selection of different individuals, in turn resulting in different judicial outcomes; or judicial behavior may be influenced by the desire to be reelected or reappointed, causing judges to cater to different groups depending on how they are selected.

Legal reformers often contend that both factors are important. Advocates of judicial elections, for example, frequently talk of "holding judges accountable" through elections, which implies that judges have an incentive under this system to cater directly to voters. Likewise, such advocates object to the appointment of judges who do not "represent the people's interests."

Because there is only weak evidence that the method of judicial selection results in different kinds of people becoming judges, economic research on judicial selection typically focuses on how judicial selection affects incentives.[38] Whether judges should be elected or appointed is probably the most discussed topic in legal scholarship.[39] This literature points to a substantial difference in outcomes between the two, caused by the differing incentives faced by judges in each system. Two excellent recent examples of this work are by economists Alex

---

[33] Eckhardt and Hilton (2007), p. 21.

[34] Hanssen (2000).

[35] Note that we are not saying that the method of judicial selection in Missouri changed during this period. Rather, the argument we are restating is that the Missouri Plan *allowed* for these changes in the composition and jurisprudence of the Missouri Supreme Court.

[36] For criticism of the "new" Ohio Supreme Court, see Owsiany (2001b).

[37] In Ohio, judges run in partisan party primaries but the general election is non-partisan. For law review articles on calls for reform, see Link (2004) or Geyh (2003).

[38] See Hanssen (2000), who argues that "[w]ith respect to judicial institutions, it does not appear that this 'self-selection' effect is important — various studies have found few significant differences in such things as where the judge went to school, the years of education, religious affiliation, etc." Also see the work of Alozie (1990) and the overview of the literature in Baum (1995).

[39] Dubois (1986).

Tabarrok and Eric Helland. Tabarrok summarizes their work in detail in Chapter 3 of this volume.

Economists Tim Besley and Abigail Payne hypothesize that more discrimination cases will be filed in states that elect their judges because: 1) voters are more likely to elect pro-worker (and anti-business) judges that will rule in their favor; and, 2) elected judges are more likely to appeal to potential voters by using their discretion to make pro-worker awards.[40] Analyzing employment discrimination charges filed in state courts over a 27-year period from 1973 to 2000, Besley and Payne found considerably more filings in states that elect their judges than in states that use a purely appointive system. Interestingly, they also found evidence that retention elections are enough to discipline appointed judges into acting like directly elected judges.

More recently, Daniel Berkowitz, Chris Bonneau, and Karen Clay looked at the effect of judicial independence on minority interests, specifically the interests of children with disabilities.[41] The authors proposed that promoting the interests of children with disabilities can be politically difficult for state judges because of the high financial cost of complying with special education litigation, and the concomitant mainstreaming of children with disabilities into regular classrooms. They found that a state's method of judicial selection helps to explain increases in special education litigation and enrollments following the passage of the Individuals with Disabilities Act (IDEA) in 1975. Controlling for a variety of other factors, Berkowitz, Bonneau, and Clay found that states with elected judges had far lower student enrollment under the IDEA than states with appointed judges. They concluded that appointed judges are more independent, and thus more able to promote minority interests that may conflict with majority preferences.

These studies are part of a large and growing literature showing that there are differences in judicial and legal outcomes between states that elect their judges and states that appoint their judges. Political scientist Melinda Gann Hall found that liberal Democratic supreme court judges in Texas, North Carolina, Louisiana, and Kentucky were more likely to vote with the conservative Republican majority if their previous election was close.[42] In a later paper, Melinda Gann Hall and Paul Brace found that Democratic state supreme court judges in elective states are less likely to overturn death penalty cases than Democratic supreme court judges in appointive states.[43] Similarly, in a previous paper, we (the authors of this chapter) used a nationwide ranking of the quality of state legal systems to conclude that judicial quality is lowest in states with partisan judicial elections.[44]

Judges appointed under the Missouri plan (or some variant) seem to be more "independent" than elected judges. This was confirmed by economist Andrew Hanssen, who noted that because more-independent judges have greater discretion, there will tend to be greater uncertainty about the outcomes of cases they decide.[45] If the outcomes could be predicted with certainty, the two parties would simply settle and go home. When the outcomes are more uncertain, however, it's more likely that each side will think they have something to gain by going to court. A higher percentage of cases going to court rather than

---

[40] Besley and Payne (2003).
[41] Berkowitz, Bonneau, and Clay (2006).
[42] Hall (1992).
[43] Brace and Hall (1993).
[44] Sobel and Hall (2007a).
[45] The idea, which Hanssen (1999) applied to the state judicial election issue, was first introduced by Priest and Klein (1984).

being settled is, therefore, an indicator that the judicial system is less predictable (and thus more independent). Hanssen looked at utility regulation cases from 1985 to 1994 and found that there is indeed more litigation where judges are appointed.[46] In later work he found that states using some form of the Missouri merit plan to select supreme court justices have far more litigation than states using judicial elections.[47] He suggests that the discrepancy could help explain the widespread support of lawyers and the American Bar Association for the Missouri Plan.

While there has been a tremendous amount of research about the differences between elected and appointed systems, there has been almost no empirical work about the differences among appointive systems.[48] The main differences among appointive systems pertain to whether a nominating commission and/or legislative confirmation are used.

The use of a nominating commission to select the slate of judicial candidates from which the governor must choose can affect which candidate is eventually chosen. In the economics literature, this process is known as agenda control.[49]

Let's consider a simple example: Suppose there are five judicial candidates (call them A, B, C, D, and E) and the nominating commission selects three for the governor to pick from. Further, suppose that the governor's own ranking of the candidates, from most to least preferred, is A, B, C, D, and E. Without a nominating commission restricting his choices, the governor would pick candidate A. With a nominating commission presenting a restricted subset of three candidates, the governor's choice will be the most preferred among the subset — a subset that might not include his most preferred candidate. If the preferences of the nominating commission differ from those of the governor, the commission can manipulate the choice set in their favor. For example, if the nominating commission most wants candidate C to be appointed, they could submit a list containing only C, D, and E, from which the governor would select C. In this case, it is the preference of the nominating commission, not that of the governor, that determines the judicial selection.[50]

When the nominating commission has the same preferences as the governor, the commission would submit their top three candidates, A, B, and C, which are also the governor's top three choices. The governor would then select candidate A, the same outcome had there been no nominating commission at all. Thus, the extent to which a nominating

---

[46] Hanssen (1999).

[47] Hanssen (2002).

[48] One exception is McLeod (2007). Unfortunately, the study's sample size is so limited that it is unclear whether the findings are best explained by differences in state law or by differences in how the states in the sample select judges.

[49] See Romer and Rosenthal (1978).

[50] According to an unattributed study made public by the Adam Smith Foundation, this is what happened in Missouri recently (2007, p. 4):

> "After reviewing all thirty applicants in just two days (giving an appallingly scant half hour interview for each applicant to the Supreme Court), the Commission forwarded three nominees to the Governor for his consideration. Two of the three were Democrats and one was a Republican. In and beyond Missouri, it is a political truism that a governor of one party, Democrat or Republican, will be loathed [sic] to appoint a person from the opposite party to the highest court. In Missouri, it has not happened in the last half century, and the last time a Governor of one party was implicitly forced to appoint a judge from the other party was nearly three decades ago during Governor Kit Bond's administration. Operating under this truism, after the Commission nominated two Democrats and one Republican, even the most generous interpretation is that the Commission had gamed the system by de facto making the choice of judge."

commission changes the outcome depends on how closely aligned its preferences are with the governor's.[51]

How likely is it that the preferences of the nomination commission and the governor will coincide? In virtually all states with a nominating commission, the governor appoints some or all of its members, so the commission will likely align with the governor to some degree. However, the term lengths of these appointments may run such that appointees from governor are choosing the candidates submitted to a subsequent governor with different preferences.

Just as a nominating commission may affect the outcomes of the judicial selection process, so may a legislative confirmation process. If the legislature, for example, would decline to confirm candidate A (the governor's most preferred candidate in the above example), the governor must submit the most preferred candidate who can garner legislative approval — perhaps candidate B or C. Again, how much this additional process matters depends on how different are the preferences of the legislature and the governor. This depends, in turn, on such factors as the rate of turnover in the state Senate, the extent to which judicial appointment is a salient electoral issue, and many others.

Thus, there is reason to believe that differences in judicial and legal outcomes among appointive states are substantially influenced by variations in the appointment methods — for example, whether they use nominating commissions, legislative confirmation, or both.

JUDICIAL SELECTION AND THE QUALITY OF STATE COURTS

In this section, we inquire whether there is evidence that a state's method of judicial selection is a significant determinant of the quality of its legal system. To do so, we must classify states into groups based on their methods of judicial selection, and then find an empirical measure of legal system quality to compare across the groups.

Based on a careful reading of the selection methods for state supreme court judges, we have identified seven major groups. Our information on selection methods comes from two sources: *Methods of Judicial Selection*, published by the American Judicature Society; and *The Book of the States*, published by the Council of State Governments.[52] There are, of course, many minor variations within each grouping, and we point the reader to the original sources for additional details on each state's method of judicial selection. A listing of the major groups, with the associated states, is given in Figure 4.3.

The first two groups are composed of those states using elections as the method of judicial selection. In the first group are the 13 states using nonpartisan elections, in which judicial candidates run for office without being identified or selected based on political party affiliation. In the second are the nine states, including West Virginia, that use some form of partisan elections in which candidates are affiliated with a political party.[53] The third group

---

[51] There are three states in which the governor must get the approval of a council for judicial appointments. In two of them, the governor appoints the members of this council, so the analysis would be similar to the case in which he appoints the members of the nominating commission.

[52] American Judicature Society (2008a) and Council of State Governments (various years).

[53] Michigan and Ohio use nonpartisan general elections, but the candidates are selected in partisan processes so they are generally classified as partisan election states.

comprises the two states that use the legislature to elect judges. The remaining four groups are composed of states using some form of gubernatorial appointment process, further differentiated according to whether a nominating commission is present and whether legislative confirmation is required. Thirteen states use a process involving only a nominating commission and the governor. Eight states add some form of legislative confirmation process to these other two steps.[54] Two states have gubernatorial appointment with legislative confirmation, but no nominating commission. Finally, the selection procedures of three states involve neither nominating commissions nor legislative confirmation, but do have some form of (usually governor-appointed) executive council that must grant approval.

Figure 4.3: States Grouped by Method of Judicial Selection

Method of Judicial Selection (number of states using it)	States Using This Method
Nonpartisan elections (13)	Arkansas, Georgia, Idaho, Kentucky, Minnesota, Mississippi, Montana, Nevada, North Carolina, North Dakota, Oregon, Washington, Wisconsin
Partisan elections (9)	**Alabama, Illinois, Louisiana, Michigan, New Mexico, Ohio, Pennsylvania, Texas, West Virginia**
Elected by legislature (2)	South Carolina, Virginia
Gubernatorial appointment from nominating commission (13)	Alaska, Arizona, Colorado, Florida, Indiana, Iowa, Kansas, Missouri, Nebraska, Oklahoma, South Dakota, Tennessee, Wyoming
Gubernatorial appointment from nominating commission with legislative confirmation (8)	Connecticut, Delaware, Hawaii, Maryland, New York, Rhode Island, Utah, Vermont
Gubernatorial appointment with legislative confirmation (2)	Maine, New Jersey
Gubernatorial appointment with council approval (3)	California, Massachusetts, New Hampshire

Note that there are many minor differences among the states within each grouping. See text and sources for additional details.

With our groups compiled, we must now find a measure of legal system quality to compare across the groups. While, unfortunately, there is no objective or widely accepted measure of the quality of state legal systems, one survey-based measure does lend itself to empirical analysis: the Institute for Legal Reform's *State Liability Systems Ranking Study*.[55] This study, conducted annually for the U.S. Chamber of Commerce by the Harris Poll, is based on a representative national sample of more than 1,500 senior attorneys, in-house

---

[54] Most states with legislative confirmation require only state senate approval.
[55] See Institute for Legal Reform (various years).

general counsel, and senior litigators at companies with annual revenues of at least $100 million. The stated purpose of the study is to derive a measure of "how reasonable, fair and balanced" the tort liability system in each state is perceived to be by American business.

The survey focuses on 10 areas: (1) overall treatment of tort and contract litigation; (2) having and enforcing meaningful venue requirements; (3) treatment of class action suits and mass consolidation suits; (4) punitive damages; (5) timeliness of summary judgment/dismissal; (6) discovery; (7) scientific and technical evidence; (8) non-economic damages; (9) impartiality and competence of judges; and, (10) predictability and fairness of juries. Based on survey responses, the index scores state legal system quality on a scale of 0 to 100. The state with the highest score is given a ranking of 1, and the other states are ranked accordingly.

While many of the factors included in this index may seem irrelevant to a state's method of judicial selection, the opposite is likely true. For example, in West Virginia the state supreme court ruled that legislation enacted by the state legislature establishing meaningful venue requirements is unconstitutional; justices elected in heavily partisan elections cast the deciding votes. It is therefore likely that the use of partisan elections for judicial selection affects West Virginia's score on questions about meaningful venue requirements. Given the broad ability of state supreme courts to interpret and overrule legislation, the composition of a state's high court (and thus the type of selection process used) can clearly have widespread consequences for the overall quality of a state's legal system.

There are potential problems with any measure of legal system quality, but the *Ranking Study* is the only empirically based index that exists across states and through time. Admittedly, the index has a bias in that it attempts to gauge how the state legal systems are viewed by large public corporations. But this bias is also one of its advantages. Most legal reforms are enacted with an eye toward promoting economic growth and development, and it is precisely the perception of the state's legal climate toward business that is being measured by this index. Other research examining this index has found that it is significantly correlated with per-capita income and other measures of economic performance across states (like poverty and unemployment rates).[56] Earlier in this chapter we presented graphical evidence showing the clear correlations between this index and measures of income and economic growth. Therefore, we can be reasonably certain that states scoring better in this index do indeed enjoy a legal climate more conducive to economic growth and prosperity.

Figure 4.4 shows the 2002 through 2007 index scores and Figure 4.5 the associated rankings, for all 50 states. The averages for the period are also given. During those six years, West Virginia earned an average ranking of 49 out of 50 — never scoring better than 49th in any year of the survey. In 2006 and 2007 in fact, West Virginia ranked dead last at 50th, with an overall index score of below 40 (out of 100) in both years. The states scoring most similarly to West Virginia in terms of being persistently ranked as having one of the worst state legal systems during this period are Alabama, Louisiana, and Mississippi. Conversely, consistently scoring at the top of this index are Delaware, Nebraska, Iowa, and Virginia. Delaware, in fact, tops the ranking in every year.

---

[56] See Sobel and Hall (2007b). See also Berkowitz and Clay (2004), who use this study to find a positive relationship between legal quality and median state income. They also showed that states with higher-quality courts have lower poverty rates, everything else being equal.

Figure 4.4: State Liability System Scores, 2002–07

State	Index Score						
	2002	2003	2004	2005	2006	2007	2002–07 Average
Alabama	37.8	31.6	34.3	35.9	44.4	50.7	39.1
Alaska	53.8	55.8	56.5	56.4	56.2	56.0	55.8
Arizona	63.2	59.7	63.8	60.9	65.1	66.3	63.2
Arkansas	49.3	44.9	52.5	50.2	54.1	56.5	51.3
California	48.6	45.6	45.2	45.5	49.8	53.5	48.0
Colorado	65.3	62.3	63.9	63.6	65.6	65.1	64.3
Connecticut	63.4	60.3	62.5	62.0	66.9	66.3	63.6
Delaware	78.6	74.5	74.4	76.0	74.9	75.6	75.7
Florida	55.2	48.6	54.1	50.9	55.2	58.2	53.7
Georgia	59.9	52.7	57.6	58.4	61.0	61.2	58.5
Hawaii	52.0	47.8	53.7	51.5	48.0	56.3	51.6
Idaho	62.4	61.8	66.2	64.2	64.0	61.3	63.3
Illinois	55.1	53.1	50.5	44.1	49.2	50.8	50.5
Indiana	62.8	65.1	64.4	65.5	65.2	68.2	65.2
Iowa	65.8	68.8	68.6	66.3	68.8	68.9	67.9
Kansas	66.0	61.0	64.4	62.6	64.5	66.7	64.2
Kentucky	53.5	54.0	56.0	54.9	58.0	60.8	56.2
Louisiana	41.3	37.3	40.5	39.1	39.0	47.3	40.8
Maine	61.0	60.9	64.1	64.2	65.5	68.9	64.1
Maryland	60.6	58.8	61.4	59.8	63.4	61.7	61.0
Massachusetts	54.0	59.1	57.7	57.8	59.0	65.7	58.9
Michigan	58.2	56.3	61.3	59.6	63.1	64.2	60.5
Minnesota	61.0	63.5	65.0	65.2	65.0	70.6	65.1
Mississippi	28.4	24.8	25.7	30.7	39.7	46.1	32.6
Missouri	56.8	55.4	52.9	51.9	57.8	60.0	55.8
Montana	49.6	56.4	51.7	54.8	54.8	57.2	54.1
Nebraska	65.4	69.3	69.1	69.7	71.5	70.0	69.2
Nevada	56.7	54.1	56.4	58.4	56.0	62.0	57.3
New Hampshire	61.9	63.2	65.2	64.0	66.0	68.2	64.8
New Jersey	55.4	56.1	60.2	57.8	61.4	63.4	59.1
New Mexico	52.8	48.6	55.1	54.5	54.2	57.5	53.8
New York	58.9	57.2	61.4	58.8	63.2	65.6	60.9
North Carolina	61.9	59.5	61.9	60.3	65.2	65.9	62.5
North Dakota	59.4	65.1	63.8	68.5	65.2	65.4	64.6
Ohio	59.4	58.6	57.2	59.5	63.5	63.9	60.4
Oklahoma	51.2	53.9	57.5	56.5	58.8	57.7	55.9
Oregon	62.5	61.2	58.4	59.6	59.8	65.7	61.2
Pennsylvania	56.2	55.9	57.5	55.5	59.3	60.8	57.5
Rhode Island	55.0	53.2	55.7	55.4	61.1	58.5	56.5
South Carolina	50.9	48.0	53.0	54.2	53.9	58.1	53.0
South Dakota	63.9	66.5	63.6	64.9	65.7	67.0	65.3
Tennessee	59.9	57.7	60.7	59.9	59.9	68.2	61.1
Texas	45.2	41.1	49.9	49.2	52.0	54.3	48.6
Utah	64.2	64.5	65.8	63.3	64.2	67.7	65.0
Vermont	60.6	59.6	61.5	60.3	62.3	62.5	61.1
Virginia	67.9	64.0	68.7	67.1	71.1	66.9	67.6
Washington	66.6	59.4	60.7	63.1	60.7	63.7	62.4
West Virginia	**35.6**	**30.9**	**31.9**	**33.2**	**37.3**	**38.0**	**34.5**
Wisconsin	62.1	62.7	64.4	62.5	62.6	67.5	63.6
Wyoming	60.7	58.0	63.8	64.7	64.2	64.7	62.7

Note: In this table, higher numbers indicate "better"-quality legal systems (i.e., a score of 100 is best, while 0 is worst).

Figure 4.5: State Liability System Rankings, 2002–07

State	State Ranking						2002–07 Average
	2002	2003	2004	2005	2006	2007	
Alabama	48	48	48	48	47	47	47.7
Alaska	37	32	33	33	36	43	35.7
Arizona	11	18	14	19	13	15	15.0
Arkansas	44	45	42	43	41	41	42.7
California	45	44	46	45	44	45	44.8
Colorado	7	12	13	13	8	21	12.3
Connecticut	10	17	18	18	5	14	13.7
Delaware	1	1	1	1	1	1	1.0
Florida	33	40	38	42	38	36	37.8
Georgia	23	39	29	28	27	31	29.5
Hawaii	40	43	39	41	46	42	41.8
Idaho	14	13	5	10	18	30	15.0
Illinois	34	38	44	46	45	46	42.2
Indiana	12	5	11	6	11	8	8.8
Iowa	5	3	4	5	4	4	4.2
Kansas	4	15	9	16	15	13	12.0
Kentucky	38	35	35	36	34	33	35.2
Louisiana	47	47	47	47	49	48	47.5
Maine	18	16	12	11	9	5	11.8
Maryland	22	23	21	23	20	29	23.0
Massachusetts	36	22	28	31	32	18	27.8
Michigan	28	29	23	24	22	23	24.8
Minnesota	19	9	8	7	14	2	9.8
Mississippi	50	50	50	50	48	49	49.5
Missouri	29	33	41	40	35	34	35.3
Montana	43	28	43	37	39	40	38.3
Nebraska	6	2	2	2	2	3	2.8
Nevada	30	34	34	29	37	28	32.0
New Hampshire	17	10	7	12	6	6	9.7
New Jersey	32	30	26	30	25	26	28.2
New Mexico	39	41	37	38	40	39	39.0
New York	27	27	22	27	21	19	23.8
North Carolina	16	20	19	20	10	16	16.8
North Dakota	25	6	16	3	12	20	13.7
Ohio	26	24	32	26	19	24	25.2
Oklahoma	41	36	31	32	33	38	35.2
Oregon	13	14	27	25	30	17	21.0
Pennsylvania	31	31	30	34	31	32	31.5
Rhode Island	35	37	36	35	26	35	34.0
South Carolina	42	42	40	39	42	37	40.3
South Dakota	9	4	17	8	7	11	9.3
Tennessee	24	26	25	22	29	7	22.2
Texas	46	46	45	44	43	44	44.7
Utah	8	7	6	14	17	9	10.2
Vermont	21	19	20	21	24	27	22.0
Virginia	2	8	3	4	3	12	5.3
Washington	3	21	24	15	28	25	19.3
West Virginia	**49**	**49**	**49**	**49**	**50**	**50**	**49.3**
Wisconsin	15	11	10	17	23	10	14.3
Wyoming	20	25	15	9	16	22	17.8

Note: In this table, lower numbers indicate "higher" ranks, or "better"-quality legal systems (i.e., being ranked 1st is best, while 50th is worst).

The main question of interest is whether there is a clear correlation between these scores (or rankings) and the method of judicial selection used by states. Using the groups described above, we calculated the average index scores and average rankings by judicial selection method. Throughout our analysis we will examine both the index scores and the associated ranking numbers. There are advantages to each. The index scores tend to provide more information because the rankings do not accurately reflect the magnitude of the differences in the underlying data. On the other hand, because the underlying questions in the survey have changed over time, the index numbers may not be directly comparable across years, whereas the rankings would be.[57] Fortunately, both measures lead to the same conclusions, so we find no reason to belabor the advantages and disadvantages of each.

Figure 4.6: Average State Legal System Quality Score by Method of Judicial Selection

Method of Judicial Selection	2002	2003	2004	2005	2006	2007	2002–07 Full Panel
Nonpartisan elections	56	55.1	56.9	57.8	58.9	61.8	61.2
Partisan elections	**50.4**	**47.3**	**48.7**	**47.8**	**51.3**	**54.2**	**53.4**
Elected by legislature	59.4	56	60.9	60.7	62.5	62.5	63.8
Gubernatorial appointment from nominating commission	60.8	60.2	61.8	61.1	63	64.4	65.3
Gubernatorial appointment from nominating commission with legislative confirmation	61.7	59.5	62.1	60.9	63	64.3	65.3
Gubernatorial appointment with legislative confirmation	58.2	58.5	62.2	61	63.5	66.2	65
Gubernatorial appointment with council approval	54.8	56	56	55.8	58.3	62.5	60.7

Notes: In this table, higher numbers indicate "better" legal systems (i.e., in the underlying data, a score of 100 is best, while 0 is worst). Full-panel averages use regression methodology to adjust for the differing mean values of the index across years.

In order to facilitate testing whether there are *statistically* significant differences among the groups, we obtain our averages and statistical confidence intervals by estimating an ordinary least squares regression, in which the index score (or rank) is used as the dependent variable and a set of indicator (0/1) variables are used for each different method of

---

[57] We use three techniques to ensure that variations in the questions do not affect our conclusions: (1) the use of the rankings rather than the index scores; (2) the use of year indicator variables in the subsequent regression analysis, to control for differences in the mean value of the index through time; and, (3) performing the analysis for each year individually, to ensure the results are robust across years.

judicial selection.[58] We perform this analysis for each year's data individually, and also for the pooled cross-section of data for the full 2002–07 period.[59] The analysis of annual data simply asks whether there are differences across states in each particular year's index score or rank, while the full period analysis asks whether these differences are consistently present during the entire period of data, from 2002 through 2007. The results of our analysis are presented in Figures 4.6 and 4.7.

To get a handle on what these numbers mean, let's look at one example from the figures in detail. Examining the first row of data in Figure 4.6 shows that states using nonpartisan elections to elect supreme court justices had an average score of 56.0 in the index in 2002, an average score of 55.1 in 2003, and so forth, on the 0- to 100-point index scale.[60] The first row of Figure 4.7 shows that during 2002, states using nonpartisan elections had an average ranking in the index of 26.4 (interpreted as an average rank of 26th out of the 50 states), and average ranking of 25.4 in 2003, and so forth.

Figure 4.7: Average State Legal System Ranking by Method of Judicial Selection

Method of Judicial Selection	2002	2003	2004	2005	2006	2007	2002–07 Full Panel
Nonpartisan elections	56	55.1	56.9	57.8	58.9	61.8	61.2
Partisan elections	**50.4**	**47.3**	**48.7**	**47.8**	**51.3**	**54.2**	**53.4**
Elected by legislature	59.4	56	60.9	60.7	62.5	62.5	63.8
Gubernatorial appointment from nominating commission	60.8	60.2	61.8	61.1	63	64.4	65.3
Gubernatorial appointment from nominating commission with legislative confirmation	61.7	59.5	62.1	60.9	63	64.3	65.3
Gubernatorial appointment with legislative confirmation	58.2	58.5	62.2	61	63.5	66.2	65
Gubernatorial appointment with council approval	54.8	56	56	55.8	58.3	62.5	60.7

Notes: In this table, higher numbers indicate "better" legal systems (i.e., in the underlying data, a score of 100 is best, while 0 is worst). Full-panel averages use regression methodology to adjust for the differing mean values of the index across years.

---

[58] The constant was omitted so that all groups could be included. In this manner, each coefficient estimate corresponds to the group mean. For the 2007 cross-sectional regression, only the indicator variables for the method of judicial selection were included. For the full panel regression of 2002 through 2007 data, the regression also includes indicator variables for each year (with 2007 omitted) to control for the differing mean values in the index across years (this also controls for any variation in the survey questions between years).

[59] Only one state, North Carolina, changed its grouping during the 2002–07 period (from partisan to nonpartisan elections in 2004), and this is appropriately coded in the data.

[60] Changes in the composition of the survey make it difficult to say why average state legal quality seems to be rising over time. Most of the increase seemed to occur in 2006, when two new elements were added to the survey, about having and enforcing meaningful venue requirements and non-economic damages.

Perhaps the most illuminating set of columns in the figures are the final two, showing the averages for the 2002–07 full panel of data. For states using nonpartisan elections, the average index score over the entire sample was 61.2, which resulted in an average ranking of 26.2 during the entire period. Using this information, it is now fairly easy to compare nonpartisan selection to the alternatives. For example, comparing the first two rows for nonpartisan and partisan elections respectively shows that for each and every year individually, as well as in the full panel, states using nonpartisan elections had higher index scores, and thus also better average rankings. (Recall that higher index scores — e.g., one closer to 100 — are better; while a lower numerical rank — e.g., being ranked 1st — is better. So the scales in Figures 4.6 and 4.7 move in opposite directions.)

For the full panel, states using partisan elections had an index score of 53.4, which is 7.8 points lower than the average index score of 61.2 for states using nonpartisan elections. The average rankings show that the average state using partisan elections ranked 38th in the index over the period, 12 spots below the 26th average ranking for states using nonpartisan elections. Therefore, based on these numbers it appears that using nonpartisan elections to select judges results in a better-quality legal system than using partisan elections.

While it is possible to strictly compare the numbers in the figures, an appropriate comparison asks whether the differences between the numbers are large enough to be considered *statistically* significant. Statistical testing takes into account not only the size of the difference in the averages, but also the number and variance among states within each group in the underlying data, to indeed ensure that at least the vast majority of states using one method all score higher (or lower) than the vast majority of states using another method. Based on conventional techniques and significance levels, our statistical tests show that in terms of average rankings a statistically significant difference does exist in the above example between these two groups (nonpartisan and partisan elections) for each and every year's data, both individually and for the entire panel. For the index scores, the difference is significant for the full panel — and for all years individually except 2002, where the difference in the average index scores is not statistically significant, although only slightly so. Therefore, it is possible to conclude *statistically* that states using nonpartisan elections do tend to score and rank better in this index of legal system quality than do states using partisan elections like West Virginia.

With one fully explained example behind us, we now consider the results in Figures 4.6 and 4.7 more comprehensively. In Figure 4.6, for the full panel of data, two methods of judicial selection tie for having the highest average index scores: gubernatorial appointment from a nominating commission and gubernatorial appointment from a nominating commission with legislative confirmation. Coming in only slightly below these top two is gubernatorial appointment with legislative confirmation but without a nominating commission. In the individual year analyses, the method receiving the highest average score varies across the years, although it is always one of these three types (although gubernatorial appointment with legislative confirmation takes the top spot in three of the six individual years). Partisan elections handily receive the worst scores both in the full panel and in every individual year.

Figure 4.8: Summary of Statistical Differences among Methods of Judicial Selection

Method of Judicial Selection	Scores and Ranks Statistically Better Than	Scores and Ranks Statistically Worse Than	Scores and Ranks Statistically The Same As
Nonpartisan elections	Partisan elections	Gubernatorial appointment from nominating commission and gubernatorial appointment from nominating commission with legislative confirmation	Elected by legislature, gubernatorial appointment with legislative confirmation, and gubernatorial appointment with council approval
Partisan elections	**None**	**Nonpartisan elections, elected by legislature, gubernatorial appointment from nominating commission, gubernatorial appointment from nominating commission with legislative confirmation, gubernatorial appointment with legislative confirmation, and gubernatorial appointment with council approval**	**None**
Elected by legislature	Partisan elections	None	Nonpartisan elections, gubernatorial appointment from nominating commission, gubernatorial appointment from nominating commission with legislative confirmation, gubernatorial appointment with legislative confirmation, and gubernatorial appointment with council approval
Gubernatorial appointment from nominating commission	Nonpartisan elections, partisan elections, and gubernatorial appointment with council approval	None	Elected by legislature, gubernatorial appointment from nominating commission with legislative confirmation, and gubernatorial appointment with legislative confirmation
Gubernatorial appointment from nominating commission with legislative confirmation	Nonpartisan elections, partisan elections, and gubernatorial appointment with council approval	None	Elected by legislature, gubernatorial appointment from nominating commission, and gubernatorial appointment with legislative confirmation
Gubernatorial appointment with legislative confirmation	Partisan elections	None	Nonpartisan elections, elected by legislature, gubernatorial appointment from nominating commission, gubernatorial appointment from nominating commission with legislative confirmation, and gubernatorial appointment with council approval
Gubernatorial appointment with council approval	Partisan elections	Gubernatorial appointment from nominating commission and gubernatorial appointment from nominating commission with legislative confirmation	Nonpartisan elections, elected by legislature, and gubernatorial appointment with legislative confirmation

An analysis of the average rankings in Figure 4.7 produces results similar to those using the underlying index scores, as would be expected. For the full panel, gubernatorial appointment from a nominating commission averages the best ranking, with gubernatorial appointment with legislative confirmation and gubernatorial appointment from nominating commission with legislative confirmation following closely behind. At the bottom of the list are partisan elections (which consistently score and rank as the worst by a wide margin), gubernatorial appointment with council approval, and nonpartisan elections.

Again, it is important to ask which of these differences, if any, are statistically significant. For each method of judicial selection, Figure 4.8 summarizes which other methods were found to have averages and rankings that were statistically different (or the same) based on our tests using the results from the full panel. All of these results were the same for both the index scores and the rankings.

Our primary interest here is in which other systems are either better or worse than (or statistically the same as) West Virginia's current system of partisan elections. When examining the full panel, we see that states using partisan elections, on average, *do statistically score and rank lower than states using all other methods of judicial selection.* Based on this analysis, West Virginia seems to have little to lose by moving away from partisan judicial elections to another method of judicial selection. That is, all other methods of selecting judges score and rank statistically better than partisan elections, suggesting that West Virginia would at least be no worse off if it wanted to experiment with selecting judges by either: (a) nonpartisan elections; (b) election by the legislature; (c) gubernatorial appointment from a nominating commission; (d) gubernatorial appointment from a nominating commission, with legislative confirmation (i.e., adding legislative confirmation to the existing process); (e) gubernatorial appointment with legislative confirmation (i.e., no nominating commission but with legislative confirmation); or, (f) gubernatorial appointment with council approval.

Two important caveats must be noted in interpreting our empirical results. First, conducting such a meta-analysis across state judicial selection methods required us to place states into groups, which may mask the impact of smaller differences within each group — for example, differences in the sizes and compositions of state nominating commissions or the type of legislative confirmation required.[61] Second, to conduct an empirical analysis requires the use of a numerical measure of state legal system quality, and we are severely limited by the uniqueness in this regard of the *State Liability Systems Ranking Study.* To the extent that this measure does not reflect the true quality of state legal systems, our analysis may suffer from bias.

CONCLUSION

Judicial selection mechanisms matter for legal system quality. Our research points toward partisan elections—the method used in West Virginia—as being inferior to all other methods of judicial selection. This probably explains why so many states—including North Carolina—

---

[61] We did attempt to see whether requiring appointed judges to run in retention elections mattered. Of the 26 states using some form of gubernatorial appointment, 16 have some form of public retention elections. The results showed that retention elections are associated with a slight reduction in the average quality of the legal system index scores, but in no case was the difference statistically significant.

have moved away from them. In fact, West Virginia is one of only a handful of states who have not yet done away with partisan elections. It is clear that viable alternatives exist, and they all involve insulating the judicial selection process from partisan politics. This can be done by moving to non-partisan elections, or by moving towards some form of appointive system.

REFERENCES

Adam Smith Foundation. 2007. The Missouri Non-Partisan Court Plan: Assessing the Summer 2007 Appellate Judicial Commission Process for Judicial Appointment to the Supreme Court of Missouri. Undated mimeo.

Ali, Abdiweli M. 2003. Institutional Differences as Sources of Growth Differences. *Atlantic Economic* Journal 31: 348-362.

Alozie, Nicholas. 1990. Distribution of Women and Minority Judges: The Effect of Judicial Selection Methods. *Social Science Quarterly* 71(2): 315-326.

American Judicature Society, 2008a. Methods of Judicial Selection. Online here: tinyurl.com/5yep6d

American Judicature Society. Judicial Selection in the States: West Virginia. 2008b. http://www.judicialselection.us/judicial_selection/index.cfm?state=WV

American Tort Reform Foundation. 2008. *Judicial Hellholes: 2007*. Washington: American Tort Reform Foundation.

Anderson, Gary M., William F. Shughart, and Robert D. Tollison. 1989. On The Incentives of Judges to Enforce Legislative Wealth Transfers. *Journal of Law and Economics* 32(1): 215-228.

Baum, Lawrence. 1995. Electing Judges. 1995. In *Contemplating Courts*, ed. Lee Epstein. Washington: CQ Press. 18-42.

Berkowitz, Daniel, and Karen Clay. 2004. Initial Conditions, Institutional Dynamics and Economic Performance: Evidence from the American States. *American Law and Economics Association 14th Annual Meeting*, Working Paper 67.

Berkowitz, Daniel, Chris Bonneau, and Karen Clay. 2006. *Judicial Independence and Minority Interests*, University of Pittsburgh, Department of Economics, Working Papers.

Besley, Timothy, and Abigail Payne. 2003. *Judicial accountability and economic policy outcomes: evidence from employment discrimination charges*, Institute for Fiscal Studies, IFS Working Papers, 2003, W03/11.

Brace, Paul, and Melinda Gann Hall. 1993. Integrated Models of Judicial Dissent. *Journal of Politics* 55(4): 914-935.

Buchanan, James M. 1974. Good Economics — Bad Law. *Virginia Law Review* 60: 483-492.

Council of State Governments. Various years. *The Book of the States*, Lexington: Council of State Governments.

Dubois, Philip. 1986. Accountability, Independence, and the Selection of State Judges. *Southwestern Law Journal* 40: 31-52.

Eckhardt, William G., and John Hilton. 2007. *The Consequences of Judicial Selection: A Review of the Supreme Court of Missouri, 1992-2007*, Federalist Society White Paper, August.

Feld, Lars P., and Stefan Voigt. 2003. Economic Growth and Judicial Independence: Cross-Country Evidence Using a New Set of Indicators. *European Journal of Political Economy* 19: 497-527.

Geyh, Charles G. 2003. Why Judicial Elections Stink. *Ohio State Law Journal* 64: 43-79.

Gray, Cheryl W. 1997. Reforming Legal Systems in Developing and Transition Countries. *Finance & Development* 34(3): 14-16.

Hall, Kermit L. 1983. The Judiciary on Trial: State Constitutional Reform and the Rise of an Elected Judiciary, 1846-1860. *Historian* 45(3): 337-354.

Hall, Kermit L. 1989. *The Magic Mirror: Law in American History*. New York: Oxford University Press.

Hall, Melinda G. 1992. Electoral Politics and Strategic Voting in State Supreme Courts. *Journal of Politics* 54(2): 427-446.

Hall, Melinda G. 2001. State Supreme Courts in American Democracy: Probing the Myths of Judicial Reform. *American Political Science Review* 95(2): 315-330.

Hall, Joshua C., and Russell S. Sobel. 2008. Is the 'Missouri Plan' Good for Missouri? The Economics of Judicial Selection. St. Louis: Show Me Institute, Policy Study #15.

Hanssen, F. Andrew. 1999. The Effect of Judicial Institutions on Uncertainty and the Rate of Litigation: The Election versus Appointment of State Judges. *Journal of Legal Studies* 28: 205-232.

Hanssen, F. Andrew. 2000. The Political Economy of Judicial Selection: Theory and Evidence. *Kansas Journal of Law and Public Policy* 9: 413-424.

Hanssen, F. Andrew. 2002. On the Politics of Judicial Selection: Lawyers and State Campaigns for the Merit Plan. *Public Choice* 110(1-2): 79-97.

Hanssen, F. Andrew. 2004. Learning about Judicial Independence: Institutional Change in the State Courts. *Journal of Legal Studies* 33: 431-473.

Hamilton, Alexander, James Madison, and John Jay. [1788] 1996. *The Federalist*, New York: Barnes and Noble Books,

Hayek, Friedrich A. 1960. *The Constitution of Liberty*. Chicago, University of Chicago Press,.

Haynes, Evan. 1944. *The Selection and Tenure of Judges*. Newark: National Conferences on Judicial Councils.

Helland, Eric, and Alexander Tabarrok. 2002. The Effect of Electoral Institutions on Tort Awards. *American Law and Economics Review* 4(2): 341-70.

Institute for Legal Reform. Various Years. *State Liability Systems Ranking Study*, Washington: U.S. Chamber of Commerce.

La Porta, Rafael, Florencio Lopez-de-Silanes, Cristian Pop-Eleches, and Andrei Shleifer. 2004. Judicial Checks and Balances. *Journal of Political Economy* 112(2): 445-470.

Link, Bradley. 2004. Had Enough in Ohio? Time to Reform Ohio's Judicial Selection Process. *Cleveland State Law Review* 51: 123-152.

McLeod, Aman L. 2007. A Comparison of the Criminal Appellate Decision of Appointed State Supreme Courts: Insights, Questions, and Implications for Judicial Independence. *Fordham Urban Law Journal* 34: 343-362.

Neely, Richard. 1988. *The Product Liability Mess*, New York: Free Press.

Owsiany, David. 2001. School Funding Decision Usurps Lawmakers Role. *Cincinnati Business Courier*, Sept. 21.

Owsiany, David. 2001. The General Assembly v. The Supreme Court: Who Makes Public Policy in Ohio? *Toledo Law Review* 32: 549-561.

Priest, George, and Benjamin Klein. 1984. The Selection of Disputes for Litigation. *Journal of Legal Studies* 13: 1-55.

Romer, Thomas, and Howard Rosenthal. 1978. Political Resource Allocation, Controlled Agendas, and the Status Quo. *Public Choice* 33(4): 27-43.

Sobel, Russell S., and Joshua C. Hall. 2007a. The Effect of Judicial Selection Processes on Judicial Quality: The Role of Partisan Politics. *Cato Journal* 27(1): 69-82.

Sobel, Russell S., and Joshua C. Hall, 2007b. The Sources of Economic Growth. In *Unleashing Capitalism: Why Prosperity Stops at the West Virginia Border and How to Fix It*, ed., Russell S. Sobel. Morgantown: The Public Policy Foundation of West Virginia.

Stratmann, Thomas, and Jared Garner. 2004. Judicial Selection: Politics, Biases, and Constituency Demands. *Public Choice* 118(no. 3-4): 251-270.

Streb, Matthew J. 2007. The Study of Judicial Elections. In *Running for Judge: The Rising Political, Financial and Legal Stakes of Judicial Elections*, editor, Matthew J. Streb. New York: New York University Press, 1-14.

Tabarrok, Alexander, and Eric Helland. 1999. Court Politics: The Political Economy of Tort Awards. *Journal of Law and Economics* 42: 157-188.

Thornburg, Elizabeth G. 2008. Judicial Hellholes, Lawsuit Climates, and Bad Social Science: Lessons from West Virginia. *West Virginia Law Review* 110: 1097-1137.

CHAPTER 5

HOW TO CHOOSE JUDGES: WEST VIRGINIA'S DIFFICULT PROBLEM
by Aman McLeod

The Rule of Law

5

HOW TO CHOOSE JUDGES: WEST VIRGINIA'S DIFFICULT PROBLEM

Aman McLeod

INTRODUCTION

West Virginia has recently been rocked by revelations that the chief justice of its Supreme Court of Appeals, Elliott "Spike" Maynard, had been photographed vacationing with Don Blankenship, who is the Chairman and CEO of coal mining giant, Massey Energy Company.[1] The furor surrounding the revelation of their relationship ultimately lead Maynard to recuse himself from two cases involving Massey Energy.[2]

Concerns that campaign contributions and the rancor and partisanship of recent judicial campaigns[3] in West Virginia are compromising the real or perceived independence of the judiciary, have led the West Virginia legislature to consider how the judicial selection process could be changed so as to better protect judges' independence.[4] Between the 2000 and 2004 election cycles, the amount contributed to state supreme court candidates who were running in those years increased by 52 percent from $1,376,534 to $2,838,905.[5] Furthermore, the 2004 election was noted for the efforts of independent advocacy groups to influence the campaign, especially And for the Sake of the Kids, which successfully spent millions to defeat incumbent supreme court Justice Warren McGraw.[6]

---

[1] Paul Nydon, *Coal Operator Says Photos Show Maynard Should Not Hear Appeal*, CHARLESTON GAZETTE, Jan. 15 2008, at 1A.

[2] Tom Breen, *Legislators Debate Judicial Elections GOP, Business Lobby Say State Should Move to Nonpartisan Balloting*, CHARLESTON DAILY MAIL, Jan. 30 2008, at 9A.

[3] E.g., Editorial, *Let's Change Judicial Selection, West Virginians Certainly Deserve a Better Way of Shaping Courts*, CHARLESTON DAILY MAIL, Nov. 8 2004, at 4A; Scott Wartman, *Court Race Muddled by Attacks*, THE HERALD-DISPATCH, Nov. 1 2004, at 1A.

[4] Breen, *supra* note 2.

[5] National Institute on Money in State Politics, data *available at* http://www.followthemoney.org/index.phtml (last visited Sept. 19, 2008).

[6] Brad McElhinny, *McGraw sues over TV ads: Case targets spots that led to justice's defeat*, CHARLESTON DAILY MAIL, Dec. 2, 2004.

West Virginia is one of only ten states that use partisan elections to select its judges at the trial or appellate level,[7] and it is one of only eight state that use partisan elections to select supreme court justices.[8] West Virginia has used this method of judicial selection for both its trial and appellate courts since 1862,[9] and although it was one of many states that used partisan elections in the Nineteenth Century, it has stayed with partisan elections as many other states have abandoned partisan elections in favor of nonpartisan elections and appointment combined with retention elections.[10] The fact that West Virginia has stayed with partisan elections while other states have chosen different systems could be interpreted as a sign of its people's attachment to this system as a means of judicial selection.

As legislators consider how to change West Virginia's judicial selection system, discussion has focused on changing to nonpartisan elections and about adopting a system of public financing for judicial campaigns.[11] This chapter will evaluate these proposals, and consider alternatives for solving some of the problems that critics of West Virginia's current system of partisan judicial elections have pointed out.

NONPARTISAN ELECTIONS:
OUT OF THE FRYING PAN AND INTO THE FIRE

The West Virginia Constitution stipulates that the judges of both the appellate and circuit courts must be chosen in elections, but it gives the state legislature the power to decide by statute whether judicial elections are partisan or nonpartisan.[12] The relative ease of switching to a system of nonpartisan elections makes this option attractive, since switching to an appointive system would require a constitutional amendment. Furthermore, the proponents of nonpartisan elections argue that this system would promote judicial impartiality and prevent judges from considering the political implications of their decisions when they are considering a case.[13] As one state senator put it "Nobody appearing before a judge should have to worry about whether they're going to get fair justice because of their party registration. Justice should be blind."[14]

The central problem with this argument, however, is that in many circumstances, knowing judges' party affiliations can help to predict how they will decide a case, regardless of the system that is used to select the judges.[15] The current theory among social scientists is

---

[7] According to the American Judicature Society, the other nine states are Alabama, Illinois, Louisiana, Michigan, New York, Ohio, Pennsylvania, Tennessee, and Texas. AM. JUDICATURE SOC'Y, JUDICIAL SELECTION IN THE STATES: APPELLATE AND GENERAL JURISDICTION COURTS: "INITIAL SELECTION, RETENTION, AND TERM LENGTH" 4-10 (2008), available online at http://www.judicialselection.us/uploads/documents/Judicial_Selection Charts1196376173077.pdf.

[8] The other seven states to use partisan elections to select their supreme courts are Alabama, Illinois, Louisiana, Michigan, Ohio, Pennsylvania and Texas. *Ibid.*

[9] AM. JUDICATURE SOC'Y, METHODS OF JUDICIAL SELECTION: WEST VIRGINIA, http://www.judicialselection.us/judicial_selection/reform_efforts/formal_changes_since_inception.cfm?state=WV (last visited Sept. 20 2008).

[10] F. Andrew Hanssen, *Learning about Judicial Selection: Institutional Change in the State Courts*, 33 J. LEGAL STUD. 431, 442 (2004).

[11] Ben Fields, *Interest Growing in Court Reform*, THE HERALD-DISPATCH, Feb. 7 2008, at 1A.

[12] W. Va. Const. Art. VIII, §§ 2,5 (2008).

[13] Fields, *supra* note 11.

[14] *Id.*

[15] *See, e.g.,* PHILIP L. DUBOIS, FROM BALLOT TO BENCH: JUDICIAL ELECTIONS AND THE QUEST FOR ACCOUNTABILITY 231-41 (1980); CASS R. SUNSTEIN ET AL., ARE JUDGES POLITICAL? AN EMPIRICAL ANALYSIS OF THE FEDERAL JUDICIARY 1-45 (2006); Melinda Gann Hall & Paul Brace, *Toward an Integrated Model of Judicial Voting*

that political party affiliation reveals something about a judge's political ideology, and that a judge's political ideology shapes how that judge interprets a law when that law is open to several plausible interpretations.[16] It follows from this theory that partisan elections give citizens easy access to important information about a how a judicial candidate will decide cases if elected. Removing judicial candidates' party affiliations from the ballot and preventing the candidates from openly associating with political parties will make it much harder for voters to understand the policy implications of supporting a particular candidate. Research shows that in low profile elections like judicial elections, voters' primary source of information about the candidates comes from the ballot,[17] and that if information about partisan affiliations is removed from the ballot the odds that a voter will cast a vote in a judicial election are reduced.[18]

Research also suggests that removing party affiliations from the ballot and preventing judges from associating from political parties will also affect the competitiveness of judicial elections and the probability that an incumbent judge will be challenged. For example, a nationwide study of state supreme court elections between 1980 and 1995 found that 61 percent of all judges in partisan election states faced challengers when they came up for reelection, whereas only 44 percent of judges in nonpartisan election states faced challengers,[19] and that supreme court races tended to be closer and incumbents had a higher probability of losing in partisan elections versus nonpartisan elections.[20] This evidence suggests that by listing party affiliation on the ballot and by allowing parties to be formally involved in election campaigns, states help voters hold judges accountable for their decisions, since the likelihood of electoral competition encourages judges to consider their constituent's desires when deciding cases, and the greater likelihood of an incumbent being challenged means that voters are more likely to have a choice in elections.

Note, too, that switching to nonpartisan elections might actually increase the need to raise money, since, on average, candidates tend to raise more in nonpartisan state supreme court races than in partisan races, all other factors being equal.[21] This might be because the candidates feel they the need to raise more money to get their messages out to voters, since the candidates cannot as easily relay on party affiliations to inform and mobilize voters.[22]

One final argument against nonpartisan elections is that the state actually has very little power to remove the influence of political parties or partisan politics from judicial elections. Of course, the state can remove partisan affiliations from the ballot, but the Constitution places serious restrictions on states' ability to limit the political speech of

Behavior, 20 AM. POL. Q. 147, 158-65 (1992); Stuart S. Nagel, *Political Party Affiliation and Judges' Decisions*, 55 AM. POL. SCI. REV. 843, 845-46 (1961); Donald R. Songer & Sue Davis, *The Impact of Party and Region on Voting Decisions in the United States Courts of Appeals*, 43 W. POL. Q. 317, 323-30 (1990); S. Sidney Ulmer, *The Political Party Variable in the Michigan Supreme Court*, 11 J. PUB. L. 352, 360-62 (1962).

[16] See Sunstein et al., *supra* note 15.

[17] Lawrence Baum, *Judicial Elections and Judicial Independence: A Voter's Perspective*, 64 OHIO ST. L.J. 13, 18-19 (2003).

[18] *Id.* at 19-20.

[19] Melinda Gann Hall, *State Supreme Courts in American Democracy: Probing the Myths of Judicial Reform*, 95 AM. POL. SCI. REV. 315, 317 (2001).

[20] Id. at 318-29.

[21] Chris Bonneau, *Campaign Fundraising in State Supreme Court Elections*, 88 SOC. SCI. Q.68, 80 (2007).

[22] *Id.*

candidates in judicial election campaigns,[23] which means that states probably cannot prohibit candidates from openly associating themselves with political parties or announcing where they stand on hotly disputed political issues like abortion. Accordingly, it is hard to keep parties or politics out of judicial elections, even in states that have nonpartisan elections.[24]

In light of the foregoing, it seems unlikely that switching to nonpartisan elections will help to prevent either the perception or the reality of politics exercising influence in the judiciary.

THE INFLUENCE OF CAMPAIGN CONTRIBUTORS

However, those who support changing West Virginia's current system for choosing judges also point to campaign contributions as a justification for changing the way that judges are selected. A national survey has shown that the public believes that contributors to judicial campaigns can buy influence,[25] and empirical evidence exists showing that campaign contributions might affect judicial decision-making.[26]

While the Constitution prohibits states from placing mandatory limits on how much a candidate can spend in an election,[27] a number of states have instituted systems of public financing for elections for various offices that are designed to limit the influence of contributors by making public funds available to qualifying candidates to fund their campaigns.[28] All of these systems are intended to entice candidates to voluntarily limit how much they raise for their campaigns with the promise of public money, however, candidates remain free to reject the public funds in order to maintain the freedom to raise and spend as much as they like. Each of these systems works in essentially the same way. Candidates must raise a certain qualifying amount in small donations from a minimum number of registered voters.[29] Once the candidates have reached the qualifying number of contributors and amount of contributions, most systems force the candidates to rely entirely on public funds, although

---

[23] *See, e.g., Republican Party of Minn. v. White*, 536 U.S. 765, at 788 (2002); *Republican Party of Minn. v. White*, 416 F.3d 738, at 756, 763-66 (8th Cir.2005).

[24] *See, e.g.*, Lewis Kamb, *Justices' Election Dilemma: Can They Be Fair? P-I Review Finds Many Potential Conflicts of Interest on High Court*, SEATTLE POST-INTELLIGENCER, Mar. 14, 2005, at A1; Conrad deFiebre, *Republican State Convention -NOTEBOOK- GOP Delegates Want Voter OK on Stadium Tax*, STAR TRIBUNE, Jun. 3, 2006, at 8A; Steven Walters, *Roggensack Elected to High Court-Silence on Issues Called Key*, MILWAUKEE JOURNAL SENTINEL, Apr. 2, 2003, at B1.

[25] JUSTICE AT STAKE CAMPAIGN, FREQUENCY QUESTIONNAIRE, OCTOBER 30 – NOVEMBER 7, 2001, 6 (2001), http://www.justiceatstake.org/files/JASNationalSurveyResults.pdf.

[26] Damon M. Cann, *Justice for Sale? Campaign Contributions and Judicial Decisionmaking*, 7 ST. POL. & POL'Y Q. 281, 288-90 (2007); Madhavi McCall, *The Politics of Judicial Elections: The Influence of Campaign Contributions on the Voting Patterns of Texas Supreme Court Justices, 1994-1997*, 31 POL. & POL'Y 314, 326-31 (2003); Eric Waltenburg & Charles Lopeman, *Tort Decisions and Campaign Dollars*, 28 SE. POL. REV. 241, 250-58 (2000); Aman McLeod, Bidding for Justice: A Case Study about the Effect of Campaign Contributions on Judicial Decision-Making," 85 U. DET. MERCY L. REV. 385, 398-400 (2008).

[27] *See, e.g., Buckley v. Valeo*, 424 U.S. 1, 12-23 (1976).

[28] The following states have currently or in the past enacted systems of public financing: California, Hawaii, Idaho, Iowa, Kentucky, Maine, Maryland, Massachusetts, Michigan, Minnesota, Montana, New Jersey, North Carolina, Oklahoma, Oregon, Rhode Island, Utah, and Wisconsin. Jason B. Frasco, Note, *Full Public Funding: An Effective and Legally Viable Model for Campaign Finance Reform in the States*, 92 CORNELL L. REV. 733, n.19 (2007).

[29] *Id.* at 743-87.

some allow candidates to continue to raise and spend private funds subject to certain limits.[30] These public finance programs are funded through a variety of methods, including state appropriations, attorney bar fees, and voluntary income tax allocations.[31]

The record of these campaign finance schemes is uneven. Some appear to have attracted a significant number of candidates, and reduced their reliance on campaign contributions,[32] while others have been less successful.[33] One lesson that can be drawn from these states' experiences with public financing of campaigns is that the amount of funding available to qualifying candidates is a critical factor in the success of these programs.[34] Unless candidates feel that the state will provide adequate funding to win an election, they are not likely to accept the contribution and spending limits tied to the receipt of such funds. For example, the availability of funds has been credited with the relative success of public campaign financing in Arizona, Maine, and North Carolina,[35] and with its failure in Wisconsin.[36] The use of multiple funding sources appears to be an effective way to create a reasonably sufficient and stable pool of funds to finance campaigns.[37]

While public financing might solve some of the problems associated with campaign contributions, its effectiveness in removing the real and perceived influence of contributors would ultimately depend on how many candidates used it, and on how much money it required candidates to raise in order to qualify for the funding, with relatively low qualifying amounts based on many small contributions being preferable.[38] That said, any attempt to pass a public financing bill would have to overcome arguments that there are far better uses for scarce government funds than political campaigns.[39]

CONCLUSION

This chapter has discussed several of the alternatives that the legislature and others are considering that are aimed at remedying problems associated with West Virginia's use of partisan elections to choose its judges. Although switching to nonpartisan elections is an unattractive option for many reasons, adopting a system of public financing for judicial elections might be effective in reducing any unfair influence that contributors to judicial campaigns might gain if enough money were made available to qualifying candidates. One option that would solve problems associated with partisan elections and campaign contributions would be to switch to an appointive system, in which judges would be appointed by the governor with or without the recommendation of a selection commission,

---

[30] *See id.* at 783-86; Aman McLeod, *If At First You Don't Succeed: A Critical Evaluation of Judicial Selection Reform Efforts*, 107 W. VA L. REV. 499, 517-19 (2005).

[31] *See* Frasco, *supra* note 28, at 743-87.

[32] *Id.* at 747-48, 757-59, 771-72.

[33] *Id.* at 785-87; McLeod, *supra* note 30 at 518-19.

[34] Frasco, *supra* note 28, at 789-90.

[35] *Id.* at 789.

[36] McLeod, *supra* note 30 at 518-19.

[37] Frasco, *supra* note 28, at 790.

[38] Another reason to ensure an adequate level of public funding for campaigns is that spending in judicial campaigns appears to be linked to the level of information that voters have about candidates. *See* Baum, *supra* note 17, at 26.

[39] *See, e.g.,* Editorial, *No on Question 3*, BANGOR DAILY NEWS, Oct. 29, 1996; Editorial, *Supporters of Public Financing Hope As Maine Goes, So Goes N.C.*, WINSTON-SALEM JOURNAL, Apr. 21, 2001; George D. Brown and Thomas R. Kiley, *Vote No on Public Funding*, BOSTON GLOBE, Nov. 2, 2002, at A15.

subject to legislative confirmation. Judges could be further insulated from political influence by giving them life tenure or by mandating that they could not serve more than a single term on the bench.[40] These options, however, would require a constitutional amendment, and would certainly be very difficult to achieve, given that no state has completely eliminated judicial elections since the mid-Nineteenth Century.[41]

Going forward, West Virginia legislators must consider what levels of impartiality and public accountability they wish to build into the state's judiciary. Partisan elections have tilted the West Virginia judiciary in favor of accountability, because they leave judges open to influence from public opinion, contributors and party leaders. Adoption for a system of partial public financing for judicial campaigns or of an appointive system of judicial selection would decrease the level of accountability in the judiciary, and enhance the possibility that judges will impartially decide the cases before them. What seems certain is that for any change to occur and be workable, it must be supported by bipartisan political consensus and broad public support which, given the nature of the issues involved, will not be easy to achieve.

---

[40] A system where judges would serve a single, lengthy, non-renewable term as been suggested by the American Bar Association's Commission on the Twenty-First Century Judiciary. See AMERICAN BAR ASSOCIATION, JUSTICE IN JEOPARDY: REPORT OF THE COMMISSION ON THE 21ST CENTURY JUDICIARY 67-73 (2003), available at https://www.abanet.org/judind/jeopardy/pdf/report.pdf (last visited Sep. 28, 2008).
[41] McLeod, *supra* note 30 at 518-19.

REFERENCES

AMERICAN BAR ASSOCIATION, JUSTICE IN JEOPARDY: REPORT OF THE COMMISSION ON THE 21ST CENTURY JUDICIARY 67-73 (2003), available at https://www.abanet.org/judind/jeopardy/pdf/report.pdf (last visited Sep. 28, 2008).

AM. JUDICATURE SOC'Y, JUDICIAL SELECTION IN THE STATES: APPELLATE AND GENERAL JURISDICTION COURTS: "INITIAL SELECTION, RETENTION, AND TERM LENGTH" 4-10 (2008), *available at* http://www.judicialselection.us/uploads/documents/Judicial_Selection_Charts_1196376173077.pdf.

AM. JUDICATURE SOC'Y, METHODS OF JUDICIAL SELECTION: WEST VIRGINIA, http://www.judicialselection.us/judicial_selection/reform_efforts/formal_changes_since_inception.cfm?state=WV (last visited Sept. 20 2008).

Editorial, *No on Question 3*, BANGOR DAILY NEWS, Oct. 29, 1996

Lawrence Baum, *Judicial Elections and Judicial Independence: A Voter's Perspective*, 64 OHIO ST. L.J. 13, 18-19 (2003).

Tom Breen, *Legislators Debate Judicial Elections GOP, Business Lobby Say State Should Move to Nonpartisan Balloting*, CHARLESTON DAILY MAIL, Jan. 30 2008, at 9A.

George D. Brown and Thomas R. Kiley, *Vote No on Public Funding*, BOSTON GLOBE, Nov. 2, 2002, at A15.

Chris Bonneau, *Campaign Fundraising in State Supreme Court Elections*, 88 SOC. SCI. Q.68, 80 (2007).

Damon M. Cann, *Justice for Sale? Campaign Contributions and Judicial Decisionmaking*, 7 ST. POL. & POL'Y Q. 281, 288-90 (2007).

Conrad deFiebre, *Republican State Convention -NOTEBOOK- GOP Delegates Want Voter OK on Stadium Tax*, STAR TRIBUNE, Jun. 3, 2006, at 8A

PHILIP L. DUBOIS, FROM BALLOT TO BENCH: JUDICIAL ELECTIONS AND THE QUEST FOR ACCOUNTABILITY 231-41 (1980)

Editorial, *Let's Change Judicial Selection, West Virginians Certainly Deserve a Better Way of Shaping Courts*, CHARLESTON DAILY MAIL, Nov. 8 2004, at 4A.

Ben Fields, *Interest Growing in Court Reform*, THE HERALD-DISPATCH, Feb. 7 2008, at 1A.

Jason B. Frasco, Note, *Full Public Funding: An Effective and Legally Viable Model for Campaign Finance Reform in the States*, 92 CORNELL L. REV. 733, n.19 (2007).

Melinda Gann Hall, *State Supreme Courts in American Democracy: Probing the Myths of Judicial Reform*, 95 AM. POL. SCI. REV. 315, 317 (2001)

Melinda Gann Hall & Paul Brace, *Toward an Integrated Model of Judicial Voting Behavior*, 20 AM. POL. Q. 147, 158-65 (1992)

F. Andrew Hanssen, *Learning about Judicial Selection: Institutional Change in the State Courts*, 33 J. LEGAL STUD. 431, 442 (2004).

Lewis Kamb, *Justices' Election Dilemma: Can They Be Fair? P-I Review Finds Many Potential Conflicts of Interest on High Court*, SEATTLE POST-INTELLIGENCER, Mar. 14, 2005, at A1

Madhavi McCall, *The Politics of Judicial Elections: The Influence of Campaign Contributions on the Voting Patterns of Texas Supreme Court Justices, 1994-1997*, 31 POL. & POL'Y 314, 326-31 (2003).

Brad McElhinny, *McGraw sues over TV ads: Case targets spots that led to justice's defeat.* CHARLESTON DAILY MAIL, Dec. 2, 2004.

Aman McLeod, Bidding for Justice: A Case Study about the Effect of Campaign Contributions on Judicial Decision-Making," 85 U. DET. MERCY L. REV. 385, 398-400 (2008).

Aman McLeod, *If At First You Don't Succeed: A Critical Evaluation of Judicial Selection Reform Efforts*, 107 W. VA L. REV. 499, 517-19 (2005)

Stuart S. Nagel, *Political Party Affiliation and Judges' Decisions*, 55 AM. POL. SCI. REV. 843, 845-46 (1961)

National Institute on Money in State Politics, data *available at* http://www.follow themoney.org/index.phtml (last visited Sept. 19, 2008).

Paul Nydon, *Coal Operator Says Photos Show Maynard Should Not Hear Appeal*, CHARLESTON GAZETTE, Jan. 15 2008, at 1A.

Donald R. Songer & Sue Davis, *The Impact of Party and Region on Voting Decisions in the United States Courts of Appeals*, 43 W. POL. Q. 317, 323-30 (1990)

CASS R. SUNSTEIN ET AL., ARE JUDGES POLITICAL? AN EMPIRICAL ANALYSIS OF THE FEDERAL JUDICIARY 1-45 (2006).

S. Sidney Ulmer, *The Political Party Variable in the Michigan Supreme Court*, 11 J. PUB. L. 352, 360-62 (1962).

Eric Waltenburg & Charles Lopeman, *Tort Decisions and Campaign Dollars*, 28 SE. POL. REV. 241, 250-58 (2000).

Steven Walters, *Roggensack Elected to High Court-Silence on Issues Called Key*, MILWAUKEE JOURNAL SENTINEL, Apr. 2, 2003, at B1.

Scott Wartman, *Court Race Muddled by Attacks*, THE HERALD-DISPATCH, Nov. 1 2004, at 1A.

Editorial, *Supporters of Public Financing Hope As Maine Goes, So Goes N.C.*, WINSTON-SALEM JOURNAL, Apr. 21, 2001.

CASES CITED

Buckley v. Valeo, 424 U.S. 1 (1976).
Republican Party of Minn. v. White, 536 U.S. 765 (2002).
Republican Party of Minn. v. White, 416 F.3d 738 (2005).

CHAPTER 6

JUDICIAL ELECTIONS: FACTS VS. MYTHS
by Chris W. Bonneau

The Rule of Law

6

JUDICIAL ELECTIONS: FACTS VS MYTHS

Chris W. Bonneau

Judicial elections, a uniquely American institution, have come under intense scrutiny in recent years. There have been several calls for the eradication of these elections by both the media and legal academics alike. However, as I will argue below, many of these claims are made on the basis of unsubstantiated empirical claims about the nature of these elections. In this essay, I am going to discuss the current state of the literature of judicial elections, focusing on elections to the state supreme court. A more detailed exploration of this topic can be found in my (with Melinda Gann Hall) recent book, *In Defense of Judicial Elections*.

MYTHS AND FACTS

Myth #1: Incumbents are subject to the whims of voters and routinely lose their reelection campaigns.

Facts: While it is true that there are some cases of incumbents losing somewhat randomly, the fact is the incumbent reelection rate for state supreme court justices is quite high. From 1990-2004, 85.7 percent of justices were reelected compared to 90.0 percent of Senators, 94.9 percent of House members, and 81.7 percent of governors. Moreover, many of those justices that lost did so for predictable reasons (scandal, out-of-touch with the preferences of the electorate, etc.). Thus, state supreme court elections are much like elections to other offices in this regard. It is true that, occasionally, an incumbent is defeated for no apparent reason. But this is true for legislative and executive races as well. Judicial elections should not be singled out for scorn just because the results of them are occasionally idiosyncratic.

Myth #2: Voters do not participate in these elections, and, when they do, they do not know enough information to make meaningful choices.

Facts: In a series of articles in the *American Journal of Political Science* (2006, 2008), Melinda Gann Hall and I show that these claims are patently false. In terms of participation, voters participate when they are more informed (either because they are more educated or because of the amount of campaign spending) and when the election is competitive. This is not surprising news. In terms of knowledge, voters are able to distinguish between more and less qualified candidates. Thus, candidates with prior judicial experience perform better with voters than do candidates without such experience. Other things being equal, we find that a quality challenger can reduce the incumbent's percentage of the vote by over 4.5 percent. Why is this the case? We argue it is because voters view lower court judges as more qualified to serve on the state supreme court than they do attorneys with no judicial experience. Not only do voters participate when they have information, they also have enough information to make informed choices in the election.

Additionally, voters overwhelmingly support the election of judges. A 2002 survey of North Carolina voters showed that 77 percent of voters claimed they were interested in the last election and 81 percent of the voters felt that judges should be elected. A 2008 survey in Minnesota indicated that 73 percent of the respondents say they "sometimes" or "almost always" vote in judicial elections and a whopping 92 percent of voters agreed (or strongly agreed) that it is important for judges to be elected by the public. At the same time, majorities of voters also said they would like more information about the candidates in these elections. However, the numbers are clear: voters like electing judges. Moreover, these two states are not anomalies: in just about every state where judges are elected and voters are surveyed, the numbers are about the same.

Myth #3: Campaign spending in judicial elections is a bad thing.

Facts: I already mentioned above how campaign spending can affect voter participation—the more spending, the higher the levels of participation. Additionally, campaign spending can make the election more competitive. In a recent article (Bonneau 2007a), I found that while spending by the incumbent was not able to raise his or her percentage of the vote, campaign spending by the challenger was able to do so. Specifically, for every 1 percent increase in challenger spending, the incumbent's level of electoral support decreases by 1.8 percentage points. This is a significant figure. Simply spending money can make the race more competitive, likely by providing voters with more information on which to base their decision. Whether you look at voter participation or electoral competition, spending in state supreme court elections enhances democracy.

Myth #4: Judges' votes are "for sale" with contributors being able to buy judges' votes.

Facts: While several studies have found a correlation between campaign contributions and votes (Banner 1988; Ware 1999; McCall 2001, 2003; Cann 2002), evidence for contributions *causing* judges' to vote a certain way is scarce (but see Cann 2007). In a recent study, Damon Cann and I (2008) examined this relationship in 3 states and found some evidence of a link in Michigan but not in Nevada or Texas. The only conclusion one can make at this point is that there is certainly a relationship between contributions and votes, but there is no systematic empirical evidence to suggest judges are voting the way they do because one of the litigants was a contributor. This area is one where more research is definitely needed and is ongoing.

Myth #5: Elections erode the independence of judges and turn them into politicians.

Facts: Judges are political. They are political beings and make political decisions. The notion that judges decide cases solely on the law and facts of the case has been widely dismissed by scholars. Further, no amount of "independence" can change this. The U.S. Supreme Court has judges appointed for life. They are as structurally "independent" as a judge can be. However, every time there is a vacancy, there is a battle between the Democrats and the Republicans over who should be confirmed. Why? Because we know that Democratic judges interpret the law and the facts differently from Republican judges. If this were not true, then it would not matter who sits on the Court. The fact that politicians, the media, and the public are all concerned about seats on the U.S. Supreme Court is prima facie evidence that judging is not the neutral, impartial enterprise some would have us believe.

Elections allow the electorate to hold judges accountable for their decisions on the bench. And this is a good thing. Recently, the Chief Justice in West Virginia (Elliott Maynard) lost his bid for reelection after photographs surfaced of him vacationing with someone (Don Massey) while that person had a case pending before the court. West Virginians decided that they did not want someone on the court that they thought was not going to be fair and impartial. If West Virginia had an appointive system, there would have been no way to get rid of Justice Maynard. (Judges are rarely impeached and removed.) But, the presence of an election allowed the voters to hold him accountable for his behavior.

Let me give another example. The U.S. Supreme Court has upheld the use of capital punishment for certain types of cases. Take a state like Texas, which has decided to use the death penalty. If I am a judge in Texas who opposes capital punishment, what is to stop me from continually voting my personal preferences and overturning death sentences—regardless of the facts of the case—if the voters are not able to hold me accountable? Without accountability, I am free to *disregard* the law with impunity. Elections can help ensure that judges comply with the duly-enacted laws of the state.

A WORD ABOUT WEST VIRGINIA

State supreme court elections in West Virginia are interesting for a couple of institutional reasons. First, there are only 5 justices on the bench. No state has a smaller supreme court. Second, justices serve for 12-year terms of office. This is the longest of any elected state. Thus, each seat becomes extremely valuable since there are so few seats and the time between vacancies can be quite lengthy. This makes every election much more important and valuable than, say, if there were a 9-member court with 6-year terms of office. More than anything else, this institutional structure contributes to the high contestation rate in West Virginia and may lead to ever-increasing campaign spending in these races.

In a recent book chapter, I looked at average spending by state and spending per capita by state from 1990-2004 (Bonneau 2007b). Of the 22 courts that elect judges in partisan or nonpartisan races, West Virginia is the 8th most expensive overall and the 5th most expensive per capita. It is important to note that the aberationally high spending election of 2004 makes West Virginia seem to be a higher campaign spending state than one would think based on prior elections. Yet, I would argue this is not evidence of any kind of problem. Since campaign spending leads to more informed voters, the amount of campaign spending can be a positive characteristic of these elections. Voters in West Virginia might be *better off* because of the amount of spending in these elections.

CONCLUSION

In sum, contrary to the rhetoric of some, judicial elections are much like elections to other branches of government. Moreover, ending elections will not remove the "politics" from the judicial selection process; it will simply shift the politics from the voters to another group (governor, legislature, etc). Judging is political and the people involved in selecting judges know this. There is just no practical way to remove politics from the process. Thus, in an inherently political process, who should be trusted to select judges? Clearly, the public thinks it should be them. Additionally, the empirical evidence suggests that voters do a pretty good job at selecting judges. There is no evidence that you get a "better" bench by appointing judges rather than having them elected. In fact, Choi, Gulati, and Posner (2007) find that while "appointed judges write higher quality opinions than elected judges do, … elected judges write many more opinions, and the evidence suggests that the large quantity difference makes up for the small quality difference." That is, the evidence suggests that elected judges may in fact actually be *better* than appointed judges. If true, this would seem to argue not only that states with elections should keep them, but that more states should institute elections for judges.

REFERENCES

Banner, Stephen. 1988. Disqualifying Elected Judges from Cases Involving Campaign Contributors. *Stanford Law Review* 40: 449-490.

Bonneau, Chris W. 2007a. The Effects of Campaign Spending in State Supreme Court Elections. *Political Research Quarterly* 60: 489-499.

Bonneau, Chris W. 2007b. The Dynamics of Campaign Spending in State Supreme Court Elections. In *Running for Judge: The Rising Political, Financial, and Legal Stakes of Judicial Elections* ed. Matthew Streb. New York: New York University Press: 59-72.

Bonneau, Chris W., and Damon M. Cann. 2008. Campaign Contributions, Judicial Decisionmaking, and Institutional Context. Paper Presented at the Annual Meeting of the American Political Science Association, August 27-31.

Bonneau, Chris W. and Melinda Gann Hall. 2009. *In Defense of Judicial Elections*. New York: Routledge.

Cann, Damon M. 2002. Campaign Contributions and Judicial Behavior. *American Review of Politics* 23: 261-274.

Cann, Damon M. 2007. Justice for Sale? Campaign Contributions and Judicial Decisionmaking. *State Politics and Policy Quarterly* 7: 281-297.

Choi, Stephen J., G. Mitu Gulati, and Eric A. Posner. 2007. Professionals or Politicians: The Uncertain Empirical Case for an Elected Rather than Appointed Judiciary. University of Chicago Law School, unpublished manuscript.

Hall, Melinda Gann and Chris W. Bonneau. 2006. Does Quality Matter? Challengers in State Supreme Court Elections. *American Journal of Political Science* 50: 20-33.

Hall, Melinda Gann and Chris W. Bonneau. 2008. Mobilizing Interest: The Effects of Money on Citizen Participation in State Supreme Court Elections. *American Journal of Political Science* 52: 457-470.

McCall, Madhavi. 2001. Buying Justice in Texas: The Influence of Campaign Contributions on the Voting Behavior of Texas Supreme Court Justices. *American Review of Politics* 22: 349-373.

McCall, Madhavi. 2003. The Politics of Judicial Elections: The Influence of Campaign Contributions on the Voting Patterns of Texas Supreme Court Justices, 1994-1997. *Politics & Policy* 31: 314-343.

Ware, Stephen J. 1999. "Money, Politics, and Judicial Decisions: A Case Study of Arbitration Law in Alabama." *Journal of Law and Politics* 25(4): 645-686.

PART II:

OTHER PERSPECTIVES ON LEGAL REFORM

CHAPTER 7

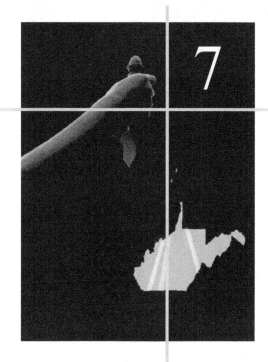

THE LAW AND ECONOMICS OF PROPERTY AND CONTRACT
by Edward J. López

The Rule of Law

7

THE LAW AND ECONOMICS OF PROPERTY AND CONTRACT

Edward J. López

A running theme in this book is that there are clear opportunities to enhance the judicial and legal systems in West Virginia to make them more conducive to economic growth and prosperity. This chapter points to some of these opportunities in the state's legal rules of property and contract. The upshot is that West Virginia can, and should, do a better job upholding the rule of law in these areas. Doing so will give consumers and businesses greater predictability and stronger incentives to make the everyday decisions that lead to economic growth and rising standards of living for all West Virginians.

The scholarly foundation for this chapter is the economics sub-discipline known as "law and economics." Nobel prize-winning economist, Ronald Coase, pioneered this field with the idea that legal rulings and regulations act like implicit prices on people's behavior. Friedrich Hayek, who won the Nobel Prize a generation earlier, also pioneered the economic analysis of the law. Hayek focused on the legal system as a set of rules that must be predictable and equally applicable to everyone in society, so that people have the opportunities to make future-oriented economic plans. The message of this chapter draws directly on the best theory and evidence available from the field of law and economics.

West Virginia ranks poorly in indices of the state's business climate and quality of the legal system, and its living standards suffer compared to other states as a result. By using the tools found in the field of law and economics, and drawing on the connection between economic growth and the rule of law, this chapter will explain how these troubling trends are related, and how West Virginia policymakers can remedy the problem by changing legal rules to improve the incentives, or implicit prices, generated by West Virginia's legal system.

THE RULE OF LAW

The rule of law is a broad concept that describes circumstances under which a society is governed not by *people*, but instead by established *rules* of interaction. Without stable rules that apply equally and predictably to all people, it is too easy for people in government to exercise their powers in arbitrary and capricious ways. The American Revolutionaries, for example, threw off the government of George III "[f]or abolishing the free system of English laws" and "establishing therein an arbitrary government."[1] In its place, the American Framers set up a government based on the rule of law.

The "law," in this context, is that body of rules and procedures that apply impartially and predictably to all people in society including (and perhaps *especially*) to government officials. When the decisions of government officials are held subject to predetermined rules, citizens in the society have a greater degree of certainty in their rights and freedoms. As Thomas Paine wrote in 1776, "[f]or as in absolute governments the King is law, so in free countries, the law ought to be King, and there ought to be no other."[2]

In countries where the "law is king," people are generally free from arbitrary and capricious acts by government officials. This makes people more able to predictably save, invest and make other sorts of long-term economic decisions that promote sustained economic growth and rising prosperity. In short, under the rule of law, government is a *protector* of rights, and that leads to a more industrious and prosperous society.

In economics, the rule of law supports capitalism first and foremost by protecting private property and enforcing contracts. When these economic institutions prevail, people's rights are more secure and predictable so it is easier for people to make economic plans that build for the future. In addition to saving and investment, other key decisions supported by property and contract include research and development, improvements to property, going to college and graduate school, forming partnerships and long-term supplier contracts, and borrowing and lending in capital markets. These innumerable every-day decisions add up to good outcomes: efficient use of resources, rising living standards, growing tax bases, and generally increasing prosperity.

However, without the rule of law economic stagnation will prevail because people lack certainty that they will retain the fruits of their labor. There is constant fear of expropriation by government officials or other private individuals through lawsuits and theft. Richard Posner, a federal judge and leading scholar of the law and economics field, writes in his classic treatise on law and economics, "the absence of legally enforceable rights would bias investment toward economic activities that could be completed in a short time; and this would reduce efficiency" (Posner 1992, p.90). The rule of law makes economic life more predictable and helps to avoid these unhappy effects.

In short, the field of law and economics helps explain how property, contract and sound legal rules support economic success. This chapter will discuss the mechanisms by which the rule of law supports the market institutions of property and contract, which in turn is why the rule of law is necessary to economic success. In fact, the available evidence points to one conclusion: without the rule of law, societies fare much worse on a number of economic indicators.

---

[1] The Declaration of Independence.
[2] Thomas Paine, The Writings of Thomas Paine, Collected and Edited by Moncure Daniel Conway (New York: G.P. Putnam's Sons, 1894). Vol. 1. Accessed from http://oll.libertyfund.org/title/343 on 2008-10-28.

MEASURING THE RULE OF LAW

What are the basic legal principles that embody the rule of law, and are these principles amenable to empirical measurement? The American Bar Association breaks down the rule of law into four attributes.

> 1. The government and its officials and agents are accountable under the law.
> 2. The laws are clear, publicized, stable and fair, and protect fundamental rights, including the security of persons and property.
> 3. The process by which the laws are enacted, administered and enforced is accessible, fair and efficient.
> 4. The laws are upheld, and access to justice is provided, by competent, independent, and ethical law enforcement officials, attorneys or representatives, and judges who are of sufficient number, have adequate resources, and reflect the makeup of the communities they serve.
> World Justice Project[3]

Several strands of research in empirical law and economics have developed methods to measure the legal principles that embody the rule of law. Most of this work focuses on the predictability of future-oriented economic decisions—for example, how secure business investment is from political manipulation. Researchers gather statistical and survey data on a broad range of factors that affect the political risks surrounding a number of economic activities. With these data in hand, researchers are able to calculate indexes to compare how well countries uphold the rule of law.

Figure 7.1 shows the top 15 and bottom 15 countries on the 2008 *Global Competitiveness Report* (*GCR*), one of the leading international rule of law indices. Some countries—like the United States, Finland, South Korea, and Japan—have very low risk because they have relatively strong rules of law. But a large number of countries—such as Bolivia, Nepal, and Uganda—have earned reputations as confiscatory states. Not surprisingly, these economies rank very low in the rule of law index.

Countries that dismantle the rule of law find it difficult to promote business investment, so their economies become plagued by stagnation and their people begin to suffer declining living standards. The authors of the *Global Competitiveness Report* explain why.

> Owners of land, corporate shares, and even intellectual property are unwilling to invest in the improvement and upkeep of their property if their rights as owners are insecure. Of equal importance, if property cannot be bought and sold with the confidence that the authorities will endorse the transaction, the market itself will fail to generate dynamic growth.
> *Global Competitiveness Report* 2008-2009, p.4.

---

[3]Verbatim from the "Rule of Law Index," World Justice Project, American Bar Association, http://www.worldjusticeproject.org rule-of-law-index/, accessed November 1, 2008.

Figure 7.1: Global Competitiveness Index for Select Countries, 2008

Top 15 Countries			Bottom 15 Countries		
Name	Rank	Score	Name	Rank	Score
United States	1	5.74	Nicaragua	120	3.41
Switzerland	2	5.61	Ethiopia	121	3.41
Denmark	3	5.58	Kyrgyz Republic	122	3.40
Sweden	4	5.53	Lesotho	123	3.40
Singapore	5	5.53	Paraguay	124	3.40
Finland	6	5.50	Madagascar	125	3.38
Germany	7	5.46	Nepal	126	3.37
Netherlands	8	5.41	Burkina Faso	127	3.36
Japan	9	5.38	Uganda	128	3.35
Canada	10	5.37	Timor-Leste	129	3.15
Hong Kong SAR	11	5.33	Mozambique	130	3.15
United Kingdom	12	5.30	Mauritania	131	3.14
Korea, Rep.	13	5.28	Burundi	132	2.98
Austria	14	5.23	Zimbabwe	133	2.88
Norway	15	5.22	Chad	134	2.85

Source: World Economic Forum, *Global Competitiveness Report*, 2008-2009, www.weforum.org.

There is a large body of empirical research by independent scholars to corroborate the claim that the rule of law and economic growth are directly correlated. A seminal paper in the 1988 *Journal of Political Economy*, for example, shows that economic growth between 1960 and 1980 was three times faster in countries that securely enforced rights to private property and contract (Scully 1988). A large number of subsequent studies have studied this initial finding and extended it to a broader set of countries and more recent data.[4] Naturally many of these studies differ on important points, yet the overarching message is clear. As discussed by Richard Posner, "there is empirical evidence showing that the rule of law does contribute to a nation's wealth and its rate of economic growth." (Posner 1998, p. 3). In short, legal institutions that protect fundamental rights to property and contract under the rule of law are a *necessary groundwork* to be able to achieve economic growth and rising prosperity.

CUES FROM LAW AND ECONOMICS

The same forces that connect economic growth to the rule of law internationally are also at work in the U.S. states. Those states with the best legal systems tend to economically outperform those with worse legal systems (see Chapter 4). Improvements to West Virginia's legal institutions, therefore, are a route to increased economic prosperity for the state.

---

[4] For a more complete list of studies that support the claim that greater rule of law leads to greater economic prosperity, see the *Economic Freedom of the World* report, available at http://www.freetheworld.com/papers.html, accessed November 1, 2008.

The most fundamental point of law and economics is that legal rules and regulations act like implicit prices on people's behavior. We know from basic economics, as well as from our own experience, that consumer demand goes down when prices increase for things like gasoline and new washer/dryer sets. Law and economics says that people follow similar thought processes when evaluating the legal implications of their decisions.

A classic example is how law and economics construes the total cost of doing business. A business firm must incur economic costs in its production and related operations—the payments to land, labor, capital, and entrepreneurship. A business firm also incurs legal costs, which get counted among the firm's "transaction costs," as they are known in law and economics (transaction costs measure the value of resources that get used in the process of forming agreements about how to use resources). Court decisions and other legal rules can influence the firm's transaction costs, and in doing so the law can alter business decisions. The question is, will the legal system encourage beneficial or harmful business decisions? The answer depends on the choice of legal rule and how it is enforced because these together determine which incentives the legal system will embody.

Economic costs of doing business tend to increase as a firm does more to decrease its legal costs. Suppose the "XYZ Drug Company" sells a medicine that helps adults who have some ailment but is harmful to children. The company knows that a fraction of its buyers will accidentally let children consume the product. Now there are options for reducing the product's risk to children, but some of these options can be very costly. A very simple step might be to install a child-proof bottle cap, but suppose the latest studies show that some fraction of children will be exposed anyway. The company could also sponsor a mass media campaign to educate buyers, but this will be very costly and still a few people won't get the message. Suppose, however, that the firm could buy a Super Bowl commercial to make certain that everyone gets the message and the firm's risk essentially disappears.

Figure 7.2 captures the interplay among a firm's economic, legal and total costs of doing business. As just described, with safer products come greater economic costs but lower legal costs. The vertical sum of these two costs is depicted in bold by the Total Costs line. The model shows why it is highly costly to make products that are either extremely dangerous or extremely safe. All other things equal, the drug company will choose some moderate risk level. If it can continue to produce and sell the medicine at the chosen risk level without losing money, then society is better off because people benefit from the treatment value of the medicine and the company earns a profit.

The Legal Cost curve in Figure 7.2 shows how legal rules can act like implicit prices on behavior. Suppose a child ingests some of the medicine despite the firm's efforts to achieve moderate risk reduction. Now suppose that a jury awards damages that greatly exceed the norm. In the model of Figure 7.2, the Legal Costs curve would shift upward, which would increase the firm's Total Costs even though its Economic Costs don't move. In this new scenario, it now makes sense for the firm to make a safer product. If it still makes the product at all. With greater total costs the firm may find that it can no longer operate without incurring losses in this market.

Figure 7.2
Economic, Legal, and Total Costs of Doing Business

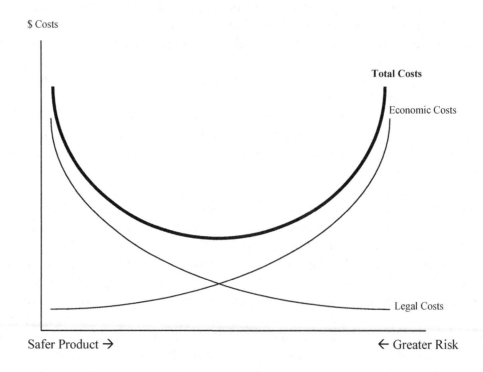

The example illustrates how the legal and regulatory rules chosen by states are significant factors in promoting economic activity that is socially beneficial. It is also important to point out that this is only a model. It does not suggest that business entrepreneurs sit down with economic graphs to decide how much risk to undertake. Likewise, there is no exact tool that policymakers can use to get the legal rules just right. That is partly because legal rules do not fully take shape in single strokes. Rather, in the form of government constructed by the American framers, a state's legal rules are written by the legislature, enforced by the state's executive branch, and interpreted by the judiciary. That is why it is the role of every government office to uphold the rule of law.

INSTILLING GOOD INCENTIVES

An efficient legal system would harbor good incentives, making it in people's interests to make decisions that wind up promoting the public interest. In many ways the common law promotes efficient outcomes. In property law, for example, sellers are urged to scrutinize forms of payment and thereby deter fraud. In contracts, efficient enforcement doctrines accommodate uncontrollable changes of circumstances in ways that minimize the waste of valuable resources. Yet too many well intentioned policies interfere with the individual decisions that make these areas of the law work efficiently to begin with. In the following sections, we will discuss how West Virginia has opportunities in property and contract law to increase the rule of law and thereby create a climate of growth for the economy.

But first, how does property law urge sellers to decrease fraud? Suppose you agree to sell your car to a man over the phone. When he arrives the next day, he claims to have only a personal check for payment. You are tired, and you need the money. What's more, you haven't gotten many calls on the car. Should you take the check?

Your better judgment would probably say no, and the common law precedent on such a case sees things the same. The high court of Mississippi ruled on the case, which was brought by the seller to recover the fraudulently purchased car. The car had exchanged hands several times before ending up on a used car lot, from which the respondents in the case purchased the car. The court reasoned that "while the ... rule may seem harsh, it is in line with the purposes of the [law], to promote commerce and business..."[5]

The direct incentive effect of the Mississippi decision is to motivate people to be cautious about acceptable forms of payment. But the ruling embodies a deeper beneficial incentive as well. The decision reinforces the rule of law because judges do not have discretion to award similarly defrauded sellers on a case by case basis. This increases the security of buyers' property rights and therefore promotes exchange and the flow of resources to higher valued uses. The rule, in this instance, simply applies equally and impartially to all persons in society. Judges are not empowered under this rule to choose winners and losers after the fact. As alluded to by the court, the stability of this rule gives buyers a greater sense of security when acquiring title to purchased property.

A similar incentive effect is found in the doctrine of contributory negligence (and its modern counterpart, comparative negligence). This doctrine motivates people to avoid accidents that damage property, while punishing would be opportunists through doctrines such as last chance avoidance. Fewer accidents means there will be less waste of resources. By upholding the rule of law and promoting the flow of resources to their highest valued uses, the Mississippi ruling does the same thing.

OPPORTUNITIES IN CONTRACT LAW

In the enforcement of contracts, there are direct opportunities for West Virginia to enhance the rule of law. Secure contract enforcement is vital to the complex types of exchange that occur in advanced economies.[6] Without contracts, exchanges would be limited to spot swaps, or between people who inherently trust each other. There would be very little division of labor, and economic activity would stagnate. But when strangers can agree to mutually beneficial terms that both sides believe will be enforced, then people can specialize according to their comparative advantages, which is elemental to productivity, economic growth, and rising living standards. Under the rule of law, contracts are enforced efficiently and that makes it in people's interests to behave in ways that serve the public interest. Unfortunately, West Virginia's rules and regulations fail in too many ways to uphold the rule of law in contract. This section presents ways in which West Virginia can improve the rule of law in contract and thus enhance the state's business climate.

---

[5] *Paschal v. Hamilton*, 363 So. 2d 1360; 1978 Miss. Cole and Grossman (2005, p.93) provide further discussion.

[6] Posner's classic text in law and economics reads: "Thus the fundamental function of contract law (and recognized as such at least since Hobbes' day) is to deter people from behaving opportunistically toward their contracting parties, in order to encourage the optimal timing of economic activity and (the same point) obviate costly self-protective measures." *The Economic Analysis of Law*, Posner (1992, p.91).

When courts hear contract actions, the question is primarily whether to enforce or discharge the contract, and if enforced what remedies to assign. To make efficient rules, the courts must ask: "Will imposing liability create incentives for value-maximizing conduct in the future?" (Posner 1992, p.95). Again, legal rules help shape people's incentives for future behavior. It is in the interests of the contracting parties, as well as in the interests of society, to reduce transaction costs. Contracting parties cannot prepare for all possible contingencies, and choosing not to specify even foreseeable contingencies can be a way to economize on transaction costs. Thus, it is inevitable that unforeseen, or unprepared for, contingencies arise for a third party to enforce. When doing so it is efficient for the courts to assign liability to the least cost avoider of the contingency, as this is how the parties would have done so had they assigned the risk when forming the contract.

Common law precedent harbors many examples in which it is efficient for courts to enforce performance, even after contingencies disadvantage one of the parties. Suppose, for example, that Dan in Dubai promises to ship Harry in Hamburg 30 tons of African spices for $500 per ton. Dan intends to ship via the Suez Canal, as all other shipping routes would be much more expensive. Unfortunately, geopolitical tensions escalate to the point of closing the Suez Canal. Dan breaches on the claim that performance has become impossible. Harry sues for specific performance. How should the court rule?

In the 1962 precedent for such as case, Britain's highest court (the House of Lords) ruled in favor of Harry.[7] Since Dan and Harry did not specify that the Suez Canal would be the one and only shipping route, the canal's closure meant that, in a legal sense, other shipping routes would be, and in fact were, possible. Hence, legally Dan is obligated to find one. Furthermore, there was no evidence that an alternative route would have ruined Dan financially. So the contingency made Dan lose some money relative to his expectations at the time of forming the contract, but the contingency didn't make Dan's performance impossible.

In other cases, performance is genuinely impossible but the efficient ruling is for the courts to enforce the contract through compensatory damage awards. Suppose I promise to send you 1,000 bottles of wine from my California winery in two weeks. One week later, my winery burns to the ground and I cannot acquire replacement wine in time to fulfill the contract. In this case, while it may be genuinely impossible for me to perform, that does not mean the contract should be discharged. Even if the fire could not be prevented, I could have insured against the regrettable event. Insurance simply replaces the risk of a major loss (my winery burning) with a much smaller but certain cost (the insurance premium). The court's ruling, in order to be efficient, must take into account whichever cost is lower. If the premium is a lower cost than the expected loss, then the risk is *insurable*, and the court's efficient ruling would be to assign liability on the party that is the lower cost insurer.

To see the same point in another way, imagine that you and I return to the point in time when we formed our agreement, only this time we decide to specify how to handle the risk of fire at my winery. If you routinely purchase wine shipments from hundreds of wineries, it may be cheaper for you to insure against the small probability that one of the wineries will catch fire. It is more likely that I will be the lower cost insurer, since I am on site and can easier calculate (and even reduce) the relevant risks. With me as the lower cost bearer of the risk, it would make sense for the contract to assign the risk to me, and the

---

[7] *Tsakiroglou & Co. Ltd. v. Noblee Thorl G.m.b.h,* House of Lords [1962], A.C. 93. Cole and Grossman (2005, p.175 ff.) offer detailed discussion.

contract would therefore include a form of insurance. Insurability is the economic rationale for assigning risks in contracts. And this is why most commercial contracts assign risks of various sorts to one of the parties, specifically the party that is the lower cost insurer.

Some contracts are clearly against the public interest and must be discharged in order for the courts to give good incentives for future behavior. Suppose, for example, that you own a restaurant and contract with the "Jim and Mary Wine Company" to supply you with California wines. Secretly, Jim agrees to send California wine labels to Mary, who agrees then to switch labels with cheap wines she acquires from New York. After shipment, you notice uneven bulges in the bottle labels and discover that someone has merely glued the fake labels over the originals. The law protects your interests, of course, and it may even punish the Jim and Mary Wine Company. But what if Jim were to sue Mary? After all, she broke her promise and Jim was harmed as a result. In the 1956 precedent for such a claim, the Supreme Court of New York threw out the conspiratorial contract, saying that it was "repugnant to public policy" and "plainly prejudicial to the public good."[8] Refusing contracts is the law's way of *not* giving people the incentives to act against the public interest.[9] In fact, the same court earlier held that "the only method by which the law can prevent such agreements from being made is to refuse to enforce them."[10]

The unifying theme of the above examples is that the courts should enforce contracts to instill good incentives, so that future contracts work to promote the public interest. Courts ought to enforce contracts against insurable risks and assign liability on the least cost avoider of the breach. Resources are wasted when inefficient producers make goods and services at high cost, and resources are wasted when people bear risks when there are other people who are lower cost insurers. On the other hand, the courts should discharge contracts whose performance would waste resources when uninsurable contingencies arise. Thus, law and economics offers a set of analytical tools to enforce contracts efficiently, which upholds the rule of law and thereby promotes economic growth.

By contrast, in recent years West Virginia's courts have ruled in novel ways relative to economically sound legal principles and common law precedent. In 2006, for example, the state Supreme Court of Appeals held that businesses without a physical presence in the state are subject to the state's franchise and corporate income taxes.[11] The Court eschewed the traditional physical presence doctrine for meeting the "substantial nexus" language in the commerce clause of the U. S. Constitution. The Court instead fashioned its own test, the "significant economic presence" doctrine, which only two other states' courts had used (see Chapter 8). In doing so, the ruling arguably departed from common law precedent.[12]

---

[8] *Mittenberg and Sampton, Inc. v. Mallor*, 1 A.D.2d 458; 151 N.Y.S.2d 748 (1956).

[9] Besides fraud, other doctrines of contract refusal include incompetence, unconscionable terms, duress, and uncontrollable circumstances such as *force majeure*. In each of these situations, resources would be wasted if the contract were enforced even in light of the performance or formation problems. Courts refuse such contracts because their enforcement would only give people bad incentives and undermine the public interest.

[10] *Coverly v. Terminal Warehouse* Co. 85 A.D. 488; 83 N.Y.S. 369 (1903).

[11] *Tax Commissioner of State v. MBNA America Bank, N.A.*, 220 W.Va. 163, 640 S.E.2d 226 (2006).

[12] The dissenting opinion of Justice Brent Benjamin reads: "There is no precedential support whatsoever for the conclusions reached by the majority decision. None. None at the state level. None at the federal level. Ignoring that our consideration here should be the effect of the tax in question on interstate commerce, rather than the type of tax it is, none of the rhetoric raised by the majority opinion explains why a state's imposition of a tax on an out-of-state corporation with no presence, tangible or intangible, on income realized from an out-of-state account does not adversely affect the nation's interstate commerce, an analysis identified by the United States Supreme Court as the cornerstone of constitutional jurisprudence. *Id.*; *Allied-Signal, Inc. v. Director, Div. of*

In 2007, West Virginia's courts continued to rule in exceptional ways, and West Virginia became home to three of the top seven verdicts across the nation that year. Large damage awards do not alone or necessarily perturb the rule of law, but unexpectedly high verdicts, which depart from the norm in significant ways, increase uncertainty of the state's business climate. Unexpectedly high damage awards make the legal costs of doing business less predictable. In Figure 7.1, for instance, firms cannot predictably estimate the position of the legal costs curve. Firms may instead estimate a high enough probability that their legal costs will be extremely high. When businesses cannot discern the rules of the game, they may just as soon decide not to do business in the state.

In addition to their high dollar amounts, the 2007 verdicts were noteworthy for their use of *punitive* damages in contract actions. This is yet another departure from the norms of legal precedent and the principles that uphold the rule of law. In the absence of evidence to the contrary, the law should assume that parties enter contracts in good faith and in the expectation of mutual gain. As Judge Posner writes in his classic treatise on law and economics: "Good faith performance...is an implied term of every contract" (Posner 1992, p.91). Thus, the common law norm is that contract remedies are intended to compensate, not punish, and therefore punitive damages are generally not awarded in contract actions. By departing from this norm, the Court again undermines the rule of law, making the business climate less predictable, and discouraging the very economic activity that creates growth and a more prosperous people.

OPPORTUNITIES IN PROPERTY LAW

West Virginia law imparts very strong powers of eminent domain to local governments, in particular for purposes of economic development.[13] Yet law and economics provides the important lesson that security in property rights is elemental to economic growth. With the specter of condemnation hanging over property owners' heads, they are less likely to invest in improving properties. Homes and businesses are less likely to be sold to new owners, thus hindering the flow of resources to higher valued uses. The reason is clear: by undermining the rule of law, strong eminent domain powers and its erratic use make it hard to predict whether property investments will be recouped, or instead taken away as part of a public economic development plan.

The authority for West Virginia's broad takings powers originates in the state's legislative, executive, and judicial branches. The statutory code of West Virginia empowers

---

Taxation, 504 U.S. 768, 112 S.Ct. 2251, 119 L.Ed.2d 533 (1992). The only state court decision on point with the specific credit card issues raised herein determined that the State of Tennessee exceeded its taxing jurisdiction in attempting to collect taxes from an out- of-state corporation on income generated by out-of-state credit accounts. *J.C. Penney National Bank v. Johnson*, 19 S.W.3d 831 (Tenn. Ct. App. 1999), *cert. denied*, 531 U.S. 927, 121 S.Ct. 305, 148 L.Ed.2d 245 (2005)." Available at *http://www.state.wv.us/ WVSCA/docs /fall06/33049d.htm*. Accessed January 26, 2009.

[13] Certain local authorities in West Virginia can forcibly transfer ownership from one private party to another in order to support economic development. The law in all 50 states and the U.S. Constitution says that the takings power is reserved only for public uses and requires condemning authorities to pay just compensation to property owners. Like every other state, West Virginia acknowledges certain traditional functions as satisfying public use, such as common carriage rights of way, public buildings, recreation and conservation. But West Virginia is relatively aggressive in letting non-traditional functions count as public use. For further discussion of West Virginia's takings law, see the chapter by Lopez, Kerekes, and Johnson (2007) in *Unleashing Capitalism*. For analysis of takings law in the 50 states, see Lopez, Jewell, and Campbell (2009).

urban renewal authorities to acquire properties through eminent domain, but only in blighted areas.[14] But the rules of the game are rigged because the urban renewal authorities themselves determine which areas are blighted[15], and the statute is very broad in defining the criteria that constitute blight.[16]

West Virginia's courts have upheld such condemnations by these local authorities. The legal precedent is a 1998 case between the Charleston Urban Renewal Authority (CURA) and the owner of a property being seized. The property itself was not blighted, but it was located within the contours of a zone that CURA had determined was a blighted area. In *CURA v. Courtland* (1998), West Virginia's Supreme Court ruled in favor of the government and this decision stands today.

To their credit, condemning authorities acknowledge the disruptive effects of using eminent domain to pursue public economic development plans. CURA's executive director, Pat Brown, said "we don't use it [eminent domain] very often, but we do use it. There is an extensive procedure, and we certainly don't want to abuse it."[17]

In reality, CURA's history is one of frequent and large-scale use of the takings power for economic development. From the 1960s through the middle of 2006, CURA condemned 523 properties for 47 development projects, 28 of which were private development projects.[18] Although CURA's condemnation rate has slowed in the past two decades, West Virginia is still a relatively aggressive user compared to other states. Since 1998, West Virginia ranks 19th in per capita properties condemned for private use.[19] CURA's property acquisitions have become so routine, the authority now performs many of the quotidian functions of a real estate company. "We do buy land that is blighted, if you will, and we also have property available for redevelopment. We usually put signs on our property. We get direct calls, referrals from the [Charleston Area] Alliance as well as the city, and we all work together."[20]

The power of eminent domain has a very long history in democratic government. Hugo Grotius, the 17th Century legal philosopher who coined the phrase, declared that the property of subjects is under the "supreme lordship" of the state, which can use and even alienate private property, but only for "public utility" and only if the state were to "make good" the loss to those who lose their property.[21] It is no surprise that Grotius cites the public use and just compensation requirements, since they go all the way to the Magna Carta

---

[14] Chapter 16 Article 18 Section 8 Paragraph (a) of the West Virginia Code reads: "An authority shall have the right to acquire by the exercise of the power of eminent domain...any real property which it may deem necessary for a redevelopment project or for its purposes under this article after the adoption by it of a resolution declaring that the acquisition of the real property described therein is necessary for such purposes."

[15] Chapter 16 Article 18 Section 8 Paragraph (b) of the West Virginia Code reads: "When an authority has found and determined by resolution that certain real property described therein is necessary for a redevelopment project or for its purposes under this article, the resolution shall be conclusive evidence that the acquisition of such real property is necessary for the purposes described therein."

[16] See Chapter 16 Article 18 Section 3 Paragraph (c) and (d) of the West Virginia Code. For more discussion, see Lopez, Kerekes, and Johnson (2007).

[17] Ann Ali, "Charleston's Past, Future Included in Redevelopment," WOWKTV.com, January 3, 2008, available online http://wowktv.com/story.cfm?func=viewstory&storyid=33134& accessed January 26, 2009.

[18] Anderson, Justin D. "Forced Property Sales Led to Many City Projects: Charleston Authority has bought 523 properties since 1960s," *Charleston Daily Mail*, May 15, 2006, p.1D.

[19] See López, Jewell and Campbell (2009) for a detailed comparative analysis of eminent domain use in the American states.

[20] Ali, *supra*.

[21] Hugo Grotius, *De Jure Belli et Pacis*, 1625.

(chapters 28 and 29, respectively). Throughout its history, eminent domain has been rightly considered to be a power of last resort, one that is inherently opposite to rule by consent of the governed. Thus it was with some justification that the U.S. Supreme Court referred to eminent domain as the "despotic power."

It undermines the rule of law when authorities routinely use powers that are intended to be of last resort. Just like the law can set implicit prices on citizens, restrictions on takings power set implicit prices on the behavior of condemnation authorities. In the language of law and economics, West Virginia sets too low a price on the use of eminent domain for economic development. With broad takings powers, local authorities face bad incentives themselves. With bad incentives, their actions are not likely to serve the public interest. However well intentioned they may be, policymakers are put in bad positions when the law allows eminent domain to be used as an expedient to ensure that planners get their way.

Other states have taken meaningful steps to restore the rule of law against the threat of broad takings powers. According to new peer-reviewed studies on this topic, almost half the states have enacted new legislation that meaningfully restricts local authorities from over using eminent domain.[22] In addition, state courts are overturning earlier decisions in nearby states with similar economic challenges, such as Michigan, Ohio, and Oklahoma. West Virginia should take the lead in such beneficial movements. To seriously restore the rule of law in this area of property, West Virginia should enact legislation to restrict the definitions of public use and blight. The Supreme Court of Appeals should overturn *CURA v. Courtland*, and the powers of local authorities to condemn properties for private use should be curtailed. These changes to the law in West Virginia would increase the implicit price to local authorities of takings for non-public uses. Doing so will restore the rule of law in this important area, giving better incentives to both property owners and local developers, and putting their individual decisions in greater harmony with the public interest and a growing state economy.

CONCLUSION

The rule of law makes economic life more predictable and helps to promote prosperity and rising living standards. Economic growth ultimately boils down to ordinary people making sound future-oriented decisions on everyday matters. For this process to work, people need good incentive structures and a reasonably predictable economic climate. Thus, it is the rightful place of the law to set the rules of the game and make economic life more predictable by protecting the security or rights to property and contract. By doing so, the legal system sets the right implicit prices for people to channel their own self-interested decisions into benefits for society. If we set good rules, people will have the right incentives to promote economic growth.

However, the law should not reward opportunistic behavior or set too low an implicit price on violating people's property and contract rights. When the objective of a state's legal system wrongly becomes to redistribute wealth, or change the winners and losers after the fact, this will distort people's incentives and create an environment where people cannot

---

[22] See recent work by Somin (2008), Morris (2008), and López, Jewell and Campbell (2009).

easily predict whether they will enjoy the benefits of their own good decisions. This severs the ties between the rule of law and economic growth. By ensuring sound and stable legal institutions, West Virginians will have the right incentives and a predictable environment for making the kinds of everyday decisions that lead to economic growth and a more prosperous West Virginia into the future.

REFERENCES

Berliner, D. 2006. *Opening the Floodgates: Eminent Domain Abuse in a Post-Kelo World.* Washington: Institute for Justice. Online: www.castlecoalition.org/pdf/publications/ floodgates-report.pdf

Cole, D. H. and Grossman, P. Z. 2005. *Principles of Law and Economics*, Prentice-Hall.

López, E. J., Jewell, R. T., and Campbell, N. D. 2009. Pass a Law, Any Law, Fast: State Legislative Responses to the *Kelo* Backlash. *Review of Law & Economics* (forthcoming).

López, E. J., Kerekes, C. & Johnson, G. 2007. Make Property Rights Stronger: Limit Eminent Domain, Chapter 7 in Russell S. Sobel (ed.), *Unleashing Capitalism: Why Prosperity Stops at the West Virginia Border and How to Fix It*. Morgantown: Public Policy Foundation of West Virginia.

Morriss, A. P. 2008. "Symbol or Substance? An Empirical Assessment of State Responses to *Kelo*," University of Illinois Law & Economics Working Paper LE07-037. Available at SSRN http://ssrn.com/abstract=1113582.

Posner, R. A. 1992. *Economic Analysis of Law* 4 ed., Little Brown and Company.

Posner, R. A. 1998. Creating a Legal Framework for Economic Development. *The World Bank Research Observer* 13(1): 1-11.

Scully, G. 1988. The Institutional Framework and Economic Development. *Journal of Political Economy* 96(3): 652-662.

Somin, I. 2008. The Limits of Backlash: Assessing the Political Response to *Kelo*, George Mason Law & Economics Research Paper No. 07-14, SSRN 976298.

CHAPTER 8

8

SHOULD WE KEEP THIS COURT?
AN ECONOMIC EXAMINATION OF
RECENT DECISIONS MADE BY THE WEST
VIRGINIA SUPREME COURT OF APPEALS

by Kristen M. Leddy, Russell S. Sobel, and Matthew T. Yanni

The Rule of Law

8

SHOULD WE KEEP THIS COURT? AN ECONOMIC EXAMINATION OF RECENT DECISIONS MADE BY THE WEST VIRGINIA SUPREME COURT OF APPEALS[1]

Kristen M. Leddy, Russell S. Sobel, and Matthew T. Yanni

There has been much discussion lately about whether West Virginia's economy could be bolstered by adopting various initiatives aimed at improving its business climate.[2] While people tend to associate a state's business climate with factors such as corporate taxes and regulations, a state's judicial system is also an important element in determining the relative attractiveness of a state to business development. State court rulings have significant effects not only on the cost of doing business in a state, but also on the predictability and risk associated with operating a business. Entrepreneurs take account of the state's business climate when deciding whether to create new jobs in West Virginia.

At the outset, it is important to discuss the proper role of the court system in a market-based economy, such as we strive for in the United States. The market-based economy relies on the market to provide information, and is the most efficient mechanism to create wealth. A market-based economy allows individuals to be secure in their persons and property, and affords individuals the ability to make decisions over the resources they control. An individual's action is only limited to the extent that individual's action violates or impinges on the rights of others. In cases where one party impinges upon the rights of another, a properly functioning legal system fairly and consistently settles disputes between parties. Court decisions, in effect, set the price (or cost) imposed for impinging on the rights of others. It is critical that courts set these prices fairly and in a predictable manner. Punishments that are too lenient will not provide the correct incentives for parties to avoid impinging upon the rights of others, and punishments that are too severe will result in an abundance of lawsuits and will discourage activities that would have created economic growth. Striking this balance is the key to the court properly arbitrating those cases before it.

---

[1] This chapter is an updated version of Kristen M. Leddy, Russell S. Sobel, and Matthew T. Yanni, *Should We Keep This Court? An Economic Examination of Recent Decisions Made by the West Virginia Supreme Court of Appeals*, FED. SOC., Oct. 2008, *available at* www.fed-soc.org/westvirginia.

[2] *See, e.g.,* UNLEASHING CAPITALISM: WHY PROSPERITY STOPS AT THE WEST VIRGINIA BORDER AND HOW TO FIX IT, (Russell S. Sobel, ed., Public Policy Foundation of West Virginia, 2007).

Economists frequently use an analogy to the board game Monopoly™ to explain the important role of the legal system, and the courts, in an economy. While the government's proper role is not to be an active player in the game, it should, and does, have the unique role of setting and enforcing the rules of the game under which the players operate. For the economic game to run smoothly, the rules must be clear, predictable, and enforced fairly. Generally, the state's legislature determines these rules, the state's executive branch enforces them, and the state's judiciary interprets them. Sometimes, however, judges depart from their interpretive function. This departure is sometimes called "judicial activism."

Arthur Schlesinger coined the term judicial activism in the late 1940s, but Schlesinger did not provide a definition of the term that scholars readily accepted.[3] While there has been little consensus on the meaning of the term,[4] a review of the scholarly literature on judicial activism yields the following common explanations of its meaning: 1) judicial conduct that exceeds the power constitutionally granted to the judiciary, 2) judicial decisions that ignore past precedent, 3) judicial decisions which "legislate from the bench," 4) the judicial exercise of broad remedial powers, and 5) judicial decisions according to the judge's personal political preferences.[5] The scholarly analysis of this term creates a framework to begin this discussion but does little to establish a uniform definition of judicial activism. In an effort to clarify the meaning of judicial activism as it relates to West Virginia, we rely on the definitions provided by West Virginia justices.

The Justices of the Supreme Court of Appeals of West Virginia used the phrase "judicial activism" a total of four times during the period from 2005 through 2008. The term does not appear in any majority opinion; rather, it appears in concurrences and in dissents. According to the various justices, "judicial activism," occurs when a court encroaches upon the authority of the legislature to bar negligent claims by employees against their employers,[6] or when a court arrogates to itself the task of seeking out and deciding an issue that no one has brought before it or argued,[7] or when a court exceeds its proper constitutional role by amending a statutory provision to remedy what it believes to be a policy inadequacy in legislative judgment,[8] or even when a court would improperly emasculate the intent and purpose of a rule of civil procedure.[9] Importantly, the justices use the term to accuse each other of judicial missteps, and to urge the other justices to refrain from activist decision-making, whatever its meaning.

The court's admonishment against judicial activism seems more than just empty rhetoric. While the court emerged as a significant entity in state policymaking since the 1960s and 1970s, the general choice of the justices is stasis according to Professor Brisbin.[10]

---

[3] *See* Keenan Kmiec, *The Origin and Current Meanings of 'Judicial Activism,'* 92 CAL. L. REV. 1441, 1443 (2004) (referring to Arthur Schlesinger's use of "judicial activism" in a *Fortune* magazine article on the U.S. Supreme Court in January 1947 as the first official usage of the term).

[4] *See* Caprice Roberts, *In Search of Judicial Activism: The Dangers of Quantifying the Qualitative,* 74 TENN. L. REV. 567, 570 (2007).

[5] *See* Kmiec at 1464-1476; Roberts, 581-600; Vincent Martin Bonventre, *Judicial Activism, Judges' Speech, and Merit Selection: Conventional Wisdom and Nonsense,* 68 ALB. L. REV. 557, 564-575 (2005); and Frank Cross and Stefanie Lindquist, *The Scientific Study of Judicial Activism,* 91 MINN. L. REV. 1752, 1762-1764 (2007).

[6] Bias v. Eastern Associated Coal Corporation (2006) (Davis, C.J., concurring).

[7] Fairmont General Hospital, Inc. v. United Hospital Center, Inc. (2005) (Starcher, J., dissenting).

[8] Worley v. Beckley Mechanical, Inc. (2007) (Benjamin, J., dissenting).

[9] Riggs v. West Virginia University Hospitals, Inc. (2007) (Davis, C.J., concurring).

[10] *See* RICHARD A. BRISBIN, JR., WEST VIRGINIA STATE GOVERNMENT: THE LEGISLATIVE, EXECUTIVE, AND JUDICIAL BRANCHES, *The West Virginia Judiciary* (Institute for Public Affairs, West Virginia University, 1993);

Brisbin's comprehensive 1993 study of the West Virginia judiciary evaluated the court's activism, finding it most likely to engage in doctrinal changes in the areas of tort law and products liability.[11] The court significantly altered the state's policies regarding the workers' compensation system, forced the state to reconstruct its prison system, established alcohol treatment programs, and provided emergency care to the state's homeless population.[12] The court revolutionized the family law system, including child custody law and prenuptial agreements.[13] Despite the court's willingness to act aggressively at the state level, it does show deference to federal court rulings, to U.S. Supreme Court rulings, and to the U.S. Constitution.[14]

In the fifteen years since Professor Brisbin's study, the state legislature made noteworthy changes in the area of tort law, such as lower caps on medical malpractice damages; limits on joint and several liability; venue restrictions; and the elimination of third-party bad-faith claims against insurance companies.[15] In the past three years, the West Virginia Supreme Court invalidated the revised venue statute, discarded a common law modification of a product manufacturer's duty to warn, upheld the imposition of a tax that may prove to violate the Commerce Clause, and refused to grant appellate review to some exorbitant punitive damages awards in commercial cases. However, it has generally upheld workers'-compensation reforms, consumer-protection and family-court-system reforms. In this study, we examine some of the most important cases that have confronted the West Virginia Supreme Court of Appeals in the years 2006 to 2008, and describe how these decisions impact West Virginia's economic climate.

The cases examined here create additional costs on companies doing (or thinking of doing) business in West Virginia. They also create cost uncertainty for businesses, which can lower the attractiveness of investing in the state. To the extent that these cases are won by the lawyers who pursue them, and their clients, this may increase the number of cases filed in the future. This draws resources away from investment and instead involves devoting resources toward litigation costs and potential wealth transfers through settlements or judgments.

THE 2008 CASE: *CAPERTON V. MASSEY*

The glare of a national spotlight shines on West Virginia's highest court, as many observers carefully watch how the U.S. Supreme Court will review the state court's ruling in *Caperton v. A.T. Massey Coal Co., Inc.* (*Massey*).[16] In *Massey*, the West Virginia Supreme Court reversed the judgment of the of the Circuit Court of Boone County and dismissed the case awarding Plaintiffs Hugh M. Caperton, Harman Development Corporation, Harman Mining Corporation, and Sovereign Coal Sales, Inc. over $50 million, including punitive damages, in

---

see also CHARLES LOPEMAN, THE ACTIVIST ADVOCATE (Praeger Publishing, 1999) (discussing the conservative history of the State's Supreme Court of Appeals prior to the 1980s).

[11] BRISBIN at 31.

[12] *Id.* at 32.

[13] *Id.* at 33.

[14] *Id.* at 33-34.

[15] Elizabeth Thornburg, *Judicial Hellholes, Lawsuit Climates and Bad Social Science: Lessons from West Virginia,* 110 W.VA. L. REV. 1097 (2008).

[16] Not reported in S.E.2d, 2008 WL 918444, 2007 W.Va. LEXIS 119 (W.Va., April 3, 2008). On November 14, 2008, the U.S. Supreme Court granted the petition for a writ of *certiorari* in this case, which will be argued on March 3, 2009.

a breach-of-contract dispute. Although the $44 million dollar punitive damage award makes the case significant in the state's contract law, several high-profile legal groups, including the American Bar Association, submitted amicus briefs,[17] asking the U.S. Supreme Court to review this case for its significance regarding recusal standards.[18]

Justice Elliott Maynard recused himself from the case after vacation photographs appeared in the media linking him with Massey CEO Don Blankenship.[19] Justice Larry Starcher similarly recused himself from the case, after comments he made about Blankenship appeared to create an impermissible bias.[20] Justice Brent Benjamin, however, did not disqualify himself from the case, even though Blankenship's campaign contributions helped Brent Benjamin defeat former Justice Warren McGraw in 2004.[21] This is a thorny issue, because Blankenship spent the money himself, in support of Benjamin. Justice Benjamin, that is to say, his campaign committee, did not receive direct campaign contributions from Blankenship, and Blankenship's expenditures were not coordinated with those of Benjamin's committee. Put more accurately, Blankenship's goal was to defeat Warren McGraw, and Benjamin benefited from Blankenship's pursuit of his goal. Does this make it improper for Benjamin to hear cases in which Massey or its CEO is a party? The U.S. Supreme Court will decide this issue.

In sparsely populated states, such as West Virginia, it is especially critical that judges fairly apply the law, given the personal relationships judges often have with case parties. For the system to work fairly, it is important that these personal or financial relationships not interfere with the fair administration of justice. An appearance that these relationships influence court decisions works to undermine the presumption of fairness and predictability in the state's legal system. The controversy associated with this case has lead to interest in reforming the method of judicial selection in the state, perhaps by moving to judicial appointment or to public funding of judicial elections.

THE 2007 CASES: *TAWNEY, DU PONT, WHEELING PITTSBURGH STEEL, AND JOHNSON & JOHNSON V. KARL*

West Virginia circuit courts awarded three of the nation's top-ten plaintiffs' verdicts in 2007.[22] All three were lawsuits against businesses. The Circuit Court of Roane County awarded the plaintiffs $404 million in their breach-of-contract claim against Columbia Natural Resources, L.L.C.,[23] the Circuit Court of Harrison County awarded the plaintiffs $251

---

[17] The Brief of the American Bar Association as *amicus curiae* in this case, *available at* http://www.abanet.org/judind/pdf/caperton_brief.pdf.

[18] *See* Lawrence Messina, *Legal Groups blast W.Va. Justice in Massey Case,* ASSOCIATED PRESS, August 5, 2008.

[19] Ken Ward, *Maynard recuses himself for the third time,* CHARLESTON GAZETTE, February 8, 2008.

[20] Paul Nyden, *Starcher recuses himself from the Massey case,* CHARLESTON GAZETTE, February 16, 2008; *see also* Justice Starcher's recusal statement, *available at* http://www.state.wv.us/wvsca/press/feb15b_08.htm.

[21] John O'Brien, *Justice Benjamin draws recusal line in major W.Va. case,* LEGAL NEWS LINE, September 12, 2008.

[22] When ranked by the dollar value of the award. *See* VerdictSearch, *Top 100 Verdicts of 2007, available at* http://www.verdictsearch.com/index.jsp?do=top100.

[23] *See* Estate of Tawney v. Columbia Natural Resources, L.L.C. (2007).

million in their toxic-tort claim against E.I. DuPont De Nemours & Co.,[24] and the Circuit Court of Brooke County awarded the plaintiff Wheeling Pittsburgh Steel Corp. $220 million in a breach-of-contract claim against the Central West Virginia Energy Co.[25]

All but one of the 2007 cases featured here included large punitive damage awards designed to punish the businesses involved. These awards are not related to the amount of damage the defendant party caused, but are instead related to the jury's interpretation of the 'badness' of the defendant party's behavior. It is much easier for jurors to internalize injuries that plaintiffs present in jury trials than it is for jurors to internalize the damage a large punitive damage award may have on the state's business climate, their future employment prospects, and their incomes. Rulings such as these can reduce the willingness of businesses to invest and/or locate in West Virginia.

A business generally faces two distinct types of risk, either of which may subject it to financial ruin. The first is economic risk, characterized by efficiency, management, and market effects. The second is legal risk, characterized by corporate exposure to lawsuits. Inefficiency and poor management risk only the businesses assets invested in the venture. The worst-case scenario is that the firm may lose all of its investment in that particular operation if it were to go out of business. The limit on economic risk for a business is then just the business assets involved or invested in that location. Legal liability, however, can impose verdicts that far exceed the amount of investment in the state, forcing the company to close or dispose of other assets and operations from other states (that had no part in the case in question) to settle the lawsuit. Thus, in cases such as those discussed here, a large national corporation conducting business in West Virginia could face not just the loss of the investment made in the state, but also the risk of a potential lawsuit that results in a verdict that reaches deeply into the total assets of the company. To avoid such exposure, a firm may choose not to have a business presence in West Virginia. We now examine each of these cases in more detail.

ESTATE OF TAWNEY V. COLUMBIA NATURAL RESOURCES

In *Estate of Tawney v. Columbia Natural Resources*, the West Virginia Supreme Court of Appeals determined the appropriate reading of the contract at issue, sent by the Circuit Court of Roane County as a certified question.[26] The approximately 8,000 plaintiffs in the case had oil and gas leases of varying forms and types with Columbia Natural Resources ("CRN"), a subsidiary of NiSource, or a predecessor in interest.[27] The oil and gas leases provided that the plaintiffs would receive payments of 1/8 of the royalty to be calculated "'at the well,' 'at the wellhead' or similar language, or that the royalty is 'an amount equal to 1/8 of the price, net of all costs beyond the wellhead,' or 'less all taxes, assessments, and adjustments.'"[28] "In light of fact that West Virginia recognizes that a lessee to an oil and gas lease must bear all costs incurred in marketing and transporting the product to the point of sale unless the oil and gas lease provides otherwise,"[29] the Supreme Court held that:

---

[24] *See* Perrine v. E.I. DuPont De Nemours & Co. (2007).

[25] *See* Wheeling Pittsburgh Steel Corp. v. Central West Virginia Energy Co. (2007).

[26] 219 W.Va. 266, 633 S.E.2d 22 (2006).

[27] *Id.* at 269, 25.

[28] *Id.* at 268, 24.

[29] *Id.*

language in an oil and gas lease that provides that the lessor's 1/8 royalty (as in this case) is to be calculated "at the well," "at the wellhead," or similar language, or that the royalty is "an amount equal to 1/8 of the price, net all costs beyond the wellhead," or "less all taxes, assessments, and adjustments" is ambiguous and, accordingly, is not effective to permit the lessee to deduct from the lessor's 1/8 royalty any portion of the costs incurred between the wellhead and the point of sale.[30]

The canon of construction that courts construe ambiguous language against the drafter supports the court's position.[31]

The interesting part of this case was the West Virginia Supreme Court's decision to refuse to hear an appeal of the $404 million verdict, the third largest verdict in the nation for 2007, of which $270 million were punitive damages.[32] Instead, the West Virginia Supreme Court "granted NiSource's request for a stay of the judgment, pending action by the U.S. Supreme Court on a petition for a writ of certiorari, which NiSource plan[ned] to file in late August."[33] Injured plaintiffs generally cannot recover punitive damages in a breach of contract action because a goal of contract law is to compensate the injured party, not to punish the breaching party.[34] The punitive damages awarded in this case represent a major departure from the standard principles of contract law.

LENORA PERRINE, ET AL. V. E.I. DUPONT DE NEMOURS & CO., ET AL.

The West Virginia Supreme Court of Appeals has announced that it will hear argument in three cases on September 24, 2008, Numbers 080721, 081461, and 081462, captioned *Lenora Perrine, et al. v. E.I. DuPont de Nemours & Co., et al. (DuPont).*[35] This includes argument in the plaintiff's appeal of partial summary judgment and DuPont's appeal of the approximately $252 million verdict.[36]

In *DuPont*, attorneys presented the Harrison County Circuit Court jury with the history of a plant built in 1911 under the ownership of Grasselli Chemical Co., Inc.[37] DuPont purchased the plant in 1928, and disposed zinc ore waste into a pile at the facility, which smoldered at high temperatures and released "toxic heavy metals into the surrounding communities."[38] In 1950, DuPont sold the plant to Meadowbrook Corp.[39] T.L. Diamond & Co., Inc. "ran the plant from 1984 until approximately 2001, when DuPont regained

---

[30] *Id.* at 274, 30.

[31] ROBERT A. HILLMAN, PRINCIPLES OF CONTRACT LAW 249 (West 2004).

[32] NiSource Reports Second Quarter Earnings, *available at* http://www.foxbusiness.com/story.markets/industries /energy/nisource-reports-second-quarter-earnings/.

[33] *Id.*

[34] HILLMAN at 134.

[35] *See* Motion docket for September 24, 2008, *available at* http://www.state.wv.us/wvsca/calendar/ sept24_08.htm.

[36] Dan Turner, *DuPont files an appeal with West Virginia Supreme Court on Spelter Lawsuit Decision*, REUTERS PRNEWSWIRE-FIRSTCALL, June 24, 2008.

[37] *Lenora Perrine, et al. v. E.I. DuPont de Nemours & Co., et al.,* No. 04-C-296; *see* VerdictSearch, *Top 100 Verdicts of 2007.*

[38] *Id.*

[39] *Id.*

operation."[40] After repurchasing the plant, DuPont "began smoothing the waste pile and covered it with a synthetic membrane to grow vegetation, which [DuPont] completed in 2004."[41] Approximately 8,000 residents sued E.I. DuPont De Nemours and Co., Meadowbrook Corp., Matthiessen & Hegeler Zinc Co. Inc., Nuzum Trucking Co., T.L. Diamond & Co. Inc., and Joseph Paushel claiming "wanton, willful, and reckless conduct."[42] At trial,

> [P]laintiffs' experts testified that the claimants were at a higher risk to cancer (skin, lung, bladder, stomach and kidney cancer) and non-cancer impairments, including decreased renal function, renal failure, plumbism (lead poisoning) and neurocognitive injury. The plaintiffs' experts opined that the class members lived in different identified zones (Zone 1A, Zone 1B, Zone 2 and Zone 3) and that each zone was at a different risk of contracting cancer. Claimants in Zone 1A had a one in 1,000 incremental increased risk of cancer; Zone 1B residents had a 5 in 10,0000 increased risk; Zone 2 had a one in 10,000 risk; and Zone 3 had a five in 100,000 risk. . . . [Plaintiffs' expert] Brown testified that it would cost $56 million to remove and replace the contaminated soils and clean affected zones. In Zone 1A, the top six inches of the soil would be scraped and replaced on 20 properties, while anything that acted as a dust trap in the homes (i.e. insulation, air conditioner, carpet) would be removed and cleansed. In the remaining zones, the cleanup would be less invasive, as homes' ventilation systems would be cleaned . . . .[43]

On the other hand,

> Defense counsel contended that the smelter did not present a public health problem, and that any risk to cancer or any other alleged diseases [were] nonexistent. This opinion was reiterated by Peter Valberg, the defense comparative risk expert, who said that it was more dangerous to smoke cigarettes and drive a car while talking on phone than to live in the Spelter area.[44]

In October of 2007, a Harrison County jury awarded the plaintiffs $196.2 million in punitive damages, $33.3 million to clean up soil and residences, $2.8 million to clean up mobile homes, $1.0 million to clean up commercial structures, and $18.4 million in lost profits.[45] On appeal, plaintiffs' argue

> that there were material questions of fact as to whether the contamination and injuries/damages due to the operation of a zinc smelter were contemplated by the original landowners and whether certain releases and easements executed in

---

[40] *Id.*
[41] *Id.*
[42] *Id.*
[43] *Id.*
[44] *Id.*
[45] *Id.*

the 1920's provide immunity for those claims. Plaintiffs seek a reversal of the circuit court's order granting partial summary judgment in favor of defendants on the Property Class members' claims and request a remand for reinstatement and adjudication of those claims upon their merits.[46]

This case presents a $251.7 million dollar award to plaintiffs who have at most "a one in 1,000 incremental increased risk of cancer."[47] Whether this value is an appropriate award is subject to debate. In any case, a site owned by multiple companies over a 100-year period has yielded plaintiffs a punitive damage award three times that of the amount needed to compensate the plaintiffs for their increased risk of injury.

PITTSBURGH STEEL CORP. V. CENTRAL WEST VIRGINIA ENERGY CO.

In a breach of contract dispute, the Brooke County Circuit Court awarded the Wheeling-Pittsburgh Steel Corp. (Wheeling-Pitt) $219.8 million in damages arising out of Central West Virginia Energy Company's "fail[ure] to deliver 104,000 tons of metallurgical grade coal per month as required under a contract that extended to 2010."[48] Central West Virginia Energy Co. (Central West Virginia Energy) is a subsidiary of Massey Energy (Massey).[49] Wheeling-Pitt had a long-term contract with Central West Virginia Energy Co. for the provision of coal, which would allow Wheeling-Pitt to operate its coke ovens nonstop.[50]

The terms of the contract included a "force majeure," or "greater forces" clause,[51] which allowed a party to breach the contract for limited amounts of time if an event occurred outside the party's control. Problems arose between Wheeling-Pitt and Central West Virginia Energy in late 2003, when "steel-making coal prices skyrocketed."[52] "Coal that had been selling for $40 a ton was going for $125 a ton or more."[53] Massey asserted that "transportation challenges . . . , a variety of geological problems, poor roof conditions, and flooding at its Southern West Virginia mines" caused the company to fail to deliver the coal to Wheeling-Pitt,[54] and that Massey and Central West Virginia Energy were protected from a breach of contract action arising under circumstances that were beyond the control of Massey and Central West Virginia Energy. Central West Virginia Energy accused Massey of "selling its steel making coal at prices far greater than its contract with Wheeling-Pitt allowed."[55]

Wheeling-Pitt sued Central West Virginia Energy and Massey for the damage their coke oven sustained in its intermittent operation, and for replacement coal purchases.[56] The Brooke County jurors awarded Wheeling-Pitt $119.8 million in compensatory damages and $50 million in punitive damages from both Central West Virginia Energy and Massey.[57]

---

[46] Id.

[47] Id.

[48] Associated Press, *Judge Orders Massey to Pay Wheeling-Pitt*, CHARLESTON DAILY MAIL, July 3, 2007, at C2.

[49] Id.

[50] Id.

[51] Ken Ward, Jr., *Massey Likely to Appeal Wheeling-Pitt Coal Verdict*, CHARLESTON GAZETTE, July 4, 2007, at A2.

[52] Id.

[53] Id.

[54] Id.

[55] Id.

[56] Id.

[57] Id.

Because the West Supreme Court of Appeals declined to hear an appeal of the verdict, Massey is appealing the case to the U.S. Supreme Court.[58]

This case provides an example of how the West Virginia courts have abandoned the concept of efficient breach of contract. Under an efficient breach, society is made better off by one party breaching an existing contract, reaping the benefits of that breach, and then compensating the injured party. Society is made better off because the breaching party creates wealth, and the innocent, non-breaching party is made whole. If the "force majeure" clause did not apply, as the jury found, then Central West Virginia Energy did owe Wheeling-Pitt an amount equal to the foreseeable damage Wheeling-Pitt sustained as a result of Central West Virginia Energy's breach. According to the jury, $119.8 million is a reasonable figure for this breach of contract. The interesting question is whether punitive damages have a place in contract law, and the West Virginia Supreme Court denied an appeal of this case to address that issue. Given the potentially large economic consequences of these large punitive awards, and the lack of legal support for awarding punitive damages in a breach-of-contract case, the Supreme Court's decision to allow the verdict to stand negatively affects the nation's view of West Virginia's business climate.

STATE EX REL. JOHNSON & JOHNSON V. KARL

Under the learned intermediary doctrine, drug manufacturers have no duty to warn consumers about the risks of taking prescription drugs because the manufacturers can rely on prescribing physicians to do so.[59] In a 3-2 decision in *State ex rel. Johnson & Johnson v. Karl,*[60] West Virginia became the only jurisdiction in the country to reject the learned intermediary doctrine in prescription medical product cases.[61]

In *Karl*, a drug manufacturer asked the Supreme Court of Appeals to issue a writ of prohibition, preventing the trial court, the Circuit Court of Marshall County, from refusing to apply the learned intermediary doctrine, in a case brought by the estate of a woman who died suddenly three days after she began taking a prescription drug made by the drug manufacturer.[62] The majority opinion cites justifications from a variety of jurisdictions which adhere to the doctrine as "largely outdated and unpersuasive,"[63] even though the rule continues to be routinely applied.[64] The court reasons that the "Norman Rockwell" depiction

---

[58] Maria Guzzo, *Massey Vows to Battle W-P to the Last,* AMERICAN METAL MARKET, May 26, 2008.

[59] *See* John A. Day, *Learned Intermediary Doctrine,* August 29, 2007, *available at* http://www.dayontorts.com/products-liability-learned-intermediary-doctrine.html.

[60] 220 W.Va. 463, 647 S.E.2d 899 (2007).

[61] *See* James M. Beck and Mark Hermann, *Headcount: Who's adopted the Learned Intermediary Rule,* July 5, 2007, *available at* http://druganddevicelaw.blogspot.com/2007/07/headcount-whos-adopted-learned.html.

[62] 220 W.Va. 463, 465, 647 S.E.2d 899, 901.

[63] *Id.* at 470, 906.

[64] *See* Ted Frank and James Beck, *West Virginia Supreme Court Strikes Down the Learned Intermediary Rule,* November 15, 2007, available at http://www.aei.org/publications/filter.all,pubID.27111/pub_detail.asp. (*citing* the following cases as examples of jurisdictions that recently applied the learned intermediary rule: *E.g.,* Ethicon Endo-Surgery, Inc. v. Meyer, ___ S.W.3d ___, 2007 WL 1095552, at *2 (Tex. App. April 12, 2007); Bodie v. Purdue Pharma LP, ___F.3d ___, 2007 WL 1577964, at *5-6, 11 (11th Cir. June 1, 2007) (applying Alabama law); Stilwell v. Smith & Nephew, Inc., 482 F.3d 1187, 1194 (9th Cir. 2007) (applying Arizona law); In re Zyprexa Prods. Liab. Litig. v. Eli Lilly & Co., ___ F. Supp. 2d ___, 2007 WL 1678078, at *28 (E.D.N.Y. June 11, 2007) (applying Pennsylvania, North Carolina and Florida law); Soufflas v. Zimmer, Inc., 474 F. Supp.2d 737, 751 (E.D. Pa. 2007); Madsen v. American Home Prodts. Corp., 477 F. Supp.2d 1025, 1033 (E.D. Mo.

of physician-patient relations no longer exists, managed care systems have reduced the amount of time doctors spend with their patients, drug manufacturers have a wealth of advertising money at their disposal to speak directly to patients, and the State's existing law of comparative contribution among joint tortfeasors adequately addresses issues of liability among doctors and drug companies when patients sue for injuries related to prescription drug use.[65]

On the other hand, the dissent argues that the issue of adequate product warnings on prescription drugs largely depends on the unique facts of each case, and the majority opinion downplays the "continuing and vital" role a physician plays in the decision to prescribe particular medications to particular individuals, based on that individual's specific needs.[66] Further, commentators suggest that the ruling may have potentially damaging effects on other doctrines, such as product identification, remote causation, and burden of proof in pharmaceutical products liability cases.[67] The results of the case arguably amount to strict liability on pharmaceutical manufacturers.

THE 2006 CASES: *MBNA* AND *RYAN V. CLONCH*

The 2006 cases highlighted here present examples of the West Virginia Supreme Court's willingness to increase tax revenue,[68] and the court's willingness to leave the bounds of the worker's compensation system to levy additional punishments on employers.[69] Both decisions decrease the predictability of West Virginia's legal system because they present sudden changes to established rules.

MBNA

In *Tax Commissioner of State v. MBNA America Bank* (*MBNA*), dealing with constitutional and tax law, the court reviewed a case in which a Delaware credit card company sought a refund of the West Virginia business franchise tax and corporate net income tax.[70] MBNA, the credit card company, had no real or tangible personal property or employees in West Virginia during the relevant two-year period, 1998 and 1999.[71] The company's business in the state included issuing and servicing credit cards, extending unsecured credit to card users, and promoting its business through mail and telephone solicitation.[72] The issue in this case was whether the imposition of West Virginia's business franchise and corporate net income taxes on MBNA violated the Commerce Clause of the U.S. Constitution.[73] The court held that the

---

2007) (applying Iowa law); Cowley v. Abbott Laboratories, 476 F. Supp.2d 1053, 1060 (W.D. Wis. 2007) (applying North Carolina law); Hill v. Wyeth, Inc., 2007 WL 674251, at *3-4 (E.D. Mo. Feb. 28, 2007); Saraney v. Tap Pharm. Prods., 2007 WL 148845, at *6 (N.D. Ohio Jan. 16, 2007); Paparo v. Ortho McNeil Pharm., 2007 WL 121149, at *3 (S.D. Fla. Jan. 10, 2007)).

[65] 220 W.Va. at 477, 647 S.E.2d at 912.

[66] *Id.* at 481, 917.

[67] *See* Frank and Beck.

[68] *See* Tax Commissioner of State v. MBNA America Bank, N.A. (2006).

[69] *See* Joseph E. Ryan v. Clonch Industries, Inc. (2006).

[70] Tax Commissioner of State v. MBNA America Bank, N.A. (2006).

[71] *Id.* at 164, 227.

[72] *Id.*

[73] *Id.*

tax scheme did not violate the Commerce Clause, reasoning that the company had a substantial economic presence in the state, sufficiently meeting the substantial nexus required to impose these taxes.[74]

On the other hand, the dissent argues that taxing a business incorporated in a foreign state, when that business has no physical presence in West Virginia, is an impermissible burden on interstate commerce, is lacking in precedential support at both the state and federal levels, and is based upon thinly-veiled-state-tax agendas and inaccurate readings of Supreme Court precedent.[75] West Virginia's Chief Justice Davis defends the majority opinion in her concurrence. She states that she sees no reason why "mom and pop" businesses in the state with relatively small gross receipts should have to pay the business franchise tax and the corporate net income tax due to their physical presence in the state, when much larger corporations, such as MBNA, that make millions of dollars doing business in the state, should not simply because they lack a physical presence.[76] As of November 30, 2006, West Virginia became the third state to use the "significant economic presence" doctrine under the Commerce Clause.[77] In June 2007, the U.S. Supreme Court declined to review the case.[78] The economic ramifications of this decision are substantial as they relate to the potential costs (in terms of the tax burden) associated with companies doing business in West Virginia. Rightly or wrongly, this decision increases the costs to out-of-state companies thinking of doing business in the state.

JOSEPH E. RYAN V. CLONCH INDUSTRIES

When an individual appeals an administrative decision on a workers' compensation issue, the appeal goes directly to the West Virginia Supreme Court of Appeals for disposition. Only five other states in the United States utilize a similar system of worker's compensation review. According to the court's statistical report for 2007,[79] seventy-three percent of the new cases filed with the court were workers' compensation cases. The court disposes of most of the compensation cases it decides to review by memorandum order, as opposed to written opinion, its primary means of disposing of non-compensation cases.[80]

Detractors of the court's workers' compensation jurisprudence, including members of the court, criticize some of its decisions as liberalizing benefit distributions beyond the legislature's original intent, driving up the cost of the workers' compensation system.[81] In *Ryan v. Clonch*, the court expanded an exception to a discovery rule, which one attorney

---

[74] *Id.* at 173, 236.

[75] *Id.* at 173-74, 236-37 (Benjamin, J., dissenting).

[76] *Id.* at 180, 243 (Davis, C.J., concurring).

[77] *See* Ryan, Inc., *West Virginia Supreme Court Finds 'Significant Economic Presence' Constitutional Under Commerce Clause in MBNA America Bank,* November 30, 2006, *available at* http://www.johnbernardllc.com/develop/West_Virginia_Supreme_Court_Finds_Significant_Economic_Presence_Constitutional.aspx. The other two states are South Carolina and New Jersey. *Id.*

[78] *See TEI urges Supreme Court to clarify nexus standard: argues in MBNA case for clear-cut physical presence standard,* TAX EXECUTIVE, May-June 2007, *available at* http://findarticles.com/p/articles/mi_m6552/is_3_59/ai_n25378288.

[79] *Available at* http://www.state.wv.us/wvsca/clerk/statistics/2007StatRept.pdf.

[80] *Id.*

[81] *See* William Wayne Repass v. Workers' Compensation Division and USX Corporation/U.S. Steel Mining Company, Inc., unpublished memorandum disposition (2002) (Maynard, J., dissenting), *available at* http://www.state.wv.us/wvsca/docs/spring02/29645d.htm.

referred to as the "narrow exception you could drive a truck through."[82] In this case, a lumber worker performing banding duties was injured when a piece of metal banding material struck him in the left eye. The employee, Mr. Ryan, filed a claim under the deliberate intent statute, which provides immunity from suit to employers unless the employee can sufficiently prove five statutory requirements, including whether the unsafe working condition violated an industry standard applicable to the process, and whether the employer had a subjective realization and appreciation of the hazardous working condition and the high degree of risk associated with it.[83] The court reasoned that even though the employer's actual subjective knowledge of the unsafe working condition was lacking, it held that the employer unconscionably violated a mandatory duty to perform a hazard evaluation pursuant to an OSHA regulation.[84] The dissent argued that the majority contravened legislative intent by using a general safety regulation to "satisfy the statutory specificity requirement of a deliberate intent cause of action."[85]

CONCLUSION

A fair and balanced legal system that enforces contracts and property rights is an essential foundation for a healthy and prosperous market-based economy. In this study, we have examined some of the cases with the largest potential ramifications for West Virginia's business climate that have faced West Virginia's Supreme Court of Appeals from 2006 to 2008. The decisions made (or refused to be made) on these cases have the potential to affect economic growth and job creation. In the end, West Virginia is in competition with the other 49 states to attract entities that will create jobs and income. Thus, it is critical to examine how West Virginia judges treat individuals and businesses relative to the treatment businesses and individuals receive in other states. If the West Virginia court system imposes more costs and uncertainty than would be present in other states, it will detract from West Virginia's ability to sustain economic growth and prosperity. To grow, West Virginia's legal system must be competitive with other states.

---

[82]Brian Peterson, *Deliberate Intent: the narrow exception you could drive a truck through*" December 27, 2005, *available at* http://legalweblog.blogspot.com/2006/12/deliberate-intent-narrow-exception-you.html; *see* Ryan v. Clonch Industries, Inc. (2006).

[83] Ryan v. Clonch Industries, Inc., 219 W.Va. 664, 669-673, 639 S.E.2d 756, 761-765 (2006).

[84] *Id.* at 673, 765.

[85] *Id.* at 675, 767.

REFERENCES

Associated Press, *Judge Orders Massey to Pay Wheeling-Pitt*, Charleston Daily Mail, July 3, 2007, at C2.

Brian Peterson, *Deliberate Intent: the narrow exception you could drive a truck through*, December 27, 2005, *available at* http://legalweblog.blogspot.com/2006/12/deliberate-intent-narrow-exception-you.html.

Caprice Roberts, *In Search of Judicial Activism: The Dangers of Quantifying the Qualitative*, 74 Tenn. L. Rev. 567, 570 (2007).

Charles Lopeman, The Activist Advocate (Praeger Publishing, 1999).

Dan Turner, *DuPont files an appeal with West Virginia Supreme Court on Spelter Lawsuit Decision*, Reuters PRNewswire – FirstCall, June 24, 2008.

Elizabeth Thornburg, *Judicial Hellholes, Lawsuit Climates and Bad Social Science: Lessons from West Virginia*, 110 W.Va. L. Rev. 1097 (2008).

Frank Cross & Stefanie Lindquist, *The Scientific Study of Judicial Activism*, 91 Minn. L. Rev. 1752, 1762-1764 (2007).

James M. Beck & Mark Hermann, *Headcount: Who's Adopted the Learned Intermediary Rule*, July 5, 2007, *available at* http://www.druganddevicelaw.blogspot.com/2007/07/headcount-whos-adopted-learned.html.

John A. Day, *Learned Intermediary Doctrine*, August 29, 2007, *available at* http://www.dayontorts.com/ products-liability-learned-intermediary-doctrine.html.

Keenan Kmiec, *The Origin and Current Meanings of 'Judicial Activism,'* 92 Cal. L. Rev. 1441, 1443 (2004).

Ken Ward, *Maynard recuses himself for the third time*, Charleston Gazette, February 8, 2008.

Ken Ward, *Massey Likely to Appeal Wheeling-Pitt Coal Verdict*, Charleston Gazette, July 4, 2007, at A2.

Kristen M. Leddy, Russell S. Sobel, and Matthew T. Yanni, *Should We Keep This Court? An Economic Examination of Recent Decisions Made by the West Virginia Supreme Court of Appeals*, Fed. Soc., Oct. 2008, *available at* www.fed-soc.org/westvirginia.

Lawrence Messina, *Legal Groups blast W. Va. Justice in Massey Case*, Associated Press, August 5, 2008.

Maria Guzzo, *Massey Vows to Battle W-P to the Last*, American Metal Market, May 26, 2008.

NiSource Reports Second Quarter Earnings, *available at* http://www.foxbusiness.com/story.markets/industries/energy/nisource-reports-second-quarter-earnings/.

Paul Nyden, *Starcher recuses himself from the Massey,* Charleston Gazette, February 16, 2008.

Richard A. Brisbin, Jr., West Virginia State Government: The Legislative, Executive, and Judicial Branches, *The West Virginia Judiciary* (Institute for Public Affairs, West Virginia University, 1993).

Robert Hillman, Principles of Contract Law 249 (West 2004).

Ryan, Inc., *West Virginia Supreme Court Finds 'Significant Economic Presence' Constitutional Under Commerce Clause in MBNA America Bank*, November 30, 2006, *available at* http://www.johnbernardllc.com/develop/West_Virginia_Supreme_Court_Finds_Economic_Presence_Constitutional.aspx.

Ted Frank & James Beck, *West Virginia Supreme Court Strikes Down the Learned Intermediary Rule*, November 15, 2007, *available at* http://www.aei.org/publications/filter.all,pubID.27111/pub_detail.asp.

TEI urges Supreme Court to clarify nexus standard: argues in MBNA case for clear-cut physical presence standard, Tax Executive, May-June 2007, *available at* http://www.findarticles.com/p/articles/mi_m6552/is_3_59/ai_n25378288.

The Supreme Court of Appeals of West Virginia docket calendar, *available at* http://www.state.wv.us/wvsca/calendar/sept24_08.htm.

The Supreme Court of Appeal of West Virginia statistical report for 2007, *available at* http://www.state.wv.us/wvsca/clerk/statistics/2007StatRept.pdf.

Verdict Search, *Top 100 Verdicts of 2007*, *available at* http://www.verdictsearch.com/index.jsp?do=top100.

Vincent Martin Bonventre, *Judicial Activism, Judges' Speech, and Merit Selection: Conventional Wisdom and Nonsense*, 68 Alb. L. Rev. 557, 564-575 (2005).

CASES CITED

Bias v. Eastern Associated Coal Corporation, 220 W.Va. 190, 209, 640 S.E.2d 540, 559 (2006) (Davis, C.J., concurring).

Caperton v. A.T. Massey Coal Co., Inc., not reported in S.E.2d., 2008 WL 918444, 2007 W.Va. LEXIS 119 (W. Va., April 3, 2008); *see also* Justice Starcher's recusal statement, *available at* http://www.state.wv.us/wvsca/press/feb15b_08.htm; *see also* the brief of The American Bar Association as Amicus Curiae in this case, *available at* http://www.abanet.org/judind/pdf/caperton_brief.pdf.

Estate of Tawney v. Columbia Natural Resources, L.L.C., 219 W.Va. 266, 633 S.E.2d 22 (2006).

Fairmont General Hospital, Inc. v. United Hospital Center, Inc., 218 W.Va. 360, 377, 624 S.E.2d 797, 814 (2005) (Starcher, J., dissenting).

Joseph A. Ryan v. Clonch Industries, 219 W.Va. 664, 639 S.E.2d 756 (2006).

Lenora Perrine, *et al.*, v. E.I. DuPont de Nemours & Co., *et al.*, No. 04-C-296-2 (W.Va. Cir. Ct., Harrison Co., 2007).

Riggs v. West Virginia University Hospitals, Inc., 221 W.Va. 646, 668, 656 S.E.2d 91, 113 (2007) (Davis, C.J., dissenting).

State *ex rel.* Johnson & Johnson v. Karl, 220 W.Va. 463, 647 S.E.2d 899 (2007).

Tax Commissioner of State v. MBNA America Bank, N.A., 220 W.Va. 163, 640 S.E.2d 226 (2006).

Wheeling Pittsburgh Steel Corp., v. Central West Virginia Energy Co., Nos. 080182 and 080183 (W. Va. Cir. Ct., Brooke Co., 2007).

William Wayne Repass v. Workers' Compensation Division and USX Corporation/U.S. Steel Mining Company, Inc., unpublished memorandum disposition (2002) (Maynard, J., dissenting), *available at* http://www.state.wv.us/wvsca/docs/spring02/29645d.htm.

Worley v. Beckley Mechanical, Inc., 220 W.Va. 633, 643, 648 S.E.2d 620, 630 (2007) (Benjamin, J., dissenting).

CHAPTER 9

9

WEST VIRGINIA LEGAL LIABILITY REFORM

by Kristen M. Leddy and Matthew T. Yanni

The Rule of Law

9

WEST VIRGINIA LEGAL LIABILITY REFORM

Kristen M. Leddy and Matthew T. Yanni

Torts scholar Kenneth Abraham defines tort as "a civil wrong arising out of contract."[1] Although Abraham describes this definition as both overinclusive and underinclusive,[2] this definition is the best simple definition that torts scholars offer. Abraham identifies five possible functions of the tort system: "corrective justice and civil redress," "optimal deterrence," "loss distribution," "compensation," and "redress of social grievances."[3] Whether the individual sympathizes with the plaintiff-friendly (or victim-friendly) school of thought or the defendant-friendly (or business-friendly) school of thought is a matter of preference. The plaintiff-friendly school values "compensat[ing] victims who have suffered grievous injuries or losses through the fault of others and the creation of an incentive for persons and firms to act to prevent potential causes of injury or death,"[4] and the defendant-friendly school values reducing the payment of compensatory and punitive damages to plaintiffs by "aboli[shing] the rule of joint and several liability, aboli[shing] the collateral source rule, limit[ing] punitive damages, and limit[ing] noneconomic damages."[5] By applying the principles of economic analysis, we attempt to divorce ourselves from these competing schools in order to explore the incentives and effects of West Virginia's tort system on the state's economy.

We begin by defining the foundations of tort law and the role of the state in protecting citizens through a sound legal system, with specific emphasis on civil liability. We next discuss some of the major complaints about West Virginia's legal system. After an exploration of these complaints, we outline three specific legal liability reforms: joint and several liability, medical malpractice liability, and venue shopping. These reforms receive significant attention because they are fair, likely to have a positive impact on the state's legal system, and relatively easy to implement.

THE FOUNDATIONS OF TORT LAW

Tort law should encourage individuals to take an efficient level of precaution in their interactions with other people and with others' property.[6] A simplified version of tort law asks

---

[1] Kenneth S. Abraham, *The Forms and Functions of Tort Law* 1.
[2] *Id.*
[3] *Id.* at 14-20.
[4] Richard A. Brisbin, Jr. & John C. Kilwein, *The Future of the West Virginia Judiciary: Problems and Policy Options*, 2, 5.
[5] ATRA's Mission: Real Justice in Our Courts.
[6] *See* Richard Posner, *Economic Analysis of Law*.

whether the tortfeasor should have done something different than what he did and whether someone or something was injured as a result. A tort cause of action is based either on a theory that the defendant negligently harmed the plaintiff or on a theory that the defendant intentionally harmed the plaintiff.

To recover in a negligence cause of action, the plaintiff must prove that the defendant owed the plaintiff a duty, that the defendant breached the duty he owed the plaintiff, that the defendant's breach caused the plaintiff to receive an injury, and that the defendant should pay the plaintiff money damages. Judge Learned Hand established that a potential tortfeasor breached his duty of reasonable care if the burden of acting to prevent an injury is less than the expected probability of loss multiplied by the expected loss (B<PL).[7] In order to minimize the social costs of negligent actions, precautions should be taken until the marginal cost of the safety improvement is equal to the marginal benefit the safety improvement provides.[8] This ideal applies equally to plaintiffs and defendants. Because "many accidents can be prevented by victims at a lower cost than by injurers,"[9] the law's aim should be "to make sure that the lower-cost avoider is encouraged to take care."[10] As such, West Virginia courts should perform detailed evaluations of whether each party was exercising due care at the time of the accident in order to ensure that the lower-cost avoider bears the liability for the action or inaction.

To recover in an intentional tort cause of action, a plaintiff must establish that the defendant intended to cause some type of contact; that the conduct was harmful or offensive to the plaintiff; and either that the defendant intended to harm or offend, or that the defendant knew that harm or offense was substantially certain to result from the contact. In applying Hand's B<PL, Posner finds that B is a negative number in an intentional tort because "rather than saving resources by injuring the victim (implying a positive B) I would save resources by not injuring the victim (implying a negative B)" since it must cost something to engage in an injurious act.[11] Posner also argues that P is much higher in an intentional tort than it would be in a negligence tort because "wanting to do someone an injury makes it much more likely that an injury will occur than if the injury would be undesired by-product of another activity."[12] Based on this analysis, Posner finds that the law is much more willing to award punitive damages in intentional tort cases than in negligence cases, because the risk of deterring socially valuable conduct by imposing additional costs on the tortfeasor is minimized in the intentional tort case where the conduct is harmful or offensive by definition. Posner also argues that there is no reason to allow a defense of contributory negligence in an intentional tort case, "since the cost of avoidance is plainly lower to the injurer than to the victim – is indeed negative to the injurer and positive to the victim. The victim cannot be the lower-cost avoider."[13]

West Virginia's liability system is designed to ensure that injured parties are compensated at least to the extent of their injuries. In some cases, this state fosters

---

[7] United States v. Carroll Towing Co.
[8] *See* Posner, *Economic Analysis of Law.*
[9] *Id.* at 172.
[10] *Id.*
[11] *Id.* at 206.
[12] *Id.*
[13] *Id.*

inefficiency by requiring tortfeasors to pay sums greater than their contribution to the injury.[14] As it relates to torts arising out of negligent actions, overcompensating victims overdeters productive activity. Unfortunately, public sentiment and the resulting legislation have placed the interests of the injured party above the prosperity of the state and its citizens. West Virginia lags behind all other states with respect to providing a fair and efficient system of injury compensation based on the *2007 U. S. Chamber of Commerce State Liability Systems Ranking Study*.[15] In the next section, we explain the economic burden placed on West Virginia by its legal liability system.

THE ROLE OF THE STATE AND WEST VIRGINIA'S LEGAL SYSTEM

The father of economics, Adam Smith, states in *The Wealth of Nations* that one of the few roles of government is to establish a fair and independent judiciary.[16] The role of the judiciary in civil law cases is to enforce contracts and settle disputes. A system that enforces contracts and creates incentives for citizens to respect the property of others creates the fundamental legal basis for long-term economic growth. A good legal system hears cases and applies established precedent in a fair, predictable, and efficient manner. Legal systems with these characteristics promote economic growth and development.[17]

West Virginia's low ranking with respect to its legal liability system is a result of the State's legislation and common-law decisions. Where the state's legislative, executive, and judicial bodies promote unfair transfers of wealth, they distort the market system and the incentives businesses face. Fortunately, some simple legal reforms have been shown to remedy this situation in other states. Adopting these reforms would lead to a more fair judicial system and greater prosperity for our state.

LEGAL LIABILITY REFORMS IN WEST VIRGINIA

We base our recommendations for legal liability reform upon the notion of fairness, the positive impact on the state's business climate, and the constitutionality of implementing the reform in West Virginia.[18] The three legal reforms considered in the following sections include 1) eliminating the doctrine of joint and several liability in all civil tort claims, 2) extending reform efforts in the area of medical malpractice liability, and 3) ending venue shopping in products liability and class action lawsuits.

---

[14] *See generally* Kizer v. Harper (2001) at n. 26. "This Court is not unmindful of the fact that Appellant, who was charged with only 1% fault, is being held liable for the full verdict under principles of joint and several liability. Despite the seeming inequity of this result, we cannot, without turning the tort law of this state 'on its head,' reach a contrary result." (quoting Miller v. Monongahela Power Co. (1999)).

[15] Institute for Legal Reform (2007).

[16] Adam Smith, *An Inquiry into the Nature and Causes of the Wealth of Nations*.

[17] Peter Boettke & J. Robert Subrick, *Rule of Law, Development and Human Capabilities*.

[18] Although it is possible to modify the West Virginia Constitution, proposing reforms that are currently unconstitutional would change the nature of this project from a practical to a theoretical one. If our goal is to help the state's economy grow, we should concentrate on those reforms that may be implemented with relative ease. We made this determination with respect to West Virginia's legal structure, not necessarily with respect to political opposition or support.

JOINT AND SEVERAL LIABILITY

'Joint and several liability' is a hybrid of 'joint liability' and 'several liability,' and provides that each defendant in a tort lawsuit may be held responsible for the full amount of damages awarded in a case.[19] This holds true even when a defendant is found responsible for only a small percentage of the damage award. Take a hypothetical case with two joint tortfeasors, in which the jury finds that one party holds a certain percentage of the liability, with the rest held by the other. Under pure joint and several liability, either defendant could be held responsible for the full amount of the judgment. This is sometimes referred to as the 'deep pockets' rule, in which potential litigants search for parties with extensive financial resources to pay large verdicts. Those best able to pay large verdicts are usually insurance companies and large businesses.

Joint and several liability unfairly requires that injured parties be compensated by parties not entirely liable for their injuries in the event one party cannot pay its proportionate share of an award. This principle is not consistent with the societies' interest in requiring that tortfeasors be required to pay only that damage they have caused. Under the doctrine of joint and several liability, tortfeasors can be required to pay for damages caused by another party. Despite the social reasons to compensate injured parties, it is both unfair and inefficient to force businesses to pay for damages they have not caused.

Proponents of joint and several liability, on the other hand, argue that it protects victims from being undercompensated if one of the defendants cannot pay his share of proportionate liability. A joint tortfeasor who pays more than his proportionate liability has a right of contribution against his co-defendant.[20] This often leads to inequitable results and procedural battles between defendants to enforce their contribution rights, particularly where one defendant remains 'holding the bag.'[21]

Currently in West Virginia, the doctrine of joint and several liability applies, except where a defendant is found 30 percent or less at fault.[22] Under this exception, the defendant's liability shall be several and not joint, and the defendant will only be liable for the damages attributable to him or her.[23] There are, however, some exceptions. Joint and several liability always applies to those who commit intentional torts; any party who acts in concert with another as part of a common plan or design resulting in harm; negligent or willful unlawful emission, disposal, or spillage of toxic or hazardous substance; or manufacture or sale of a defective product.[24] Also, on motion, a court can order reallocation of any uncollectable amount among the other parties, though defendants less than ten percent at fault will not be subject to reallocation.[25] In cases involving medical professional liability, West Virginia has adopted several liability.[26] Under several liability, the defendant is responsible only for the value of damages he caused.

---

[19] Joint liability refers to liability shared by two or more parties, while several (or proportionate) liability refers to liability where parties are liable only for their respective obligations.

[20] *See, e.g.*, Haynes v. City of Nitro (1977), in which the right of contribution is the defendant's ability to pursue another defendant who fails to pay her proportionate share.

[21]*See* Edward M. Koch, The Pennsylvania Supreme Court Declares the Fair Share Act Unconstitutional.

[22] W.Va. Code Ann. §55-7-24.

[23] *Id.*

[24] *Id.*

[25] *Id.*

[26] W.Va. Code Ann. §55-7B-9.

Courts in neighboring states are split in their decisions on the application of joint and several liability. Ohio applies modified joint and several liability, in which joint and several liability only applies to economic losses if the defendant is more than 50 percent liable for unintentional torts or any percentage liable for an intentional tort.[27] Tennessee has eliminated joint and several liability.[28] In June 2002, the Pennsylvania Legislature passed the Fair Share Act, which applied several liability unless a defendant's proportionate negligence was greater than sixty percent, with some exceptions.[29] However, in September 2006, the Supreme Court of Pennsylvania affirmed a decision which made the Fair Share Act unconstitutional, returning Pennsylvania to pure joint and several liability.[30] Maryland and Virginia apply pure joint and several liability as long as the injury to the plaintiff is indivisible.[31] Fortunately, states applying pure joint and several liability are in the minority because about two-thirds of the nation has either abolished joint and several liability or restricts its application to defendants that are at least fifty percent liable for a plaintiff's injury.[32]

A small reform, on par with Ohio's system, would require West Virginia to further restrict its application of joint and several liability to defendants with proportionate negligence of fifty percent or more. At best, West Virginia should enact a state law which extends several liability from cases involving medical professional liability to all civil cases, in which each defendant will only be liable for its proportionate share of the plaintiff's loss. Proportionate liability will alleviate the threat of holding businesses accountable for substantial judgments not incurred by their actions.

MEDICAL MALPRACTICE LIABILITY

In 2003, West Virginia enacted HB 2122, reforming its liability system with respect to the responsibilities of medical professionals.[33] Reducing state medical malpractice from joint and several liability to pure several liability, in 2005, was an important victory for both patients and medical staff. By limiting medical malpractice liability to pure several liability, West Virginia has provided for patient care and helped to attract and retain high quality doctors and their staffs.

Despite recent successes, there are still important reforms outstanding to decrease the burden medical malpractice places on the State and its medical providers. We propose to limit expert medical testimony to that of established professionals in the same field as the defendant in medical malpractice cases. This helps to curtail the use of medical experts in trial that do not have expert knowledge of pertinent issues at hand, and are not sufficiently familiar with standard procedures in that field. Implementing these reforms will help to reduce the burden placed on both the state court system and the medical professionals named as tortfeasors.

---

[27] Ohio Rev. Code Ann. §2307.22.

[28] *See* McIntyre v. Balentine (1992).

[29] 42 Pa.C.S.A. §7102.

[30] *See* DeWeese v. Cortes (2006).

[31] *See* Consumer Protection Division v. Morgan (2005) and Maroulis v. Elliot (1966), in which a plaintiff's injuries are indivisible if they cannot be split between defendants.

[32] *See* American Tort Reform Association, Joint and Several Liability Rule Reform; *see also* Dave Lenckus, Courtrooms Playing Role in Reforming Tort System.

[33] Don Sensabaugh & Michele Grinberg, HB 2122: Medical Professional Liability Reform.

VENUE SHOPPING

We recommend the imposition of meaningful venue requirements to help eliminate venue shopping and 'jackpot justice' in West Virginia, as well as reduce the State's burden in providing a location for these trials to be held. In 2003, it seemed that West Virginia was well on its way to accomplishing just that. In that year, the West Virginia Legislature amended the state's venue statute to restrict access to the state courts for non-residents unless a substantial part of the acts or omissions giving rise to the claim occurred in the State or the plaintiff could not obtain jurisdiction against a defendant where the claim arose.[34] Furthermore, each plaintiff had to independently establish that the venue was proper.[35] The Legislature amended the venue rules to stem abuse of West Virginia's courts by nonresidents who viewed the state as a 'magnet jurisdiction.' Magnet jurisdictions are plaintiff-friendly jurisdictions with generous juries, particularly for asbestosis cases,[36] where nonresidents can take advantage of liberal consolidation laws. This increases the pressure plaintiffs can place on defendants and increases the size of a potential verdict.

Unfortunately, this significant legislative reform measure was declared unconstitutional in 2006 by the West Virginia Supreme Court in *Morris v. Crown Equipment Corp.* In *Morris*, the Supreme Court of Appeals held that a plaintiff cannot be denied the right to bring a products liability lawsuit in this state against a West Virginia corporation and an out-of-state corporation merely because the plaintiff is the resident of another state.

In 2007, the West Virginia Legislature responded to the Court's decision in *Morris* by adopting the doctrine of *forum non conveniens*, and repealing the parts of the 2003 venue reform statute which the Supreme Court of Appeals held unconstitutional as violating the Privileges and Immunities Clause of the U.S. Constitution.[37] Under this doctrine, if a defendant is a corporation, venue is proper where the corporation's principal place of business is, and if it is not in the state, then where the corporation does business.[38] If the corporation is organized under West Virginia laws, but has its principal place of business elsewhere, then venue is proper in the circuit court of the county in which the plaintiff resides, or the circuit court of the county in which the seat of government is located has jurisdiction over actions against the corporation.[39] The Chamber of Commerce has stated that the venue reform statute is 'fatally flawed' and contains loopholes which make it significantly weaker than the 2003 venue reform statute.[40] It is not West Virginia's responsibility to provide a venue for plaintiffs' attorneys to exploit. To the extent that it does, the state fosters a perception of unfriendliness towards businesses and entrepreneurs.

OTHER POTENTIAL AVENUES OF REFORM

In this section, we cover additional reforms that do not merit a full and thorough treatment

---

[34] W.Va. Code Ann. §56-1-1(c).

[35] *Id.*

[36] See, *e.g.*, State *ex rel.* Mobil Corp. v. Gaughan (2002).

[37] *See* http://www.state.wv.us/wvsca/Amicus/LegisSummaries/HB2956.htm.

[38] W.Va. Code §56-1-1 (amended by H.B. 2956, Reg. Sess. (W.Va. 2007)).

[39] *Id.*

[40] Online at: http://www.instituteforlegalreform.com/media/pressreleases/20070425_HP_WestVirginia.cfm (last visited 12/10/08).

because they are less effective in their capacity to improve the state's legal climate than those reforms already analyzed. We address the contentious issues of punitive damages and the collateral source rule. We also discuss the problems with medical monitoring, and explain why awarding damages for medical monitoring is harmful to West Virginia's economy.

LIMITING PUNITIVE DAMAGES

According to the Institute for Legal Reform's *2007 U.S. Chamber of Commerce State Liability Systems Ranking Study*,[41] punitive damages reform is the most important issue to improve the litigation environment. Punitive damages are damages awarded to a plaintiff, in addition to compensatory damages, when the defendant is found to have acted with recklessness, malice or deceit. These damages are intended to punish and deter blameworthy conduct.

Fortunately, punitive damages compose a very small part of the tort system. They are awarded in less than four percent of all tort injury verdicts.[42] Nonetheless, controversy surrounds punitive damages because there is no generally accepted principle that governs the amount that should be awarded. The determination of punitive damages is left to the jury. Significantly, juries often have little guidance and wide latitude in how to assess damages, and courts are reluctant to interfere with the province of the jury even when an award is excessive.[43]

West Virginia imposes no statutory limits on punitive damages awards, and the standard for determining whether to award punitive damages is a preponderance of the evidence. This level of proof is required in most civil cases, and it means that the finder of fact in a case must find only that the facts are more probably one way than another. Eleven other states employ this standard.[44] Thirty-one states require a higher level of proof, clear and convincing evidence; two states mostly prohibit punitive damages; and five states prohibit punitive damages altogether.[45] Because punitive damages are designed to punish, we recommend that West Virginia judges require that the jury find at least clear and convincing evidence before allowing a punitive damages award.

THE COLLATERAL SOURCE RULE

Defendants disfavor the collateral source rule because it prevents defendants from disclosing payments to plaintiffs made by collateral sources at trial. Defendants would like to introduce evidence at trial showing that insurance or another similar source has already compensated the plaintiffs for part or all of the damage arising from the defendant's conduct. Allowing otherwise, defendants argue, would permit the plaintiff to make a double recovery, once from his insurer and then a second time from the defendant. If the role of compensatory damages is to compensate the plaintiff for the full value of his or her injuries, then, plaintiffs may be made more than whole if they receive a compensatory payment greater than the value of their injuries.

---

[41] http://www.instituteforlegalreform.com.

[42] *See* National Center for State Courts, http://ncsconline.org.

[43] Anna Bamonte Torrance, Legal Obstacles to Tort Reform in Pennsylvania.

[44] *Id.*

[45] *Id.*

On the other hand, Posner argues that the economic purpose of the negligence system is not compensation, but is the deterrence of inefficient accidents.[46] "To permit the defendant to set up [the plaintiff's] insurance policy as a bar to the action would result in underdeterrence."[47] If insurance companies bear the burden of paying for a defendant's wrongful actions, then the defendants will be underdeterred in their decision to invest in caution or safety. Furthermore, subrogation eliminates plaintiff's double recovery. In exchange for lower premiums, plaintiffs frequently assign insurance companies the right to recover from the plaintiff's award the value of payments the insurance company made to the plaintiff arising from the defendant's conduct.

West Virginia has statutorily modified the collateral source rule, such that its courts permit collateral source evidence in medical malpractice actions after the jury verdict but before damages have been awarded.[48] This reform would appear to mitigate against excessive recoveries in medical malpractice actions, and it could potentially be extended to other types of tort cases, such as personal injury or wrongful death actions. However, this is not a pressing area of reform for West Virginia because of the private remedy of subrogation largely operates to eliminate any double recovery.

MEDICAL MONITORING DAMAGES

"A medical monitoring claim seeks to recover the anticipated costs of long-term diagnostic testing necessary to detect latent diseases that could develop as a result of tortious exposure to toxic substances in the environment. Medical monitoring has long been part of recoverable damages when there is present physical injury."[49] After a controversial decision in 1999, however, plaintiffs in West Virginia courts can bring a claim for medical monitoring damages if wrongfully exposed to an injurious or toxic substance *absent* present physical injury.[50] This decision also authorizes the award of lump sums to plaintiffs.[51]

To permit medical monitoring damages for plaintiffs who lack a present physical injury creates a number of potential problems, including allowing the plaintiff to recover damages even when the plaintiff cannot prove that he or she suffered an actual physical injury, much less that the defendant caused it.[52] Some potential problems include astronomical and unpredictable liability for defendants, widespread and serious abuse by plaintiffs (who may be awarded a lump sum payment with no requirement that the money be spent on medical monitoring), and a legal system clogged with unreliable and trivial claims.[53]

This potential source of legal reform is ripe for legislative change. Some suggestions include requiring the proof of an actual injury for monitoring or eliminating the alternative of lump sum awards, requiring that plaintiffs actually spend the award money on medical monitoring, or even eliminating medical monitoring damages altogether.

---

[46] Posner, *Economic Analysis of Law*, at 200.

[47] *Id.*

[48] W. Va. Code § 55-7B-9a.

[49] David T. Peterson, Recent Developments in Medical Monitoring Claims in Mass Tort Litigation.

[50] Bower v. Westinghouse (1999) (emphasis added).

[51] *Id.*

[52] *Id.*

[53] Victor E. Schwartz and Mark A. Behrens, *Judicial Activism in the Civil Justice System: Problems and Solutions*, 5.

CONCLUSION

We conclude that West Virginia is in need of meaningful legal liability reform if the state's residents wish to promote a healthy business climate and the long-term economic growth that it generates. This chapter outlined the major avenues for meaningful legal liability reform in West Virginia and covered the issues of joint and several liability, medical malpractice liability, and venue requirements with suggestions for their improvement. We hope that readers better understand the pertinent issues in the legal liability reform, because we believe that reform has great potential to further the interests of the state.

REFERENCES

Adam Smith, *An Inquiry into the Nature and Causes of the Wealth of Nations* (Random House 1937) (1776).

American Tort Reform Association, Joint and Several Liability Rule Reform, *available at* http://www.atra.org/show/7345 (last visited 12/10/08).

ATRA's Mission: Real Justice in Our Courts (2008), *available at* http://www.atra.org/about/ (last visited 12/10/08).

Anna Bamonte Torrance, Legal Obstacles to Tort Reform in Pennsylvania (2001), *available at* http://www.physiciansnews.com/law/601torrance.html (last visited 12/10/08).

Dave Lenckus, Courtrooms Playing Role in Reforming Tort System, *available at* http://www.businessinsurance.com/cgi-bin/article.pl?articleId=14140&a=a&bt=curbing (last visited 12/10/08).

David T. Peterson, Recent Developments in Medical Monitoring Claims in Mass Tort Litigation (2007), *available at* www.envinfo.com/webcasts/toxic-tort/peterson.pdf (last visited 12/10/08).

Edward M. Koch, The Pennsylvania Supreme Court Declares the Fair Share Act Unconstitutional (2006), *available at* http://www.whiteandwilliams.com/CM/News Alerts/Pennsylvania-Supreme-Court-Declares-Fair-Share-Act-Unconstitutional.asp (last visited 12/10/08).

George A. Barrett & Michael L. Brookshire, *Assessing Damages in Personal Injury and Wrongful Death Litigation*, 16(3) J. Forensic Econ. 315 (2004).

Goodwin Procter, *Products Liability and Mass Torts Alert* (2007), *available at* http://www.goodwinprocter.com/~/media/3ED1F81C51E0421BBDAA54A09C57765 B.ashx (last visited 12/10/08).

Institute for Legal Reform (2007), *available at* http://www.instituteforlegalreform.com/ (last visited 12/10/08).

Kenneth S. Abraham, *The Forms and Functions of Tort Law* (Foundation Press 3d. ed.2007) (1997).

Peter Boettke & J. Robert Subrick, *Rule of Law, Development and Human Capabilities*, 10 Sup. Ct. Econ. Rev. 109 (2004).

Richard A. Brisbin, Jr. & John C. Kilwein, *The Future of the West Virginia Judiciary: Problems and Policy Options*, W. Va. Pub. Affairs Rep. 2, 5 (2007), *available at* http://www.polsci.wvu.edu/ipa/par/reporter24_2.pdf.

Richard Posner, *Economic Analysis of Law* (Aspen Publishers 2007).

Victor E. Schwartz & Mark A. Behrens, *Judicial Activism in the Civil Justice System: Problems and Solutions*, 5, Litigation News (Federalist Society for Law and Public Policy Studies 1999).

West Virginia Chamber of Commerce press release, *available at* http://www.institutefor legalreform.com/media/pressreleases/20070425_HP_WestVirginia.cfm (last visited 12/10/08).

CASES CITED

Bower v. Westinghouse, 206 W.Va. 133, 522 S.E.2d 424 (1999).

Consumer Protection Division v. Morgan, 387 Md. 125, 874 A.2d 919 (2005).

DeWeese v. Cortes, 588 Pa. 738, 906 A.2d 1193 (2006).

Haynes v. City of Nitro, 161 W.Va. 230, 240 S.E.2d 544 (1977).

Kizer v. Harper, 211 W.Va. 47, 561 S.E.2d 368 (2001).

Maroulis v. Elliot, 207 Va. 503, 151 S.E.2d 339 (1966).

McIntyre v. Balentine, 833 S.W.2d 52, 60 USLW 2764 (1992).

Miller v. Monongahela Power Co., 184 W.Va. 663, 671, 403 S.E.2d 406, 414 (1999).

Morris v. Crown Equipment Corp., 219 W.Va. 347, 633 S.E.2d 292 (2006).

State *ex rel*. Mobil Corp. v. Gaughan, 211 W.Va. 106, 563 S.E.2d 419 (2002).

United States v. Carroll Towing Co., 159 F.2d 169, 1946 A.M.C. 35 (2d Cir. 1947).

CHAPTER 10

APPEALING CHANGES: A CASE FOR EXPANDING APPELLATE REVIEW IN WEST VIRGINIA'S JUDICIARY
by Matthew R. Bowles and Mark A. Sadd

The Rule of Law

10

APPEALING CHANGES: A CASE FOR EXPANDING APPELLATE REVIEW IN WEST VIRGINIA'S JUDICIARY

Matthew R. Bowles and Mark A. Sadd

James Madison wrote that "[t]he merit of the founders of our republics lies in the more accurate views and the practical applications of the doctrines of [self-government]. The rights of man as the foundation of just Government had been long understood; but the superstructures projected had been sadly defective."[1] So much for planning ahead. In the wake of West Virginia's founding, the architects of its court system in the 19th Century likewise did not anticipate the ever-expanding web of laws, the rise of the regulatory state and the volume and complexity of consumer and commercial relationships and conflicts in the 21st Century.

The superstructure of West Virginia's judicial branch has failed to develop concomitantly with the economic, social and regulatory demands that society now places on them. When it becomes clear that the courts have insufficient capacity to properly resolve conflicts and to dispense justice, it is our obligation to evaluate and, when the case is demonstrated, to modify our judicial superstructure to meet current demands and to plan for future ones.

In this chapter, we argue that West Virginia's sole appellate court, the Supreme Court of Appeals of West Virginia, simply does not have sufficient capacity in personnel and resources to perform its critical functions within the judicial branch. This is particularly true in relation to the important roles that are expected of a court system in the American tradition.

We call for the creation of an intermediate appellate court in West Virginia in conjunction with the creation of an appeal of right for most civil and criminal matters.[2] The

---

[1] Letter to N. P. Trist, February—, 1830, Madison, James. 1865. IV, page 58, Letters and Other Writings of James Madison, Published by order of Congress. 4 volumes. Edited by Philip R. Fendall. Philadelphia: Lippincott.

[2] Currently, West Virginia is almost alone among the States in that it has only discretionary appellate review of alleged lower court error. When we use the term "appeal of right," we mean a litigant's absolute right to have his

first part of this article will draw a blueprint for reinforcing the State's judicial superstructure. The second part of this article will highlight some shortcomings that are inherent in the judicial branch in West Virginia relative to and as a consequence of the complexities of modern government and life. Finally, the third part of this article will articulate the need for an intermediate appellate court in West Virginia and the creation of an appeal of right by demonstrating that these additions to the judiciary's superstructure will redress the present shortcomings and promote stability and effective government.

This article seeks to frame an argument for thinking about fundamental changes to West Virginia's judiciary and to suggest a point of departure for public debate to fortify the judicial system as a critical superstructure of the State's government.[3]

PART I: FOLLOWING THE BLUEPRINT

We have come to expect judges, courts and the judiciary to fulfill essential functions in society. By design and convention the judiciary is viewed as the last resort for the protection of civil liberties, including free speech, religious practice and property rights. The courts are often the last venue for ensuring public access to the executive and legislative branches and challenging public corruption and the usurpation or abuse of power by public institutions and officers. The judiciary is entrusted with the dispensation of criminal and civil justice in accordance with evolving social norms. The courts have vast dominion and power over a wide range of issues – legal, political, economic and otherwise. The judicial branch is arguably the most powerful coordinate in the tripartite system of government.

Despite its preeminence, the judiciary is, for all practical purposes, solely responsible for reviewing and correcting its own work. This is accomplished, if it is accomplished at all, principally through appellate review. If error occurs in a civil or criminal proceeding in the circuit courts, it is only in West Virginia's sole appellate court, the Supreme Court of Appeals, that the judiciary is able to correct it.[4]

It is not the judiciary's functions but rather its systemic efficacy that is the subject of this article. Does the judiciary perform its critical functions to their greatest potential? If its performance is satisfactory, how does it improve or excel?[5] For while the other more political branches of government in the American tradition regularly check the exercise of power of each other, the checks exercised against the judicial branch are only narrowly and infrequently exercised. Governors do not pardon wrongly convicted citizens very often and

---

case and the court's adjudication of it reviewed on the merits at least once in an appellate court, thus, an appeal of right on the merits.

[3] Our readers will note that we have used statistics gathered from various sources and that we have attempted to uniformly use numbers from 2006 because that year is the last year of widely reported statistics on these issues. However, we note that the *West Virginia Supreme Court of Appeals 2007 Annual Report* has already been released and is available online. We would invite our readers to compare these to the 2007 numbers of the Supreme Court of Appeals.

[4] We acknowledge the appearance of the opportunity for a litigant to seek a circuit court's reconsideration of what it believes is a mistaken prior ruling or decision; but, self-reversals or changed minds are not common in the State's circuit courts.

[5] Peter Drucker (2004), the management genius and consultant, wrote: "Checking the results of a decision against its expectations shows executives what their strengths are, where they need to improve, and where they lack knowledge or information."

have throughout American history enforced the rulings of courts in all but the most extreme circumstances without much question and even less resistance. The legislative branch, thankfully, does not often react to rulings of the judicial branch by cutting funding or reducing the number of judges or courts. The judiciary in the American tradition is left largely to police itself. Its *de facto* obligation to self-regulate is principally moral and only underscores the ever-increasing importance of appellate courts in the American tradition.

For this reason we have chosen to evaluate the need for changes to the superstructure of the appellate level of the judiciary in West Virginia. Commentators have variously emphasized attributes of the appellate level of the American judicial system; however, it is our view that appellate courts should serve three principal purposes.

A. The Correction of Prejudicial Error by the Judicial Branch

One principal purpose of any appellate system is to provide the opportunity for sufficient review and correction of error by the courts of original jurisdiction.[6] Despite their best efforts, which often include long hours and few resources, circuit courts and other courts of original jurisdiction cannot achieve perfect resolutions of conflicts or deliver perfect opinions in each and every case. Error and mistake will occur. Exactly when, where and how often such error occurs is unknown, underscoring the importance of sufficient review.

Identifying and calculating the kind and incidence of error in any judicial system would be highly difficult to undertake with any satisfactory degree of accuracy. As to frequency, there are numbers that might purport to measure instances in which appellate courts reversed lower court decisions. These likely would represent only a small fraction of the instances in which litigants would have appealed error but for countervailing factors, such as time, money and the evaluation of success, each of which has nothing to do with the legal merits of an appeal. The cost of pursuing an appeal as measured in legal fees alone might be (and usually is) significant. The direct cost, as significant as it might be, does not accurately represent the whole cost to an aggrieved party. A litigant who believes that he is a victim of judicial error must also consider the business, political and emotional costs of pursuing an appeal within a context of uncertainty and risk. This is especially true in West Virginia, which, unlike most other states, does not afford an appeal of right to litigants. It is certainly plausible that uncertainty, risk, cost and the lack of appeal of right all discourage appeals by disgruntled litigants. For the same reasons that many cases settle before trial, we postulate that many, and perhaps most, litigants do not pursue appellate review even where they believe that a lower court committed substantial error.

A look at some emblematic statistics is instructive. In June 2006 the Bureau of Justice Statistics in the Office of Justice Programs within the United States Department of Justice published a report of data on appeals from civil trials conducted in 46 large counties.[7] The study found, among other things, that in 2001 about 15 percent of verdicts in civil trials were appealed to an intermediate appellate court. Of these appeals, 43 percent were withdrawn, dismissed or transferred and 57 percent were decided on the merits.[8] Of those cases decided

---

[6] *Appellate Court Performance Standards and Measures*, National Center for State Courts and the Appellate Court Performance Standards Commission, Roger A. Hanson, Project Director. June 1999, at 3.

[7] Cohen, Thomas H., Bureau of Justice Statistics *Appeals from General Civil Trials in 46 Large Counties* 2001-2005, NCJ , June 2006, 212979 at 1.

[8] Cohen, Thomas H., *supra* Note 8, NCJ 212979 at 1.

on the merits, about one third were reversed, modified or remanded.[9] Thus, for every 100 cases decided by trial in the counties covered by the study, 15 were appealed, 8.5 were decided by an appellate court on the merits and 2.8 were reversed, remanded or modified. Even where the parties had already incurred the initial expenses and external costs of a trial and then an appeal, 60 percent of those appeals that were not decided on the merits were withdrawn by one or both of the parties. This suggests powerful influences, other than direct costs, on the decisions of many litigants in pursuing appeals.[10]

Various states have reported reversal numbers even higher than the Department of Justice found. For instance, the Supreme Court of Mississippi reported in its 2006 Annual Report that of the 585 general civil appeals resulting in decisions on the merits in Mississippi Appellate Courts that year, 163 or 28 percent were reversed.[11] The State of Texas reported that in 2006 its appellate courts reversed, modified or remanded 768 cases, affirmed 1,463, dismissed 1,985, disposed of 1,150 and consolidated 74 cases.[12] Assuming that every case that was dismissed, disposed of or consolidated was free of error (some of these cases were likely voluntary dismissals or withdraws) the first level appellate courts in Texas had a reversal rate in 2006 of roughly 14.1 percent.

Given that these numbers widely vary and that, for the reasons already mentioned, they might not reflect all instances of error because of the pressures against pursuing an appeal, estimating the average error rate for courts of original jurisdiction is educated guesswork at best. But, what is difficult to dispute is that any judicial system, including West Virginia's, has a substantial error rate. It would be foolish to suggest otherwise.[13] The inherent error involved in the administration of justice in lower courts reveals the corresponding need for an appellate court (or courts) to ensure these errors are corrected and that justice is as perfectly achieved as is possible.

B. Ensuring the Even, Fair and Consistent Application of the Law

Ensuring the just application of the law begins in the courts of original jurisdiction. Multiple courts of original jurisdiction over the same subject matter, sitting in different venues within a jurisdiction governed by the same law, with different presiding judges, will often reach different conclusions on the same issues. This is an unsurprising outcome. Some people think differently than others. Democrat judges sometimes think differently than Republican judges. Religious judges sometimes think differently than irreligious ones and so on. West Virginia has 31 circuit courts and more than 60 circuit court judges. No two of them think exactly alike. Thus, another primary purpose of an appellate system, often little appreciated, is the unification of the law within a jurisdiction through the correction of departures from a standard or norm of law.

The development of common law has been the traditional means to unify the reading and application of the law within a jurisdiction. Common law is expressed in opinions of an appellate court that result from real cases and controversies. Therefore, the critical elements in

---

[9] *Id.* at 1.

[10] *Id.* at 4. We acknowledge that some losers in trial courts pursue appeals merely as settlement leverage against the prevailing parties.

[11] As of 1/1/2009, report available online at: http://www.mssc.state.ms.us/reports/SCTAnnRep2006.pdf.

[12] As of 1/1/2009, report available online at: http://www.courts.state.tx/pubs/AR2006/toc.htm.

[13] "The history of human opinion is scarcely anything more than the history of human error." Voltaire, quoted in Krieger (2002).

creating an adequate body of common law are, first, appeals pursued by litigants on issues where the rule of law is unclear or misapplied, and, second, published opinions that future litigants and judges may rely on.

It might be presumed, perhaps incorrectly, that losing litigants with legitimate concerns will fill the appellate pipeline with cases that will generate guidance, interpretation and common law for others who come after them. However, as mentioned before, a number of circumstances weigh against a litigant's decision to appeal when he believes a lower court has committed one or more errors. In addition to the internal factors mentioned above (business, political and emotional) that influence a litigant's decision to appeal, there also might be external factors. These external factors include the litigant's perception of and confidence in his lawyer, the litigant's perception of his chances to prevail on the merits and the litigant's perception of the political or jurisprudential leanings of an appellate court. Some of these factors might, depending on the circumstances, increase or decrease the likelihood of a litigant to seek an appeal. But we postulate that one external factor will almost always decrease the likelihood of an appeal: Whether the appeal itself is discretionary or available by right. Since 2004 West Virginia remains the only state to provide an appeal solely at the discretion of its appellate court in 100 percent of cases decided in its lower courts.[14] Thus, we further postulate that litigants in West Virginia, as a matter of course, will be less likely to appeal error because of the uncertainty that these appeals will actually be heard.

In addition to hearing a sufficient number of appeals, the second key to achieving the goal of ensuring the even, fair and consistent application of the law is the volume and value of written appellate opinions. In discussing the importance of written opinions, two commentators have stated:

> ... fully reasoned written opinion[s] serve[] a number of vital functions. For instance, a published opinion enhances predictability. Even if the opinion does no more than restate existing legal doctrine, it can show how the doctrine applies to different facts. Publication thus increases certainty by increasing the stock of precedents. Publication also hardens precedents because it is easier for a court to ignore one inconvenient precedent than ten.[15]

Many of West Virginia's sister states have realized and emphasized the importance of building a foundation of published jurisprudence to promote certainty and uniformity with regard to the application of the law. When Nebraska created an intermediate appellate court in 1991 to serve its citizens and relieve pressure on its overburdened supreme court, its legislature did not require that its judges issue opinions.[16] For a time the judges of that intermediate appellate court issued only orders to dispose of cases.[17] After the first month of oral argument the six judges "concluded that written opinions were beneficial for the attorneys, the parties, and citizens of Nebraska." They stated that they believed that "opinions assist the attorneys and the parties in understanding the reasoning behind the judges'

---

[14] Murray, Peter L., *Maine's Overburdened Law Court: Has the Time Come for a Maine Appeals Court?* 52 Me. L. Rev. 43 at 69 (2000). Please see footnotes 48 and 49 *infra* dealing with New Hampshire's adoption of mandatory appeals.

[15] Richman, William M. & William L. Reynolds, *Elitism, Expediency, and the New Certiorari: Requiem for the Learned Hand Tradition.* 81 Cornell L. Rev. 273, 282 (1996).

[16] Miller-Lerman, Lindsey, *The Nebraska Court of Appeals*, 27 Creighton L. Rev. 146, 154 (1993).

[17] 27 Creighton L. Rev. at 154.

decisions and offer guidance to future litigants."[18] It is this idea that an opinion serves to guide future litigants and citizens, recognized by Nebraska as an important reason for the issuance of appellate opinions, that is critical when considering the importance of appellate opinions to the judicial branch as a whole and not simply to the litigants presently involved.

Countless factual situations are possible that are beyond the ability of any law-making body to anticipate. Many situations that boil over into litigation are likely to be repeated, either because they represent an economically important issue or because a litigant demonstrates a means by which a particular statute or regulation may be molded to his objectives.[19] Some of these repeating issues are famous for their longevity and, because they have been the subject of litigation for so long, the rules governing the application of the law to them are considered to be cornerstones of common law: *Hadley v. Baxendale* for the foundations of consequential damages; *Palsgraf v. Long Island Railroad Co.* for duty and proximate cause; *Pennoyer v. Neff* and *International Shoe Co.* for personal jurisdiction. Leaving aside first year law school lessons, it becomes apparent that all laws go through the same processes by which they are issued, then prodded, poked and challenged upon a variety of facts until it becomes settled, altered or negated. Although a statute controls from the first day it becomes law, the law becomes settled only through the gauntlet of litigation that reduces the uncertainty that undermines its reliability. When considered in light of both internal and external costs of litigation, it is this stage of settled law that brings predictability to the system of rules on which citizens and businesses rely.

Commentators have decried the paucity of published opinions at the Federal level and suggested that it is exactly a lack of well-reasoned opinions that adds uncertainty to the law. "[W]hat makes for an unpredictable outcome [in litigation] is not an oversupply of circuit decisions, but the absence of a circuit precedent that is closely on point or, less commonly a fact-specific rule of law that by its nature requires case-by-case evaluation."[20] The fair application of the law is dependent upon the consistency with which similar facts produce similar outcomes. This consistency is built by a clear common law that covers an adequate number of issues and the continued and repetitive enforcement of the elements of the common law. We also argue that a sufficient body of appellate opinions on a variety of issues is the only means to ensure the consistent application of the law over time and throughout a jurisdiction such as a state. Ensuring this kind of consistency and reliability is a primary purpose of a judicial branch.

C. To Inspire and Maintain Public Confidence in the Justice System

It is true that an appellate court system must be consistent and apply a predictable collection of jurisprudence. It is also true that an appellate court system must appear upright and just to serve as a basis for public confidence that wrongs will be redressed and that litigants will have a fair opportunity for a hearing. Former Chief Justice Warren Burger said that "[a] sense of confidence in the courts is essential to maintain the fabric of ordered liberty for a free people."[21] Some commentators have suggested that furthering such a public image is

---

[18] *Id.*

[19] Lawyers are paid, in part, to use the language of the law to achieve the greatest results for their clients.

[20] 81 Cornell L. Rev. at 310.

[21] See North Dakota Judicial System Annual Report 2007, available, as of 1/1/2009, online at http://www.court. state.nd.us/court/news/ndcourts2007a.pdf.

dependent upon the issuance of written opinions by appellate courts. Others have hinted that public confidence is maintained by continuing the tradition of oral arguments at the appellate level. Whatever the means, as the State Justice Institute has explained, preserving the public's confidence and belief in the justice system should be an important goal in any court system.[22]

Courts of last resort have an important role to play in maintaining the public confidence. By design, most courts of last resort in the states are not intended to decide cases in the volume needed to build and maintain public confidence in the system as a whole. This is because courts of last resort take up most cases, not because of the individual litigants or facts involved, but because the issues are likely to be repeated and the case offers a good opportunity to issue guidance on an issue. Advocating for more written opinions from the intermediate federal courts in their article, *Elitism, Expediency, and the New Certiorari: Requiem for the Learned Hand Tradition*, authors William Richman and William Reynolds argue that published opinions play an important role, not just in the development of common law but in the maintenance of public confidence in the judicial branch. Published opinions, they suggest, enhance predictability, hold judges accountable for their reasoning, increase accessibility regarding the law and further the social goal of "assuring that the complaints of every litigant – small or large, rich or poor – are given equal treatment" by the most powerful officials in the judicial branch.[23] A court of last resort, in most instances, does not have the resources, nor was it intended, to provide each and every litigant equal treatment or an equal review of each and every case.

The need for accessibility, openness and accountability of the court system, for all litigants, has also been advanced as an argument for increasing the number of cases heard during oral argument by appellate courts with commentators arguing that "from an institutional standpoint, it is important for the appellate process to be public and for the parties to feel that they have had a chance to interact directly with the judges and to be heard."[24]

The same reasoning may also be applied in an argument advancing the need for an appeal of right. It might be argued that a discretionary decision not to hear an appeal involves some review of a case and at least tacit approval of the outcome by an appellate court. But such denial of requests for appeal do not inspire confidence that any serious consideration was given by appellate judges on the merits of the issues. We suggest that access to an appeal on the merits is one characteristic that is essential to maintain public confidence in the judiciary. "Making appellate court systems accessible to the public and to attorneys protects and promotes the rule of law. Confidence in the review of the decisions of lower tribunals occurs when the appellate process is open to those who seek or are affected by this review or wish to observe it."[25]

---

[22] See Generally *Appellate Court Performance Standards and Measures*, State Justice Institute and the Appellate Court Performance Standards Commission, Roger A. Hanson, Project Director. June 1999, at 10-13.

[23] 81 Cornell L. Rev. at 281, 296 (1996).

[24] 52 Me. L. Rev. 43, 58.

[25] *Appellate Court Performance Standards and Measures* at 10.

PART II: THE SYSTEMIC SHORTCOMINGS OF WEST VIRGINIA'S JUDICIAL SUPERSTRUCTURE

We suggest that the combination of a system using 100 percent discretionary review and a single appellate court shouldering the appellate responsibility for the entire jurisdiction of West Virginia has led to unappealing (pun intended) circumstances: (i) a litigant in West Virginia is less likely to appeal even where a tribunal has committed substantial error; (ii) the litigant is less likely to have his appeal heard on the merits; and, (iii) on the whole, West Virginians, relative to other jurisdictions, have insufficient expressions of common law for guidance in the myriad of complex economic and social issues that they confront. To be clear, it is the system under which West Virginia uses a single appellate court that must undertake to complete all of the functions and objectives of a sufficient judicial superstructure that hamstrings the Supreme Court of Appeals. The Supreme Court of Appeals, irrespective of the effort or work ethic of its justices, does not have the resources to address the variety of important functions required of the judicial branch.

A. Nearly Complete Lack of Error-Correction Review

A primary purpose of any appellate court system must be the provision for sufficient review to correct prejudicial error by the courts of original jurisdiction.[26] As discussed earlier, even the best trial court judges cannot be expected to deliver perfect rulings in each and every case that comes before them. Because no other branch of government is involved with the correction of judicial error, it is all the more important that the appellate level of the judicial branch hear and consider cases to correct error to the extent possible in the administration of justice. This point should be obvious.

The Supreme Court of Appeals, according to its own statistics, heard only approximately 179 appeals of roughly 1,222 considered in 2006[27] or less than 15 percent (workers compensation appeals have been excluded on both sides of this statistic because circuit courts do not exercise original jurisdiction over these matters). According to the summary of the circuit court filings in 2006, available as a portion of the Supreme Court's 2006 Annual Report, 47,998 cases were filed in circuit court in 2006.[28] That means that only approximately 179 cases of 47,998 heard by West Virginia circuit courts in 2006, or less than one half of one percent, enjoyed the benefits of an appeal on the merits.[29]

---

[26] *Appellate Court Performance Standards and Measures,* at 3.

[27] The 2006 Annual Report of the Supreme Court of Appeals, is available, as of January 1, 2009, on the Office of the Clerk of the Supreme Court of Appeals of West Virginia's website: http://www.state.wv.us/wvsca/clerk.htm The report provides both the number of filed appeals (at pages 1 and 2), and the number of petitions reviewed or considered in 2006 (at page 5). The chart on page 5 reports that 2006 saw 2,589 petitions reviewed, leaving 1,222 (after excluding the 1367 workers compensation cases). The Supreme Court reports on the same chart, on page 5, the percentage of cases in each category it accepted for appeal. By converting the percentages into real numbers, adding each category and rounding to the nearest whole number – we arrived at approximately 179 cases granted appeal in 2006.

[28] Report available online at: http://www.state.wv.us/wvsca/circuits.pdf.

[29] Although we are mindful that not all cases are filed in circuit court and appealed, or given the opportunity to request an appeal, in the same calendar year we cite the 2006 numbers purely as an example and would point our readers to the very similar number of filed circuit court cases since the creation of the Family Courts in January 2002. This information is also available in the Circuit Court Summary.

With such an exceedingly low rate of review, circuit court judges in West Virginia do not need to seriously worry about being corrected or reversed. Any such concern of circuit court judges is perhaps overwhelmed by the odds against the event of such an outcome. The initiative and willingness of a litigant to pursue justice are also likely weakened in a system that forces his interests to be largely determined by a single trial judge with little oversight. In sum, a trial court outcome in West Virginia is virtually unassailable.

The impact on a litigant's opportunity to appeal has direct implications for the individual litigants in addition to the societal impacts of an inactive judiciary. Statistics provided by the State Justice Institute in their final report issued November 17, 2006, entitled *West Virginia Circuit Court Judicial Workload Assessment*, bring the direct impact on litigants into focus.[30] This study, used in part to determine the sufficiency of judicial resources, assigns "case weights" to each type of action heard by West Virginia circuit courts. Case weights are intended to measure the number of minutes that a judge needs to dispose of an average case of a particular type and are calculated either by actual surveys of circuit court judges or estimates by an expert panel.[31] According to the State Justice Institute, the case weight is an accurate reflection of the typical amount of time judges take to resolve cases of a specific type.[32] A look at the case weights in West Virginia circuit courts is eye-opening: Felony cases are disposed of, on average, in 166 minutes.[33] General civil matters are disposed of in 174 minutes.[34] Additionally, the State Justice Institute concludes that in the majority of West Virginia's judicial circuits, judges are handling more than a single judge should be expected to handle.[35]

When considered together, the short period of time spent by circuit court judges in West Virginia on the average case, the excessive workloads of the average circuit court judge, and the systemic lack of opportunity for appeal means that the case of the average litigant in West Virginia was adjudicated by a judge who spent mere minutes on the matter and was overworked in so doing. The icing on this unpalatable cake is that the litigant has a razor-thin chance to obtain relief or even review in an appellate court.

B. Petitions Reviewed and Denied Do Not Advance Any Discernable Goal of a Meaningful Judicial Superstructure

Litigants in West Virginia are entitled to pursue an appeal to the Supreme Court of Appeals, but unlike other states, are not guaranteed to have that appeal heard on the merits. Thus, it is unsurprising that West Virginia's high court has one of the highest petition rates for discretionary review in the United States. We argue that the simple petition for review is wholly inadequate to advance any of the goals of a sound judiciary.

Although a petition for review involves some briefing of the facts in and the law applicable to a case, it is unclear whether the justices give substantial attention to those cases that they refuse to accept. Commentators looking into matters of judicial expediency in other states have found that "[t]he task of determining whether to exercise discretionary review is

[30] Report available online at: http://www.state.wv.us/wvsca/circuits/CircuitFinalReport.pdf.

[31] State Justice Institute, *West Virginia Circuit Court Judicial Workload Assessment, Final Report*, Nov. 17, 2006. Brenda K. Uekert Project Director at 6-7.

[32] *West Virginia Circuit Court Judicial Workload Assessment* at 7.

[33] *Id.* at 3.

[34] *Id.* at 3.

[35] *Id.* at 4.

an important element of the supreme court's workload, but the time expended per individual case is very small[.]"[36]

Even if one would argue that each petition for appeal receives a thorough review, it would be an assumption that would be difficult to verify. It would also be doubtful given that the Supreme Court of Appeals itself regularly claims that it is one of the busiest appellate courts in the nation.[37] Moreover, a denial of a particular petition for appeal does not advance any of the articulated purposes of the judiciary because (i) it does not build confidence in the system by assuring the litigants that the matter was given a full review; (ii) it does not explain the reviewing court's reasoning in refusing to hear the matter so that the parties feel confident that their arguments were addressed; and (iii) it does not provide any sense or guidance for future litigants to rely on or on which citizens, government agencies and businesses may pattern their future behavior.

The concept of "summary affirmance," or affirming a lower court's actions without opinion is similar to a denial of discretionary review and has been criticized in the Federal system for just such failure to advance the purposes of that judiciary. "Summary affirmance without oral argument is indistinguishable from a denial of certiorari. In each case there is no argument, no opinion, no precedent, no accountability, and no assurance that any ... judge has devoted enough time to the case to determine whether the decision is correct..."[38] Similarly even under the unlikely scenario that the review of a petition could be considered meaningful error correction review by a justice or more than one justice (as opposed to by their law clerks), such review and denial of the petition would not promote the perception of adequate error correction because it is issued without stated reasoning.[39] Therefore, petitions filed and not accepted for appeal do nothing to advance the purposes of the judicial system in West Virginia.

C. Inadequate Number of Published Opinions

According to its 2006 Annual Report, the Supreme Court of Appeals disposed of 2,721 cases in 2006.[40] Of these 2,304, or roughly 85 percent, were disposed by the high court's refusing to grant the petition for appeal. Four other categories, counted separately by the Supreme Court under the heading of "disposal", including dismissal, withdraw of petition, mootness, or disposed by order, total another 174 cases, leaving 243 cases spread over three categories.

We, thus far, have argued that written opinions of an appellate court are not only important to improve the fairness of a judicial system and to increase confidence of the public in the outcomes it produces, but necessary to provide future litigants and the public at large with guidance as to the law on various issues that regularly arise. The 243 cases in 2006, remaining after eliminating those petitions that were refused, dismissed, withdrawn, moot and disposed by order, represent those instances worth examining to determine their potential for fulfilling the goals of a sound judicial branch.

---

[36] Cope, Gerald B. Jr., *Discretionary Review of the Decisions of Intermediate Appellate Courts: A Comparison of Florida's System with those of the other State and the Federal System*, 45 Fla. L. Rev. 21, 30 (1993).

[37] See generally *Supreme Court of Appeals of West Virginia – 2006 Statistical Report*, at 5.

[38] 81 Cornell L. Rev. at 294.

[39] "Often, the less there is to justify a traditional custom, the harder it is to get rid of it." Mark Twain, cited in Holms and Baji (1998).

[40] *Supreme Court of Appeals of West Virginia – 2006 Statistical Report*, at 4. Note again the discrepancy in language, "disposed" in 2006 as opposed to "considered" or "reviewed."

First: Memorandum Orders. In 2006, the Supreme Court of Appeals reports that it issued 122 "Memorandum Order[s]" without providing much, if any, data or summary of the typical contents or issue disposition of a memorandum order. In 2007, the Annual Report of the Supreme Court of Appeals relates that most of the workers compensation appeals that the Supreme Court of Appeals accepts are disposed of by memorandum orders.[41] Looking at the petitions reviewed in 2006, we see that 1,367 workers compensation petitions were considered and approximately 109, or 8 percent as reported by the Court, were granted review. Based on the Supreme Court of Appeals' reporting of its own habits in 2007, we can surmise that the vast majority of the 122 memorandum orders issued by the Court in 2006 were related to workers compensation. We have not considered workers compensation appeals throughout this treatment because they are not heard by the circuit courts; therefore, we cannot consider these 122 memorandum orders as sufficient expressions of the opinion of the Supreme Court of Appeals that would fulfill any of the judiciary's goals we have identified.

Of the 243 cases that the Supreme Court of Appeals disposed of in 2006, then, we are now reduced to 121 that are available to fulfill the substantive goals.

Second: Per Curiam Opinions. In 2006 the Supreme Court of Appeals issued 61 *per curiam* opinions. The extent to which these opinions serve the goals of a judiciary is debatable and worth discussing, if only because they represent nearly half of the remaining cases.

In their article "The West Virginia Supreme Court of Appeals" Richard Brisbin Jr., and John C. Kilwein, of the West Virginia University Department of Political Science, state that *per curiam* opinions of the Court are often issued in "less significant and routine cases" that "[n]ormally … raise no novel issues of law and … that demand no clarification of existing law."[42] The Supreme Court of Appeals has ruled that "[p]er curiam opinions have precedential value as an application of settled principles of law to fact necessarily differing from those at issue in signed opinions."[43] The Supreme Court of Appeals also has stated that when new points of law are announced, they will be announced in signed opinions, but that a *per curiam* opinion has value in guiding lower courts regarding the application of existing law to various facts and circumstances.[44]

Thus, *per curiam* opinions in West Virginia seem to be of mixed value in advancing the goals of a sound judicial system.

On one hand, the Supreme Court of Appeals recently announced that *per curiam* opinions can, and should, provide guidance to lower courts in the application of various points of law. This change from prior prohibitions certainly helps solidify existing precedent and, to the extent that it applies existing determinations of the meaning of the law to additional fact patterns, it helps to add certainty to the law. On the other hand, a *per curiam* opinion fails in adding certainty to the law in that it only deals with an already settled issue where presumably there was some existing basis for certainty. *Per curiam* opinions also fail to identify the author of the opinion and thus do not allow lawyers to gauge the leanings of

---

[41] *Supreme Court of Appeals of West Virginia – 2007 Statistical Report*, at 4. Report available online at: http://www.state.wv.us/wvsca/clerk/statistics/2007StatRept.pdf.

[42] Brisbin, Richard A. Jr. Ph.D., and John C. Kilwein Ph.D, *The West Virginia Supreme Court of Appeals*. As of 1/1/2009 available online at: http://www.polsci.wvu.edu/ipa/par/report_10_2.html.

[43] Syl. Pt. 3, *Walker v. Doe*, 208 W. Va. 319, 540 S.E.2d 536 (2001).

[44] Syl. Pt. 2-3, *Walker v. Doe*, 208 W. Va. 319, 540 S.E.2d 536 (2001).

the high court on any particular issue. Because authorship is not claimed, a *per curiam* opinion serves as less assurance that a particular case was given the kind of careful consideration and well-reasoned drafting that would be assured if a particular justice was signing her name.

It is our position that *per curiam* opinions are better than every other means of disposition currently in use by the Supreme Court of Appeals, except signed opinions, and that these opinions do serve to promote some of the goals advocated here. But still they fail to well serve every goal of a sound judicial superstructure.

Third: Signed Opinions. Signed opinions are the gold standard of appellate disposition of cases. Signed opinions fulfill all of the goals of a judiciary. They increase the stock of precedent, guide future litigants, give certainty to the law, enhance predictability, harden precedent, increase access to the high court, hold lower court judges accountable for their decisions and encourage well-reasoned decisions.[45] Issuing signed opinions is perhaps the most important function of appellate courts.

The Supreme Court of Appeals issued 60 signed opinions in 2006 and 47 signed opinions in 2007.[46] Although the Annual Reports of the Supreme Court of Appeals emphasize the number of petitions compared to other states, the real comparison (in light of the relative lack of worth of a considered but rejected petition and the absolute necessity of published opinions in advancing the goals of a judiciary) should be the number of signed opinions in relation to those of other states.

The Supreme Court of New Hampshire, until recently, was arguably the most similar state judicial branch to that of West Virginia. New Hampshire also has no intermediate appellate court and, until 2004, heard a nearly completely discretionary docket.[47] That has changed. Since the beginning of 2004, New Hampshire's high court has accepted most appeals from the State's lower courts on a mandatory basis.[48] In 2003, the last year that New Hampshire had a primarily discretionary docket, the New Hampshire Supreme Court issued 186 written opinions despite processing fewer appeals and serving a population smaller than that of West Virginia.[49] In 2006, the New Hampshire Supreme Court issued 158 opinions, even as it accepted cases on a mandatory basis, and thereby increased the number of appeals accepted.[50]

In addition to New Hampshire, the Supreme Court of Appeals has compared itself, in both the 2006 and 2007 Annual Reports, to several other states that are among the few remaining states without intermediate appellate courts. These courts also report issuing a

---

[45] 81 Cornell L. Rev. at 282-283.

[46] *Supreme Court of Appeals of West Virginia – 2006 Statistical Report*, Pg. 4; *Supreme Court of Appeals of West Virginia – 2007 Statistical Report*, at 4.

[47] See generally 52 Me. L. Rev. at 69.

[48] See New Hampshire Supreme Court Rule(s) 3, 7 available as of 1/1/2009 online at: http://www.courts.state. nh.us/rules/scr/index.htm. Also see New Hampshire Supreme Court Judicial Duties online at: http://www. courts.state.nh.us/supreme/index.htm. See also Footnote 49. We note that the Supreme Court of Appeals of West Virginia Statistical Reports from 2006 and 2007, as cited previously herein, describe New Hampshire as having a 100 percent discretionary docket. We believe that this information in these reports is outdated and would refer readers to the citations listed in this footnote to compare the discrepancies.

[49] State of New Hampshire Judicial Branch, 2003-2004 Report. *Justice Moving Forward: A Time For Change* at pages 6-7. Available online, as of 1/1/2009 at: http://www.courts.state.nh.us/supreme/rpt03.04.pdf.

[50] See the 2005-2006 Biennial Report of the New Hampshire Judicial Branch, *State of New Hampshire Judicial Branch: Mapping the Future*. Available online at http://www.courts.state.nh.us/press/report06_web.pdf. See also footnote 49.

number of opinions in 2006 far in excess of that of the Supreme Court of Appeals. North Dakota, for instance, disposed of 226 cases by issued opinion in 2006;[51] Delaware's Supreme Court issued 79 (2007)[52] and Montana's high court disposed of an astounding 352 cases by written opinion (2007).[53]

Even if one adds the total number of *per curiam* opinions of the Supreme Court of Appeals, every state mentioned above, save Delaware, issued more opinions than West Virginia in 2006 despite having smaller populations and fewer requests for appeal. We note that it is not clear from the reporting of these courts whether the number of opinions includes *per curiam* opinions. The exception is Delaware whose high court's 79 opinions represent only those assigned to an individual justice (with *per curiam* opinions reported separately), meaning that it too issued more signed opinions than the Supreme Court of Appeals.

There is something to be said for advocating quality over quantity. Some contend that the number of high quality, major opinions that can be produced in a year by an appellate judge is between 25 and 30, with a few suggesting that 35 is a reasonable output.[54] The Supreme Court of Appeals issued only 12 per justice in 2006. In 2007 the Supreme Court of Appeals issued only 47 signed opinions or 9.4 per justice.

West Virginia's judicial branch needs to promote the certainty of the law and guidance to its citizens and businesses through the publishing of more opinions. An intermediate appellate court would add another court that could lend weight to existing precedent and demonstrate to lower courts how to apply existing rules to various factual scenarios. These expressions of the proper application of law would not only promote the goals of the judicial branch but would free the Supreme Court of Appeals from its enormous burden of simple case disposition and allow it to focus on issuing guidance through more signed opinions from each justice on a variety of issues under West Virginia law.

PART III: A REVISED JUDICIAL SUPERSTRUCTURE IN WEST VIRGINIA

Other states have created intermediate appellate courts to help fulfill the societal goals of their judiciaries. Two of the more recent additions to the growing number of states with intermediate appellate courts have been Nebraska and Mississippi, both of which added intermediate appellate courts in the 1990s.[55]

All things considered, we propose the creation of the Court of Appeals of West Virginia in conjunction with a right of first appeal in most cases. The Court of Appeals would issue written opinions, thereby increasing the body and variety of common law within the

---

[51] See North Dakota Judicial System Annual Report 2007, available online at http://www.court.state.nd.us/court/news/ndcourts2007a.pdf.

[52] 2007 Statistical Information for the Delaware Supreme Court, available online at: http://courts.delaware.gov/AOC/Annual%20Reports/FY07/?SupremeDispoBrkdwn.pdf.

[53] 2007 State of the Judiciary Address, Chief Justice Karla M. Gray, p.9 of the Transcript, Available online at: http://www.montanacourts.org/state_judiciary/2007.pdf. While it is possible that these other states make different determinations as to what constitutes an opinion for the terms of their reporting, the numbers are so staggering as to suggest a serious discrepancy beyond any calculation anomalies.

[54] 52 Me. L. Rev. 43 at 63.

[55] 52 Me. L. Rev. 43 at 72.

jurisdiction. With a new Court of Appeals, the right of first appeal from the circuit courts would be available and fairly administered. First, it would ensure greater opportunity for justice or sense of justice for litigants in specific cases and reduce uncorrected judicial error. Second, it would enhance the consistent application of the law throughout the state and increase public confidence in the judicial branch. An appeal of right would bring West Virginia in step with virtually every other state and satisfy the American Bar Association standard that "a party to a proceeding heard on the record should be entitled to one appeal of right from a final judgment..."[56]

This new intermediate appellate court would calendar, resolve and clear first appeals from West Virginia's circuit courts and administrative agencies. Much like intermediate courts in other states it would entertain the initial appeal, assume responsibility for error correction, ensure that rules and procedures have been followed and that the correct law has been applied in every case.[57]

In January 2004, when the New Hampshire high court instituted a right of appeal in most instances, that state experienced a small increase in the total number of appeals filed, from 842 in 2003 to 898 in 2004, but a huge increase in the number of appeals reviewed or "accepted" from 347 in 2003 to 645 in 2004.[58] We believe that West Virginia could expect a similar increase and surmise that the increased review of appeals along with the attendant consequences in the form of opinions generated, errors corrected and public confidence fostered would help to fulfill the goals of a sound judiciary that are stressed in this article. Unlike in New Hampshire, the Supreme Court of Appeals would not be left to shoulder this increased burden alone, but instead would be assisted by the new Court of Appeals. The two courts could work together to accomplish the important goals of a modern judiciary. At the same time, the Supreme Court of Appeals could focus its own efforts on only those cases and appeals it deems most worthy of its attention.

A new intermediate appellate court could be designed in different ways to handle these cases. Intermediate appellate courts are now found in most states. Many states have different systems specifically tailored for their needs.[59] The most familiar model is the Federal system with separate courts of appeals, each with its own districts or geographic jurisdictions.[60] Florida is an example of a jurisdiction patterned after the Federal model.[61] Other states have designed specialized courts to deal with certain subject matter or specifically with criminal matters.[62]

---

[56] 52 Me. L. Rev. at 58 citing ABA Standards Relating to App. Cts. §3.10 (1994). We note that the extent to which states offer an appeal of right is varied and therefore difficult to compare; however, without an exhaustive analysis, it appears clear that following the institution of mandatory review in most instances in New Hampshire, that West Virginia remains the only State with a completely discretionary docket. Virginia has an intermediate appellate court that handles appeals in criminal matters, domestic relations, and administrative appeals including workers compensation. Some of these appeals are by right and some are at the discretion of its intermediate court. The Supreme Court of Virginia has a mostly discretionary docket. The Commonwealth, although complex in terms of what may be appealed as a matter of right, is likely the state, other than West Virginia, with the fewest opportunities to appeal as a matter of right.

[57] See generally 45 Fla. L. Rev. 21 at 28-34.

[58] State of New Hampshire Judicial Branch, 2003-2004 Report. *Justice Moving Forward: A Time for Change* at pages 6-7. Available online, as of 1/1/2009 at: http://www.courts.state.nh.us/supreme/rpt03.04.pdf.

[59] 45 Fla. L. Rev. 21 at 31-33.

[60] *Id.*

[61] *Id.*

[62] *Id.* at 31-32.

Another approach — the one we advocate — would be a single, state-wide Court of Appeals. Because West Virginia is relatively small, it is this approach that has the greatest potential to reduce the costs associated with administration of the Court of Appeals and reduce the potential for conflicts between various geographically based subdivisions of the same court.

We envision a single Court of Appeals with no divisions or circuits. It would seat no fewer than nine judges who would preside in rotating panels of three. The Court of Appeals would be based in Charleston. Panels could travel to other cities and towns on a regular or as-needed basis. Since the panels would be rotating, different judges would make the trip each time for different cases, precluding the development of geographical associations with particular judges.

A single state-wide intermediate appellate court works elsewhere. Nebraska saw verifiable results when it created its intermediate appellate court in 1991 and appointed six judges with mandatory appellate jurisdiction in most instances.[63] Following the creation of this court, due in large part to the shifting of appellate burdens, the Nebraska Supreme Court increased the average length and number of issues addressed in its opinions.[64] Furthermore, the Nebraska Supreme Court was able to increase its reversal rate (presumably catching an increased percentage of existing error); decrease the percentage of its dispositions accomplished by memorandum order; and file more dissenting and concurring opinions during the same time.[65] We surmise that the creation of a Court of Appeals in West Virginia would have much the same effect. It would fulfill the goals of the judiciary in and of itself. It would free the Supreme Court of Appeals to increase the volume and value of its work product and develop the role of the judiciary in West Virginia as an authoritative source and guide to citizens, litigants, lawyers and judges.

Many different variations are available to select qualified individuals to fill the new judgeships that would be created on this intermediate appellate court. The present system involving elections could be used or modified. Judges could be appointed by the Governor and confirmed in some manner by the Legislature. Although appellate appointments are a new concept for the judicial branch in West Virginia, they have worked well in other jurisdictions where they take various forms. By way of example, appointments could be for a set term without the possibility of reappointment, or they could be for a set term followed by a state-wide, unopposed, simple retention vote for an additional term. We leave the manner of selecting judges for an intermediate appellate court for another day. Nonetheless, we suggest those considering a selection system should articulate the ways their proposals will serve the stated goals of a sound judiciary.

We have articulated three goals for a consistent and adequate judicial superstructure. There are others, perhaps less important ones. In every event, the goals to be served should befit West Virginia's particular needs. Some might believe that the type and volume of civil, criminal and administrative cases in West Virginia do not merit the creation of an intermediate appellate court. We disagree. Comparisons with peer states strongly support our position. Further, the case for an intermediate appellate court is even stronger based on fundamental concerns for quality of review and current systemic inadequacies. Assuming the creation of an appeal of right, we believe the case for an intermediate court in West Virginia

---

[63] 52 Me. L. Rev. 43, at 73.

[64] 52 Me. L. Rev. 43, at 73.

[65] *Id.*

is complete. The question is not whether a certain number of cases are filed, pending or processed. Rather the only issue is whether the superstructures of the West Virginia judiciary are accomplishing the goals that West Virginians deserve and expect of their courts.

REFERENCES

Appellate Court Performance Standards and Measures 1999. Williamsburg: National Center for State Courts and the Appellate Court Performance Standards Commission.

Brisbin, Richard A. Jr., and John C. Kilwein. 1993. The West Virginia Supreme Court of Appeals. *West Virginia Public Affairs Reporter* 10. Online at: *http://www.polsci.wvu. edu/ipa/par/report_10_2.html*

Cohen, Thomas H. 2006. *Appeals from General Civil Trials in 46 Large Counties* 2001-2005. NCJ 212979. Washington: U.S. Department of Justice.

Cope, Gerald B. Jr. 1993. Discretionary Review of the Decisions of Intermediate Appellate Courts: A Comparison of Florida's System with those of the other State and the Federal System. 45 Fla. L. Rev. 21.

Drucker, Peter. 2004. What Makes an Effective Executive. *Harvard Business Review* 82: 58-63.

Gray, Carla M. 2007. 2007 State of the Judiciary Address. Online at: http://www.montana courts.org/state_judiciary/2007.pdf

Holms, John P., and Karin Baji. 1998. *Bite-Size Twain: Wit and Wisdom from the Literary Legend*. New York: St. Martin's Press.

Krieger, Richard Alan. 2002. *Civilization's Quotations: Life's Ideals*. New York: Algora Publishing.

Madison, James. 1865. Letter to N. P. Trist, February—, 1830. In Philip R. Fendall (ed.), *Letters and Other Writings of James Madison*. Philadelphia: Lippincott.

Miller-Lerman, Lindsey. 1993. The Nebraska Court of Appeals. 27 Creighton L. Rev. 146

Murray, Peter L. 2000. Maine's Overburdened Law Court: Has the Time Come for a Maine Appeals Court? 52 Me. L. Rev. 43.

National Center for State Courts. 2006. *West Virginia Circuit Court Judicial Workload Assessment*. Online at: http://www.state.wv.us/wvsca/circuits/CircuitFinalReport.pdf.

North Dakota Judicial System Annual Report 2007. Online at http://www.court.state.nd.us/ court/news/ndcourts2007a.pdf.

Richman, William M., and William L. Reynolds. 1996. Elitism, Expediency, and the New Certiorari: Requiem for the Learned Hand Tradition. 81 Cornell L. Rev. 273.

State of New Hampshire Judicial Branch. 2004. *Justice Moving Forward: A Time For Change 2003-04 Annual Report*. Online at: http://www.courts.state.nh.us/supreme/rpt03.04.pdf

State of Delaware, Administrative Office of the Courts. 2007. *2007 Annual Report of the Delaware Judiciary*. Online at: http://courts.delaware.gov/AOC/Annual%20Reports/ FY07/?index.htm.

State of New Hampshire Judicial Branch. 2006. *State of New Hampshire Judicial Branch: Mapping the Future 2005-06 Annual Report*. Online at http://www.courts.state.nh.us/ press/report06_web.pdf.

State of Texas, Office of Court Administration. 2006. *Annual Statistical Report for the Texas Judiciary.* Available online at: http://www.courts.state.tx.us/pubs/ar2006/toc.htm.

Supreme Court of Appeals of West Virginia, Office of the Clerk of the Supreme Court. 2006. *2006 Statistical Report.* Online at: http://www.state.wv.us/wvsca/clerk.htm.

Supreme Court of Appeals of West Virginia, Office of the Clerk of the Supreme Court. 2006. Summary of Circuit Courts. In *2006 Statistical Report.* Online at: http://www.state.wv.us/wvsca/circuits.pdf

Supreme Court of Mississippi. 2007. *2006 Annual Report.* Available online at: http://www.mssc.state.ms.us/reports/SCTAnnRep2006.pdf.

CASES CITED

Walker v. Doe, 208 W. Va. 319, 540 S.E.2d 536 (2001).

CHAPTER 11

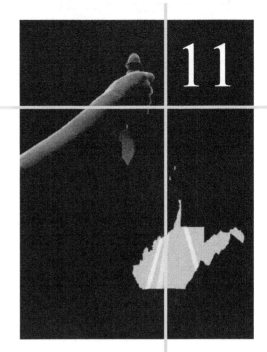

DELIBERATE INTENT, A UNIQUE CAUSE OF ACTION IN WEST VIRGINIA FOR EMPLOYEE ON-THE-JOB INJURIES: IS IT REALLY NEGLIGENT INTENT?

by Ronda L. Harvey

The Rule of Law

11

DELIBERATE INTENT, A UNIQUE CAUSE OF ACTION IN WEST VIRGINIA FOR EMPLOYEE ON-THE-JOB INJURIES: IS IT REALLY NEGLIGENT INTENT?

Ronda L. Harvey

When an employee is injured on the job in West Virginia, the employee does not need to go to court and prove liability against his employer to recover damages. Instead, the employee can file for workers' compensation benefits which pay for his medical treatment and lost wages while he is recuperating.

Most employers in West Virginia are required to maintain workers' compensation insurance, and in turn, are immune from lawsuits stemming from on-the-job injuries. The employer's immunity, however, is lost if the employee can show that his employer deliberately injured him.

The question of what is considered a deliberate injury has been the subject of tremendous debate in both the civil court system and legislative arena for the past three decades. Many believe that West Virginia's current standard is too broadly interpreted, resulting in too many workers' compensation lawsuits, and an unnecessarily high cost of doing business in the state.

This chapter examines the history of West Virginia's legislation and case law regarding deliberate intent, and offers suggested reforms that could help to improve the situation to result in more predictability and fairness in the way these cases are decided.

HISTORY OF CASE LAW AND LEGISLATION REGARDING DELIBERATE INTENT

The West Virginia Workers' Compensation Act was enacted in 1913.[1] The intent of the act is two-fold: (1) to provide injured workers with automatic benefits for work-related injuries,

---

[1] 1913 W.Va. Acts 64.

regardless of fault, and (2) to insulate employers from the unpredictability of civil tort litigation. The system was designed to be mutually advantageous for both the employer and the employee. The employer contributes to the fund from which employee benefits are paid and in return, the employee and his dependents give up their common law right to sue for any work-related injury. Workers gain because they are guaranteed compensation even if the injury was their fault, while employers gain because they are no longer subject to the costs of frequent litigation and civil tort damages.

From its inception, the West Virginia Workers' Compensation Act specifically granted employers immunity from private tort liability for work-related injuries unless the injuries occurred as the result of the "deliberate intention" of the employer to injure the employee.[2] For 65 years, the "deliberate intention" exception contained in the Act was construed narrowly by the courts. Tracking the legislative language, the courts typically required an injured employee to show a specific intent of the employer to cause the injury. In the late 1970s, however, deliberate intent litigation took a noticeable turn away from this narrow interpretation.

In 1978, the West Virginia Supreme Court of Appeals decided the landmark case of *Mandolidis v. Elkins Industries, Inc.*[3] In *Mandolidis*, the court refused to uphold the employer's immunity from a civil lawsuit in the absence of actual intent to injure, instead holding that "willful, wanton, or reckless" conduct which resulted in a workplace injury fell within the "deliberate intention" exception.[4]

The employee in *Mandolidis* was a machine operator who lost two fingers and part of his right hand when he was operating a ten-inch table saw that did not have a safety guard. The employee alleged the deliberate intention exception applied. The court considered the following facts:

(i)   the employer's table saws were not equipped with safety guards,

(ii)   the employer had removed the safety guards because they slowed production,

(iii)   the operation of the table saws without the safety guards was a violation of both federal and state standards,

(iv)   a federal OSHA inspector had tagged the employer's table saws and ordered that they not be used,

(v)   the employer removed the OSHA tags and continued the operation of the table saws without the guards,

(vi)   prior injuries to other employees had occurred from use of table saws without the required safety guards,

---

[2] W.VA. CODE § 23-4-2(c)(2)(Supp. 1991).
[3] 246 S.E.2d 907 (W.Va. 1978). The decision reviewed three lower court cases consolidated for appeal, but, unless otherwise noted, the discussion in this chapter centers on the facts of the case involving Mr. Mandolidis and his employer.
[4] *Id.* at 914.

(vii) former employees had been discharged for refusing to use the table saws without the guards,

(viii) current employees were led to believe that the refusal to use the table saws without the guards would result in either their termination or suspension, and

(ix) the employer knew injuries would be sustained through use of the table saws without the guards and deliberately chose to require use of the saws without the guards for the purpose of maximizing its profits.

While these facts may appear egregious, the trial court "determine[d] that the deliberate intent to injure ... is lacking."[5] The trial court granted summary judgment because the facts did not show that the defendant employer acted with "deliberate intent."[6] On appeal the Supreme Court disagreed, and overturned the summary judgment holding that "willful, wanton and reckless conduct" is actionable under the deliberate intent exception. This decision changed the standard of proof for a deliberate intent civil action[7] and opened the proverbial floodgates for three decades of intense, confusing and costly litigation.

Foreshadowing the future, Justice Richard Neely expressed concern in his dissent, noting that "violation of a safety statute alone does not constitute intentional injury; unsafe working conditions do not constitute intentional injury; failure to follow recommended procedures or to take standard precautions, do not constitute intentional injury."[8] Justice Neely prophetically predicted that "the tone of the majority opinion invites nuisance lawsuits, a high percentage of which will be settled (particularly by small employers) in preference to sustaining the cost of litigation."[9]

Some cases were tried and appealed. An article in the 1982 West Virginia Law Review[10] examined six of the early cases that were tried under *Mandolidis*: *Smith v. A.C.F. Industries*,[11] *Haverty v. Norris Industries*[12] and *Littlejohn v. Conrail*[13] (brought in federal court); and *Cline v. Joy Manufacturing Co.*,[14] *Mooney v. Eastern Associated Coal Corp.*,[15]

---

[5] *Id.* at 918.

[6] *Id.*

[7] From the date of the enactment of the Workers' Compensation Act, the phrase "deliberate intention" was strictly interpreted by the West Virginia Supreme Court. Indeed, just a few years prior to the *Mandolidis* decision, the West Virginia Supreme Court decided *Eisnaugle v. Booth*, 226 S.E.2d 259 (W. Va. 1976). The first syllabus in *Eisnaugle* states: "Neither gross negligence nor wanton misconduct are such to constitute deliberate intention ..." 226 S.E.2d at 259. The law in West Virginia then, prior to *Mandolidis,* held that in order to go to trial on the issue of "deliberate intent," a plaintiff must allege and support a set of facts which, if proved, would demonstrate advance notice or knowledge of a situation "from which the natural and probable consequence reasonably to be anticipated was death to the employees." *Mandolidis*, 246 S.E.2d at 911-12; *Maynard,* 175 S.E. at syl. pt. 1.

[8] *Id.* at 922.

[9] *Id.* at 923.

[10] David A. Mohler, Note, *In Wake of Mandolidis; A Case Study of Recent Trials Brought Under the Mandolidis Theory – Courts are Grappling with Procedural Uncertainties and Juries are Awarding Exorbitant Damages for Plaintiffs.* 84 W.Va. L. Rev. 893 (1982).

[11] Civil Action No. 80-3063 (S.D. W.Va. Feb. 1, 1980).

[12] Civil Action No. 78-2262 (SD. W.Va. Jul. 21, 1978).

[13] Civil Action No. 79-2404 (S.D. W.Va. Oct. 11, 1979).

[14] Civil Action No. 79-C-8036 (Cir. Ct. Mingo Cty. Mar. 19, 1979).

[15] Civil Action No. 79-C-6648 (Cir. Ct. Boone Cty. 1979).

and *Marcum v. Windsor Power House Coal Co.*[16] (brought in state circuit court). The article notes that these cases alone resulted in over $6 million in verdicts against employers.[17] Several other civil actions that were brought under *Mandolidis* did not make it to a jury, but were settled instead.

While the large verdicts in deliberate intent cases often make headlines, there are other less-obvious costs associated with deliberate intent litigation. In addition to any monetary verdicts, businesses must spend resources defending against these lawsuits, even if the lawsuit is decided in the business's favor. Even more importantly, the threat of large civil verdicts often leads to cases being settled out of court for inflated amounts. Thus, the cost of doing business in West Virginia is increased not only by the verdicts, but also by the costs of defending against these cases and out-of-court monetary settlements.

In an attempt to reign in deliberate intent litigation, in 1983 the Legislature amended West Virginia Code § 23-4-2. The amended section included language explicitly and unambiguously stating that "willful, wanton, or reckless" conduct is not sufficient, standing alone, to destroy an employer's statutory immunity under the West Virginia Workers' Compensation Act. The amendment also established a five-part test and required the employee to prove each element before the employee could pierce an employer's immunity.[18]

The second element required a showing that the employer had "subjective realization" of the specific unsafe working condition and the high degree of risk it presented. By including this element, the legislature demonstrated an intent to depart from the typical negligence

---

[16] Civil Action No. 80-C-152 (Cir. Ct. Brooke Cty. 1980).

[17] The jury in only one of the six cases examined, *Haverty v. Norris Industries, Inc.* returned a defense verdict.

[18] W. VA. CODE § 23-4-2 (c)(2)(ii)(Supp. 1991).

(2) The immunity from suit provided under this section and under section six-a [§ 23-2-6a], article two of this chapter, may be lost only if the employer or person against whom liability is asserted acted with "deliberate intention." This requirement may be satisfied only if:

(i) It is proved that such employer or person against whom liability is asserted acted with a consciously, subjectively and deliberately formed intention to produce the specific result of injury or death to an employee. This standard requires a showing of an actual, specific intent and may not be satisfied by allegation or proof of (A) conduct which produces a result that was not specifically intended; (B) conduct which constitutes negligence, no matter how gross or aggravated; or (C) willful, wanton or reckless misconduct; or

(ii) The trier of fact determines, either through specific findings of fact made by the court in a trial without a jury, or through special interrogatories to the jury in a jury trial, that all of the following facts are proven:

(A) That a specific unsafe working condition existed in the workplace which presented a high degree of risk and a strong probability of serious injury or death;

(B) That the employer had a subjective realization and an appreciation of the existence of such specific unsafe working condition and of the high degree of risk and the strong probability of serious injury or death presented by such specific unsafe working condition;

(C) That such specific unsafe working condition was a violation of a state or federal safety statute, rule or regulation, whether cited or not, or of a commonly accepted and well-known safety standard within the industry or business of such employer, which statute, rule, regulation or standard was specifically applicable to the particular work and working condition involved, as contrasted with a statute, rule, regulation or standard generally requiring safe workplaces, equipment or working conditions;

(D) That notwithstanding the existence of the facts set forth in subparagraphs (A) through (C) hereof, such employer nevertheless thereafter exposed an employee to such specific unsafe working condition intentionally; and

(E) That such employee so exposed suffered serious injury or death as a direct and proximate result of such specific unsafe working condition.

"should-have-known" standard and instead apply a standard that measures the particular employer's knowledge of the alleged unsafe condition.

The intent of the legislative exception was understood fully by both sides. Indeed, the International Executive Board of the United Mineworkers of America referred to the amendment as "anti-union," and refused to hold its 1983 convention in Charleston, West Virginia because of the passage of the amendment.[19]

Despite the Legislature's efforts, the amendment barely slowed the maelstrom of deliberate intent civil lawsuits. Injured employees were rushing to file their lawsuits. While exact data on the number of lawsuits filed is not available, at least 37 of the many deliberate intent lawsuits filed for the first seven years after the 1983 amendment were appealed from the trial court level. This gave the Supreme Court ample opportunity to follow the Legislature's intent, and narrowly construe the statutory amendment to reduce costly civil litigation. The Supreme Court, however, failed to construe the deliberate intent statute narrowly. In fact, on December 20, 1990, the Court issued an opinion in *Mayles v. Shoney's, Inc.*[20] declaring that the amendment broadened the deliberate intent exception to employer immunity. Prior to *Mayles*, no opinions of the West Virginia Supreme Court of Appeals even inadvertently implied that the 1983 amendment had expanded the deliberate intent exception.

Moving forward, the state Supreme Court continued deciding cases under the new-found premise that the amendment expanded the exception.[21] The business community made some additional attempts to amend the legislation over several years, and in 2005 the deliberate intent exception was changed again to its present language which requires a showing that the employer had "actual knowledge" as opposed to "subjective realization" that the specific unsafe working condition existed. The 2005 amendment was yet another effort to narrow the deliberate intent exception. However, litigation continues unabated in this murky area of the law. Although the phrases essentially mean the same, the phrase "actual knowledge" is a more plain, concise and understandable phrase that is consistent with the tenor of the statute which attempts to define the act of the employer that constitutes a deliberate intent injury.

---

[19] *See UMW to Hold Convention in Pittsburgh*, UPI, Mar. 8, 1983, LEXIS, Nexis Library, UPI.

[20] 405 S.E.2d 15 (W.Va. 1990). In *Mayles*, a fry-cook at a Captain Ds restaurant was seriously injured when a bucket of hot cooking grease, which he was carrying to a disposal bin, spilled upon him causing severe burns. The employee's testimony at trial revealed that no one instructed him to wait for the grease to cool down, rather, the grease was always immediately disposed of while it was hot. Further, evidence indicated that an alternate, safer route to the disposal unit was not used because the bucket was too hot and heavy, and the other routes were too long. Certain employees had expressed concerns regarding the unsafe manner in which the hot grease was disposed, but these concerns had not been reported to the unit manager. Finally, testimony revealed that in 1983 another employee had suffered a foot injury in the same manner as the plaintiff. The current manager testified that he was never informed of a prior injury. The lower court in *Mayles* entered judgment on a jury verdict for the plaintiff, and the Supreme Court, with Justice Margaret Workman writing the majority opinion, affirmed the decision. The *Mayles* opinion construed the sufficiency of the evidence as to each requirement involved in the statutory five-part test of West Virginia Code § 23-4-2 and determined that all five elements were met. In the most surprising aspect of the *Mayles* decision, the Court admitted with candor that this was not the case that could probably have prevailed under the extremely narrow concept of deliberate intent enunciated in the *Mandolidis* decision. *Id.* at 23.

[21] In the post-1983 amendment case of *Blake v. John Skidmore Truck Stop, Inc.*, 493 S.E.2d 887, 892 (1997), the West Virginia Supreme Court noted with irony that "the legislature, in an apparent effort to narrow the parameters of civil liability for employers, has indeed broadened the concept by enactment of the five-part test of W. Va. Code § 23-4-2(c)(2)(ii)."

HOW DOES WEST VIRGINIA'S DELIBERATE INTENT CAUSE OF ACTION COMPARE TO OTHER STATES?

No other state has established an exception to an employers' workers compensation immunity from civil suit for workplace injuries as broad as West Virginia's.[22] Many states have no "deliberate intention" exception to employer immunity.[23] The states that do have such an exception require a *specific* intent to injure.[24] Cases from other jurisdictions involve a variety of statutes that contain slightly different terminology, but the cases generally fall into two categories: (1) cases rejecting recklessness or gross negligence and requiring a specific intention to cause an injury or death; and (2) cases holding that an employer can be liable for deliberate intention where the employer's conduct is willful, wanton, or reckless.[25] The latter category is similar to the West Virginia standard established by *Mandolidis* prior to the 1983 amendment of West Virginia Code § 23-4-2.

In some states that have no statutory deliberate intent exception, courts have held that at least under certain circumstances, a tort action may be brought against an employer for an "intentional" injury because the state's workers' compensation system covers only "accidental" injuries.[26] Thus, in some states that have no statutory exception for deliberate injuries, the injured employee may still be allowed to recover damages outside workers' compensation benefits.[27] These cases, however, uniformly require showing that the employer had a specific intention to cause the injury.[28]

DELIBERATE INTENT'S PRACTICAL IMPACT ON BUSINESS IN WEST VIRGINIA AND A REVIEW OF THREE KEY CASES

Business and industry in West Virginia have suffered a huge financial blow from the expansion of the deliberate intent exception. The *quid pro quo* compromise envisioned by the founders of workers compensation has been all but annihilated with the expanded interpretation of the deliberate intent exception. Not only must an employer fund workers compensation benefits for its injured employees, the employer also must bear the cost of defending a civil suit and pay its employees an additional amount for settlement or jury verdicts. Given the complexity of these cases, defense costs can be extremely high. In 2008, the West Virginia Chamber of Commerce estimated an average of over $275,000 in defense costs per civil action.[29]

---

[22] *See*, David B. Harrison, annotation, *What Conduct is Willful, Intentional, or Deliberate Within Workmen's Compensation Act Provision Authorizing Tort Action for Such Conduct*, 96 A.L.R. 3d 1064 (1979 & Supp. 1997).

[23] *Id.* at 1069.

[24] *Id.* at 1071-1090.

[25] *Id.* at 1068.

[26] *Id.* at 1071.

[27] *Id.*

[28] *Id.*

[29] *"Deliberate Intent" Lawsuits Threaten State No-fault Workers' Comp.*, West Virginia Chamber of Commerce, Chamber Links (Feb. 7, 2008).

In addition to defense costs, the various interpretations of the deliberate intent statutory language make it difficult for employers to avoid deliberate intent civil actions. Employees are emboldened by the case law expansions and file civil suit for workplace injuries more often; trial court judges are reluctant to grant summary judgment even though the statute specifically mandates it; and employers can not effectively predict or anticipate what may comply with the statutory language to plan ahead and adequately safeguard the workplace and protect themselves from suit.

We now turn to a discussion of a few cases that highlight West Virginia's lenient interpretation of the deliberate intent exception.

A. *Blake v. John Skidmore Truck Stop, Inc.*

In 1997, the West Virginia Supreme Court of Appeals rendered a significant opinion in *Blake v. John Skidmore Truck Stop, Inc.* that extended deliberate intent liability against employers for the criminal acts of a third party.[30] Specifically, a criminal's act of repeatedly stabbing a store clerk while robbing the store's cash register was actionable.[31] Significantly, the case was before the Supreme Court on the appeal of the employee who lost at the trial stage when the trial court granted a directed verdict at the end of the employee/plaintiff's case. The case was tried a second time, resulting in a complete and final verdict for the defendant/employer. Thus, the employer was forced to incur trial costs twice and was found not liable for deliberate intent. In his dissent, Justice Elliott E. "Spike" Maynard reflected that "this Court's decision in *Skidmore* guarantees that another meritless action, rightfully dismissed by the circuit court, will now go to trial."[32] He further stated that:

> A lack of security measures in a convenient store in rural West Virginia, which has the lowest crime rate in the nation, simply does not constitute a specific unsafe working condition with a high degree of risk and a strong probability of serious injury or death. This is especially so in light of the apparent lack of evidence that the convenient store has a history of being robbed.[33]

One commentator noted that the majority's opinion in *Skidmore* "appears representative of a trend in favor of employees."[34] The trend did not stop with *Skidmore*.

B. *Roberts v. Consolidation Coal Co.*

The trend in favor of employees continued in 2000 when the Supreme Court eviscerated the traditional common law defenses available in other tort actions. In *Roberts v. Consolidation*

---

[30] 493 S.E.2d 887 (W.Va. 1997).

[31] *Id.* at 896-97.

[32] *Id.* at 898.

[33] *Id.*

[34] *Philip R. Strauss, Deliberate Intention Claims Based on Third-Party Criminal Acts: Blake v. John Skidmore Truck Stop, Inc.*, 101 W.Va. L. Rev. 515 (1999).

Coal Co.,[35] the Supreme Court held that neither a defense of the employee's contributory negligence nor a defense of the employee's deliberate intent, as that term is construed by West Virginia Code § 23-4-2(c)(2), is available to employers when the cause of action asserts deliberate intent.[36]

The Court rationalized that West Virginia Code § 23-4-2(c)(1) was enacted "to establish a system which compensates even though the injury or death of an employee may be caused by his own fault."[37] The Court identified self-inflicted injury and injury caused by intoxication as the only two statutory defenses available to employers.[38] Based on the plain statutory language, the Court held that contributory negligence is not available to employers as a defense in deliberate intent cases.[39] In addition, the Court held that an employer may not assert that the employee's deliberate intent contributed to their injury since the statute does not use that term in reference to employees.[40]

The *Roberts* decision invites the argument that acts of the employee or failure of the employee to act cannot be presented as evidence. Notably, however, the *Roberts* case does not bar evidence by the employer relating to proximate cause and, indeed, such a holding would be legally untenable. The *Roberts* decision simply stands for the proposition that: "when an employee asserts a deliberate intention cause of action against his/her employer, ... the employer may not assert the employee's contributory negligence as a defense to such action."[41]

C. *Ryan v. Clonch Industries, Inc.*

Most recently, the West Virginia Supreme Court of Appeals reviewed the subjective realization/actual knowledge requirement of the deliberate intent statute in *Ryan v. Clonch Industries, Inc.*[42] In the *Ryan* case, Mr. Ryan was employed as a "banding man" in a lumberyard owned by the defendant. The job duties of a banding man included cutting metal banding from a coil, placing the bands around pallets of lumber, tightening the bands and crimping the ends together.[43] On his third day as a banding man, Mr. Ryan was struck in the left eye by a piece of metal banding when he was in the process of cutting it.[44] Mr. Ryan brought a deliberate intent action under the five element test. He alleged the defendant's failure to provide him with safety glasses was a specific unsafe working condition. To prove the third element – violation of a specific safety regulation, Mr. Ryan relied on the defendant's admitted violation of a certain OSHA regulation requiring the employer to inspect the workplace and assess what personal protective equipment was necessary. The

---

[35] 539 S.E.2d 478 (W. Va. 2000).

[36] *Id.* at syl. pts. 8 and 9. Mr. Roberts was injured while working in one of the defendant's mines. The longwall mining shield malfunctioned and Mr. Roberts attempted to restart the shield electronically. When that attempt failed, he tried to manually restart the machine. When the shield resumed operation, Mr. Roberts was crushed. Both his back and neck were severely damaged, and he was unable to return to work. Ultimately, the jury found Mr. Roberts 49% responsible for his injuries, and defendant at fault for the remaining 51%.

[37] *Id.* at 493, quoting West Virginia Code § 23-4-2(c)(1).

[38] *Id.*

[39] *Id.* at 496.

[40] *Id.* at 496.

[41] 539 S.E.2d at 496.

[42] 639 S.E.2d 756 (2006).

[43] 639 S.E.2d at 759.

[44] 639 S.E.2d at 769.

defendant argued that Mr. Ryan could not prove actual knowledge because the defendant had not performed the workplace assessment required by the OSHA regulation and thus had no actual knowledge that safety glasses were necessary for the task Mr. Ryan was performing. The West Virginia Supreme Court held that "where the defendant employer has failed to perform a reasonable evaluation to identify hazards in the workplace *in violation of a statute, rule or regulation imposing a mandatory duty to perform the same*, the performance of which may have readily identified certain workplace hazards, the defendant employer is prohibited from denying that it possessed 'a subjective realization' of the hazard asserted."[45]

This holding increases an employer's difficulty to show a lack of actual knowledge of the unsafe working condition and invites an argument well beyond its holding. Employees now argue that *Ryan v. Clonch* places a general requirement on employers to inspect the workplace. If an employee is injured, the injury was the result of the employers' failure to inspect the workplace, discern the unsafe working condition and correct it. This argument is compelling and difficult for an injured employee to resist; however, the employee's argument is flawed because it changes the fundamental nature of the deliberate intent civil action. Essentially, the argument changes the actual knowledge element to a "should have known" or negligence standard. The argument also extends the holding of *Ryan v. Clonch* beyond its limits. Even under *Ryan v. Clonch*, an employer's failure to inspect negates the actual knowledge defense only when a regulation contains an affirmative duty to inspect.

The decisions in *Skidmore, Roberts* and *Ryan v. Clonch* serve as examples of how West Virginia's deliberate intent statute is being applied, and highlight some of the issues in need of reform. The widespread calls for reform from the business community are echoed by the president of the West Virginia Coal Association, who in 2005 stated that "deliberate intent is a serious problem affecting the entire business community in West Virginia."[46] Some legislators have even gone on record saying that deliberate intent is "a substantial deterrent to coal companies."[47]

CAN AN EMPLOYER OBTAIN INSURANCE FOR DELIBERATE INTENT?

The business community has also expressed concern over the lack of insurance for deliberate intent.[48] For several years after *Mandolidis* and even after the 1983 amendment, insurance companies were not sure how to deal with a deliberate intent claim brought under policies issued to employers. Specific insurance for deliberate intent did not exist, and insurance companies viewed deliberate intent as an intentional act which was excluded under liability polices. Some insurance companies began offering "stop-gap" insurance to cover deliberate intent actions.

The "Employers' Excess Liability Fund" was established under Article 4C in Chapter 23 of the West Virginia Code as a vehicle to provide coverage for employers that may be subjected to liability for excess damages because the injury of an employee resulted from the deliberate intention of the employer. This fund and its obligation was transferred to

---

[45] 639 S.E.2d at 766.
[46] *Id.*
[47] WBOY news posting; Tort Reform Debate Resumes (March 3, 2005).
[48] *Id.*

BrickStreet[49] on January 1, 2006. BrickStreet was required by law to offer coverage for deliberate intent until at least June 30, 2008. While BrickStreet is no longer required to offer the coverage, at least at the publication of this chapter, BrickStreet has continued to offer the coverage.

A memo from the West Virginia Office of the Insurance Commissioner (OIC) dated May 27, 2008, expressed concern "that the coverage be generally available for the employers of this state."[50] New private carriers entering the market after July 1, 2008 were not required by statute to offer the type of coverage as part of their workers' compensation policies, and deliberate intent actions are not covered by employers' liability policies. The Office of the Insurance Commissioner is encouraging private carriers to offer deliberate intent coverage and will provide guidelines to insurers on how to structure the plans.

While insurance coverage would apparently help businesses cope with the costs of deliberate intent litigation, it is important to remember that insurance coverage is not free. In fact, to be actuarially sound the average premium will has to at least equal the average litigation payout. Therefore, while the insurance may lower the risk faced by businesses over the timing and amounts, it does nothing to fundamentally lower the overall costs of deliberate intent litigation on the business community. In addition, these insurance policies have limits on coverage, so they don't even completely eliminate the risk component as an employee may be awarded damages in excess of the amount covered by the employer's insurance.

SUGGESTIONS FOR REFORM

Since the enactment of the deliberate intent statute, reforms have been suggested during most legislative sessions. Meaningful reform is difficult because few legislators want to be perceived as thwarting or removing an employee's right to sue his or her employer. Major reform could occur if courts would simply apply the statutory requirements and strike employee's civil actions that do not meet all five required elements. This type of reform starts with the West Virginia Supreme Court of Appeals. If the West Virginia Supreme Court of Appeals begins to uphold summary judgments and apply the statute as written instead of interpreting the elements broadly, the trickle down effect would cause trial courts to also apply the required elements in their strictest form.

Several legislative reforms have been suggested. One reform involves clarification of the third element which requires a showing "that the specific unsafe working condition was a violation of a state or federal safety statute, rule or regulation…of a commonly accepted and well-known safety standard within the industry or business of the employer[.]" The clarifying language would expressly exclude equipment or operator's manuals, maintenance manuals, or similar product manuals. In addition, the clarifying language would include a provision

---

[49] BrickStreet Insurance is a private company borne out of the former West Virginia Workers' Compensation Commission, which was the state's only provider of workers' compensation coverage. BrickStreet became a privately held mutual Jan. 1, 2006, and assumed many of the obligations of the former state-run system. Beginning July 1, 2008, the workers' compensation insurance market in West Virginia opened to other private carriers, and BrickStreet was relieved of some of its mandatory coverage responsibilities.

[50] Memorandum to Attendees of April 8, 2008 Carrier Conference Regarding Deliberate Intent, W.Va. Ins. Comm'r. (May 27, 2008).

stating that the "statute, rule, regulation or standard" specifically applied to the alleged unsafe working condition.

Another reform that has been suggested involves clarifying whether a deliberate intent cause of action may be brought against a supervisor. The reform would include language that specifically excludes a supervisor or management personnel from being named individually in an action filed under the statute.

CONCLUSION

To experience sustained economic growth, West Virginia must have a competitive business climate. The growth of deliberate intent litigation stands in the way of that goal. As long as our neighboring states continue to have legal systems that better handle workplace injury claims, West Virginia will be at a competitive disadvantage in attracting and retaining industrial jobs.

Attempts have been made to reform deliberate intent law in West Virginia, and some positive changes have occurred. However, often these positive legislative steps have been undone in the court system. Accordingly, more reform is needed to ensure that an employee's right to recovery is interpreted in a fair and predictable manner that does not unduly harm the economic prosperity of all West Virginians by creating an uncompetitive business climate.

References

Harrison, David B. 1979 & Supp. 1997. What Conduct is Willful, Intentional, or Deliberate Within Workmen's Compensation Act Provision Authorizing Tort Action for Such Conduct. *96 A.L.R. 3d 1064, 1068-1069, 1071-1090.*

Mohler, David A. 1982. In Wake of Mandolidis; A Case Study of Recent Trials Brought Under the Mandolidis Theory – Courts are Grappling with Procedural Uncertainties and Juries are Awarding Exorbitant Damages for Plaintiffs. *84 W Va. L. Rev. 893.*

Strauss, Philip R. 1999. Deliberate Intention Claims Based on Third-Party Criminal Acts: *Blake v. John Skidmore Truck Stop, Inc. 101 W.Va. L. Rev. 515.*

UMW to Hold Convention in Pittsburgh, UPI, Mar. 8, 1983, LEXIS, Nexis Library, UPI.

WBOY News Posting; Tort Reform Debate Resumes (March 3, 2005).

West Virginia Chamber of Commerce, Chamber Links. Feb. 7, 2008. "Deliberate Intent" Lawsuits Threaten State No-fault Workers' Comp.

West Virginia Insurance Comm'r. May 27, 2008. Memorandum to Attendees of April 8, 2008 Carrier Conference Regarding Deliberate Intent.

Cases and Laws Cited

Blake v. Skidmore Truck Stop, Inc., 493 S.E.2d 887 (1997).

Cline v. Joy Manufacturing Co., Civil Action No. 79-C-8036 (Cir. Ct.. Mingo Cty. Mar. 19, 1979).

Eisnaugle v. Booth, 226 S.E.2d 259 (W. Va. 1976).

Haverty v. Norris Industries, Civil Action No. 78-2262 (S.D. W.Va. Jul. 21, 1978)

Littlejohn v. Conrail, Civil Action No. 79-2404 (S.D. W.Va. Oct. 11, 1979).

Mandolidis v. Elkins Industries, Inc., 246 S.E.2d 907 (W.Va. 1978).

Marcum v. Windsor Power House Coal Co., Civil Action No. 80-C-152 (Cir. Ct. Brooke Cty. 1980).

Mayles v. Shone's, Inc., 405 S.E.2d 15 (W.Va. 1990).

Mooney v. Eastern Associated Coal Corp., Civil Action No. 79-C-6648 (Cir. Ct. Boone Cty 1979).

Roberts v. Consolidation Coal. Co., 539 S.E.2d 478 (W.Va. 2000).

Ryan v. Clonch Industries, Inc., 639 S.E.2d 756 (2006).

Smith v. A.C.F. Industries, Civil Action No. 80-3063 (S.D. W.Va. Feb. 1, 1980).

W.Va. Code § 23-4-2(c).

West Virginia Workers' Compensation Act, (1913 W.Va.).

CHAPTER 12

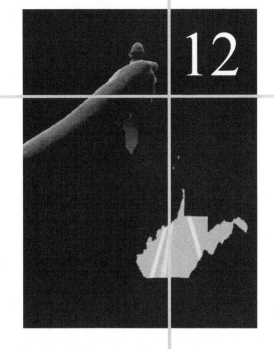

MEDICAL LIABILITY REFORM IN WEST VIRGINIA: IS IT WORKING? WILL IT LAST?

by Evan H. Jenkins and Juliet A. Terry

The Rule of Law

12

MEDICAL LIABILITY REFORM IN WEST VIRGINIA: IS IT WORKING? WILL IT LAST?

Evan H. Jenkins and Juliet A. Terry

Medical professional liability in West Virginia has had a tortured existence, particularly in the last two decades. Since the creation of the Medical Professional Liability Act in 1986, health care providers and lawyers have been at war on where to draw the line between stemming excessive, costly litigation and keeping the courthouse doors open for legitimately injured patients. Compounding this protracted dilemma is the insurance industry, which is affected not just by claims and litigation but also market forces.

This chapter first reviews what led to the 2001 (H.B. 601) and 2003 (H.B. 2122) reforms, then uses the best available data to determine whether the reforms succeeded in achieving their intended purpose or if the critics of reform were accurate in their claim the reforms would have no positive impact.

This chapter includes:

- Reports containing data on the number of medical liability lawsuits that are filed in each of the state's 55 counties on a monthly basis for the last eight years showing the impact of the reforms on lawsuit frequency;
- Data compiled by the West Virginia Insurance Commission for the last eight years tracking a key indicator of an insurance carrier's financial performance;
- Rate filing data tracking changes in the premium rates charged both before the reforms were enacted and after; and
- Licensure statistics dating back more than 10 years from the West Virginia Board of Medicine showing the number of newly licensed West Virginia physicians.

The final section of this chapter is devoted to a review of decisions by the West Virginia State Supreme Court of Appeals on the constitutionality of the various components of the Medical Professional Liability Act.

THE ROAD TO REFORM

Suing doctors for medical negligence is not a particularly novel concept. Decades ago, the late West Virginia lawyer Hale J. Posten predicted malpractice lawsuits would become more common. In a 1935 West Virginia Lawyer Quarterly article, Posten foretold of an evolution unfolding: "As the practice of medicine in its various branches tends to become a business rather than a personal relation, and the paternal position of the family physician fades into the limbo of forgotten things, it is likely that actions against doctors for their acts of negligence in the exercise of their art will become more, rather than less, frequent."[1]

Over the years, the health care delivery system has changed dramatically with many factors such as government regulation and insurance payor restrictions coming between the traditional doctor-patient relationship. Posten was more correct than he could have realized when predicting more lawsuits against physicians. While the law on medical malpractice litigation dates back to 19th century English common law, the last few decades have seen significant attention paid by states to medical liability.[2] When an insurance crisis hit the country in the 1980s, one of the cost drivers identified was medical liability litigation, and West Virginia lawmakers created the Medical Professional Liability Act. The MPLA was not a barrier to litigation — it provided structure with some limitations. Ohio County Circuit Court Judge Arthur M. Recht recalled the legislation during a newspaper interview in 2000. "The Medical Professional Liability Act of 1986 was a piece of legislation that responded to concerns in the health care community. It created a highly structured framework for the handling and disposing of medical and professional liability," Recht said.[3]

Years after passage of the MPLA, however, it became clear to the medical community that the availability and affordability of medical liability insurance remained a problem in West Virginia. The cost for insurance began skyrocketing in the late 1990s and early years of this decade, but the medical and legal communities could not agree on why rates were spiking. The warring sides blamed an uptick in medical malpractice litigation and related costs or insurance industry mismanagement and profiteering among the many possible causes. What cannot be denied, however, is that insurance companies were paying far more in claims than they anticipated.

From 1993 to 2007 in West Virginia, insurance carriers paid out more than $500 million in medical liability lawsuit settlements, with the average amount exceeding $200,000 per claim.[4] In the past 15 years, more than $40 million was awarded in court judgments, and in each of 20 cases, juries awarded more than $1 million to plaintiffs.[5]

In West Virginia, malpractice carriers tracked by the National Association of Independent Insurers (now the Property Casualty Insurance Association of America) posted combined ratios ranging from about 122 percent to as high as 160 percent in the 1990s,

---

[1] Posten, Hale J. "The Law of Medical Malpractice in West Virginia." 41 W.Va. L.Q. 35 (1935), as quoted in "Simplifying the Law in Medical Malpractice: The Use of Practice Guidelines as the Standard of Care in Medical Malpractice Litigation," by Sam McConkey IV, W.Va. L. Rev. 491 (Winter 1995).

[2] Budetti, Peter P. and Teresa Waters. "Medical Malpractice Law in the States." Henry J. Kaiser Family Foundation, May 2005.

[3] Terry, Juliet A. "Health Care Goes to Court." Wheeling News-Register, May 14, 2000.

[4] West Virginia Insurance Commission 5 percent Market Share report, November 2008.

[5] Ibid.

meaning carriers were not earning enough in premiums to cover losses.[6] This kind of financial performance led to rate increases in West Virginia approved by the Insurance Commission because they met state law requirements as adequate to cover liabilities without being discriminatory, unjust or artificially high.[7]

By the end of the 20th century, the issue hit the state Capitol, but before taking action, lawmakers challenged the insurance industry to document their justification for the premium rate increases. The insurance companies claimed the crisis was being driven by the state's litigious environment and that state lawmakers needed to enact legislation to reform West Virginia's civil justice system. Reform opponents claimed the insurance carriers' claims were driven by corporate greed or mismanagement coupled with low return on investment and suggested the crisis could best be resolved through tighter restrictions and more regulations on the insurance industry.

Regardless of the true culprit behind the steeply rising rates, however, the availability and affordability of medical liability insurance became more than merely challenging. The number of companies selling this line of insurance dwindled, and their rates became cost prohibitive, forcing some doctors to limit the scope of their practices to leave out higher risk components such as delivering babies. Other physicians pulled up the stakes completely and left West Virginia for regions where insurance was less expensive.

Information from the West Virginia Board of Medicine validated claims that physicians were leaving the state. In addition, state law requires all indemnity payments from lawsuit settlements or verdicts be reported to the physician's licensing board. This information was useful in validating the claim settlement and judgment data reported by the insurance companies to the Insurance Commission.

Policymakers concluded the affordability and availability crisis was being driven in large part by the state's litigious environment, which caused the financial performance of the insurance carriers selling medical liability coverage to deteriorate, forcing them to raise premium rates significantly or stop selling this line of insurance altogether. The high rates and/or limited insurance availability made West Virginia an unattractive place to practice medicine, thus affecting the physician resource available to care for West Virginia patients.

By 2001, the U.S. Department of Health and Human Services identified 50 West Virginia counties as wholly or partly designated as medically underserved areas and found health professional shortage areas in each of the state's 55 counties.[8] Some communities were left with no physicians trained to deliver babies. Others had no neurosurgeons, meaning all serious head trauma injury cases had to be transported to another hospital, delaying urgently needed treatment and displacing patients and family members from their communities.

Continued concerns about doctors' ability to find and afford liability insurance fueled an expansion to the Medical Professional Liability Act in 2001. Those changes were not a panacea, however, and in early 2003, the spotlight continued to shine brightly on the need for more dramatic medical liability reform, and the Legislature responded with a sweeping overhaul of the MPLA.

---

[6] A combined ratio measures the profitability of an insurer. Expressed as a percentage, it measures what an insurer must pay to cover claims and expenses per dollar of earned premium. Essentially, a combined ratio of 100 percent indicates a break-even point. Anything beyond 100 percent indicates a loss.

[7] West Virginia Insurance Commission 5 percent Market Share report, November 2004.

[8] West Virginia Department of Health and Human Resources. "Burden of Cardiovascular Disease in West Virginia." July 2001.

In total, the Legislature enacted a series of reforms in 2001 and 2003 that took the 1986 Medical Professional Liability Act and brought it into the 21st century.[9] The reforms were designed specifically to address this insurance affordability and availability crisis that impacted West Virginia patients' access to care. Lawmakers approved tax credits to help offset the high insurance rates. The state's own governmental insurance program, the Board of Risk and Insurance Management (BRIM) was directed to begin selling medical liability insurance coverage to non-governmental, private practicing physicians. Following a period of mounting losses in the state's own insurance program, the 2003 reforms directed the closure of the expanded BRIM program and created, with a significant state subsidy, a physician-led mutual insurance program to provide insurance coverage for physicians.

The statutorily created West Virginia Mutual Insurance Co. now insures more than three-quarters of the physicians who purchase private sector insurance in West Virginia. By design the company is led by a board that is made up of a majority of West Virginia practicing physicians. Its structure as a mutual insurance company means that each policyholder has an ownership interest. To date, through the board's leadership efforts and an experienced professional management team, the company has built a strong operation that serves as the foundation of the medical liability insurance marketplace in West Virginia.

The elements of the 2001 and 2003 reforms that were debated most hotly centered on changes to the state's civil justice system and on how lawsuits alleging negligence against physicians and other health care providers would be handled in state courts.

The 2001 reform legislation, for example, added a new requirement designed to weed out meritless lawsuits by requiring that a screening certificate of merit be obtained from an independent, qualified health care provider who reviewed the facts of the case and believed a breach in the standard of care may have occurred. A notice of intent to sue and the certificate of merit must be served on the physician before a lawsuit was filed to show that the claim may be legitimate and give the parties an opportunity to reach a settlement.

The 2003 reforms included a provision that prohibited a patient from using the court system to obtain double recovery (collateral source) for the same injury and another provision limited a physician's financial exposure only to his or her percentage of fault (several liability) determined by a jury. The Legislature also reduced from $1 million to $250,000 the cap on the amount a jury could award for noneconomic damages and imposed a new $500,000 total damages cap in certain cases relating to trauma care. These and other civil justice reform provisions contained in the 2001 and 2003 legislation were designed to impact both insurance affordability and availability.

As alluded to above, it is a massive understatement to say the policy discussion and legislative debate over the passage of both sets of reforms were heated. Reform advocates said the actions were necessary to preserve access to health care by bringing fairness and balance to the court system. Critics claimed the changes amounted to "special rights" for doctors and would limit or restrict a patient's rights to have a medical negligence claim fully adjudicated. Central to the critics' opposition to many of the reforms enacted was their belief that the changes would not result in lower insurance rates or improved access to care.

Have the reforms worked? Several key measures indicate the MPLA is functioning as it was intended. The question remains, however, whether the latest incarnation of the MPLA will withstand constitutional scrutiny. When asked to decide the constitutionality of various provisions of the Medical Professional Liability Act, justices of the West Virginia Supreme

---

[9] W.Va. Code, 55-7B.

Court of Appeals have shown their stripes over the years and made it clear how they feel about certain portions of the act. But much of the case law on medical malpractice dates back to a Court makeup that no longer exists, so predicting how the current or future Court will view the reforms is difficult.

One of the most controversial components of the Medical Professional Liability Act dates back to when it first was created in 1986 — the imposition of a $1 million limit on noneconomic damages arising from a malpractice lawsuit.[10] Since its enactment, the "cap" on pain and suffering, as many have termed it, has generated volumes of praise and criticism. The Supreme Court first upheld the cap in 1991 in *Robinson v. Charleston Area Medical Center*.[11] Several years later, the Supreme Court heard a new challenge to the cap in *Verba v. Ghaphery*.[12] Like in *Robinson*, the challenge in *Verba* attacked the cap's constitutionality on equal protection grounds. While under intense scrutiny, the Supreme Court upheld the noneconomic damage cap in December 2000, affirming its holdings in *Robinson*.

Two of the most controversial changes made in 2003 involved reducing the noneconomic damage cap down to $250,000 and imposing a $500,000 total cap on damages stemming from trauma care rendered in an emergency situation.[13] The constitutionality of those two changes has yet to be decided in the courts, but some of the 2001 reforms already have made their way to the Supreme Court. Although the justices have refused so far to address the constitutionality of the new pre-suit requirements, the majority has indicated a willingness to throw procedural requirements aside if they prevent a plaintiff from bringing a lawsuit. Former Justice Elliott E. "Spike" Maynard, in fact, warned that the majority opinion in one case "may result in the complete gutting of a portion of the 2001 medical malpractice reforms."[14]

MEASURING PROGRESS

LAWSUIT FILINGS

Liability insurance rates are impacted heavily by three factors: claim frequency (number of suits filed), severity (average size of settlements and jury awards) and "shock losses" (judgments exceeding $1 million). Prior to 2001, medical liability insurance companies conducting business in multiple states, including West Virginia, reported that while severity and shock losses were on par in West Virginia compared to other states, they did see a significantly higher rate in the number of suits filed per insured in West Virginia.

In an effort to weed out meritless lawsuits some believed were being filed in the state, the 2001 medical liability reform legislation included a requirement that, with few exceptions,

---

[10] The language of W. Va. Code, 55-7B-8, as amended in 1986: "In any medical professional liability action brought against a health care provider, the maximum amount recoverable as damages for noneconomic loss shall not exceed one million dollars and the jury may be so instructed."

[11] *Robinson v. Charleston Area Medical Center Inc.* 186 W.Va. 720, 414 S.E.2d 877 (W.Va.1991).

[12] *Estate of Marjorie Verba v. Ghaphery, M.D.* 543 S.E.2d 347 (W.Va. 2000).

[13] W.Va. Code, 55-7B-8 and 55-7B-9c (2003).

[14] *Hinchman v. Gillette.* 618 S.E.2d 387 (W.Va. 2005) (Maynard, concurring in part and dissenting in part, filed July 11, 2005).

any medical liability suit filed must contain a certificate of merit from an independent medical expert indicating that there is evidence that medical negligence may have occurred.

Another reform measure contained in the 2001 legislation was a $165 increase in the filing fee on any suit against a health care provider alleging medical negligence under the Medical Professional Liability Act. The extra filing fee is collected by the circuit clerk of the county where the lawsuit is filed and forwarded monthly to the West Virginia State Treasurer for deposit in the Medical Liability Fund.

The State Treasurer's collection report provides a clear picture of claim filing activity in every county throughout the state on a monthly basis and a way to document the impact of the 2001 and 2003 reforms on lawsuit filing frequency in West Virginia.

Figure 12.1: Medical Liability Lawsuit Filings[15]

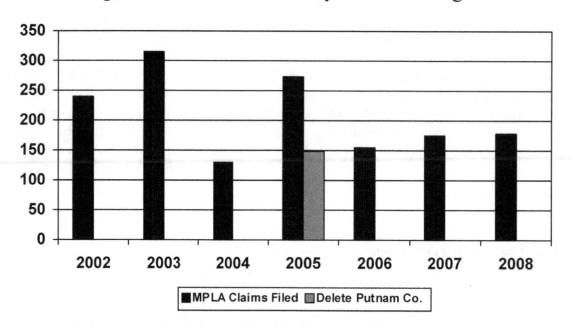

In 2002 and 2003, MPLA claim filings against health care providers in West Virginia were 239 (11 months of filing data) and 315 respectfully. Following the full implementation of the 2001 and 2003 reforms, medical liability lawsuit saw a sharp decline beginning in 2004 with an annual total of only 130, a 59 percent drop from the prior year total. Filing totals for 2005 were 273, significantly higher that the 2004 total; however, much of the increase from the prior year can be attributed to the lawsuits filed in one county (Putnam County) relating to a specific health care provider. Reducing the annual statewide total by the claim filings in Putnam County shows the 2005 filing total of 147 is in line with the 2004 historic low number. From 2006 to 2008, the claim filing report show continued low annual totals (154, 174 and 178, respectively).

In addition to the drop in lawsuit filings, a 2006 annual report by the Insurance Commission on the medical liability insurance marketplace documented a rise in the number of claims being dismissed, attributing these positive trends also to the pre-filing certificate of

---

[15] Medical Liability Fund 2002-2008 West Virginia State Treasurer's Office Reported by Month Collected, as reported in the West Virginia Insurance Commission 5 percent Market Share report, November 2008.

merit requirement. The Insurance Commission's report stated: "We believe that this screening process [pre-filing certificate of merit] explains the sharp and maintained rise in the percentage of dismissals seen beginning in 2002. Additionally, in 2002, we have seen a sharp drop in the percentage of claims settled. ... Overall, the number of claims filed has ... decline[d] over 50%."[16]

INSURANCE COMPANY FINANCIAL PERFORMANCE

While there was little public sympathy for the poor financial performance reported by the insurance companies in the late 1990s, the public did become engaged when physicians were driven out of state or out of practice because of skyrocketing insurance premium rates. Double-digit premium rate hikes year after year were needed to make up for the companies' mounting losses.

An important indicator of a carrier's financial performance is its combined ratio. This number is reported as a percentage of each premium dollar the insurer spends on claims and expenses and does not include any return on investment. A decrease in the ratio means financial results are improving; an increase means that they are deteriorating. When the ratio is over 100 percent, the insurer has an underwriting loss. An easy way to understand this ratio is to consider that if a carrier receives $1 in premium and pays out $1 in claims and expenses, the carrier has a 100 percent direct combined ratio.

The West Virginia Insurance Commissioner collects this information from the insurance companies doing business in the state and issues a report annually that tracks the direct combined ratio. The report indicates a 165 percent direct combined ratio for 1999 in West Virginia, meaning that for every dollar collected in premium, the carriers paid out $1.65 in claims and expense. It is not difficult to understand why carriers began increasing premium rates in the late 1990s to cover the mounting underwriting losses. The carrier's poor financial performance was also a deterrent to new carriers wanting to start doing business in West Virginia.

Following the passage of the 2001 and 2003 reforms, the direct combined ratio showed steady improvement moving from significant underwriting losses to underwriting profits in recent years. Another significant observation is how the carrier's financial performance was much worse in West Virginia compared to national averages prior to the reforms but now demonstrates better performance here than in other states.

A slip in the carriers' reported financial performance in 2007 was pointed out as a possible anomaly in the November 2008 report. Two companies left the West Virginia insurance market that year, and their financial performance for 2007 skewed the overall market performance, according to the Insurance Commission. The report said that absent those two companies, the "West Virginia market would have more closely reflected the experience of the countrywide market in 2007, were it not for those exits and the great impact that it created upon these percentages for our relatively small market."

---

[16] West Virginia Insurance Commission 5 percent Market Share Report, November 2006.

Figure 12.2: Direct Combined Ratio,
Nationwide and West Virginia[17]

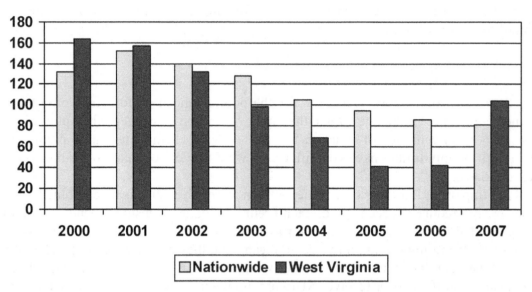

Another measure of insurance carriers' financial performance is the direct operating ratio, which further reflects dividends paid and investment gains and losses.

Figure 12.3: Direct Operating Ratio,
Nationwide and West Virginia[18]

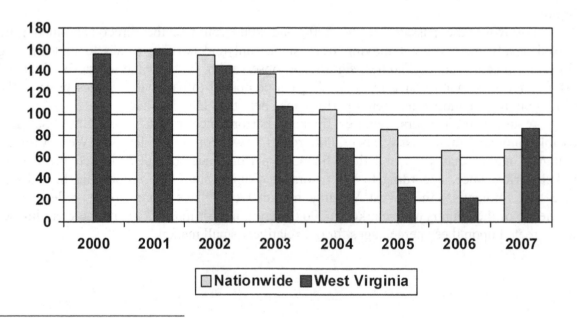

---

[17] West Virginia Insurance Commission 5 percent Market Share report, November 2008. Direct combined ratios do not take into consideration reinsurance recoveries or payments for reinsurance coverage.
[18] Ibid.

Again, the exit of two companies in 2007 skewed direct operating ratio results for that year, but overall, the chart above demonstrates that after accounting for dividends and investment gain, medical malpractice produced an operating profit in West Virginia annually from 2004 to 2007. Averaging financial performance from 2000 to 2007, the industry posted a total direct operating ratio of 98.9 percent; in West Virginia, carriers combine for a total direct operating ratio of 85.7 percent, meaning the medical liability insurance industry remains profitable overall in West Virginia and specifically more profitable than that of the countrywide average.[19]

The improved financial performance reflects the impact the 2001 and 2003 reforms have had on the state's civil justice system. The 50 percent drop in medical liability lawsuit filings in recent years, due in large part to the certificate of merit requirements, coupled with the other civil justice reform measures can be credited for a reduction in the carriers' claims expense.

PREMIUM RATE REDUCTIONS

Carriers have responded to their improved financial performance in West Virginia by reducing physician premium rates.

Figure 12.4: Annual Premium Base Rate Change in Percentage[20]

	Effective Date	Percent Requested	Percent Granted
West Virginia Mutual Insurance Co.	1/1/2009	0	0
	3/1/2008	-0.01	-0.01
	1/1/2008	0	0
82.15 percent WV market share	1/1/2007	-15	-15
	1/1/2006	-5	-5
	1/1/2005	10.2	10.2
	7/1/2004	initial filing	initial filing
Woodbrook Casualty Insurance Co.	11/1/2008	-8.3	-8.3
	11/1/2007	-10.7	-10.7
	10/20/2006	-2.8	-2.8
(formerly Medical Assurance of WV Inc.)	10/20/2005	-1.1	-1.1
	10/20/2004	18.5	14.5
7.63 percent WV market share	10/3/2003	17.3	13
	7/1/2002	23	16
	9/14/2001	30	18
	8/1/2000	35	35

[19] West Virginia Insurance Commission 5 percent Market Share report, November 2008.
[20] Ibid.

The state's largest carrier, the West Virginia Mutual Insurance Company, has more than 82 percent of the market. Just 18 months after its initial rate filing it reduced rates in January, 2006 by 5 percent. The Mutual reduced rates again the following year by another 15 percent. In addition to these base rate reductions, the carrier has instituted a number of credits available to physicians that can reduce the actual premium rate by an additional 15 to 20 percent. In total, premium rates charged by the Mutual, depending on the physician practice specialty, have dropped 25 to 45 percent in just the last few years.

The state's second largest carrier, Woodbrook Casualty Insurance Co., reported since October, 2005 four consecutive premium rate cuts totaling over 22 percent.[21] According to Insurance Commission records, Woodbrook's annual rate reductions the last few years have had the net effect of lowering medical liability insurance rates to the equivalent of what they were in 2002-2003.[22]

IMPROVED ACCESS TO CARE

A more stable liability system and lower premium rates have brought a renewed sense of optimism and improved outlook on the attractiveness of practicing medicine in West Virginia. Data from the West Virginia Board of Medicine clearly demonstrates a turnaround in the number of physicians seeking licensure to practice medicine in the state.

Figure 12.5: Annual Total of Newly Licensed Physicians by the West Virginia Board of Medicine[23]

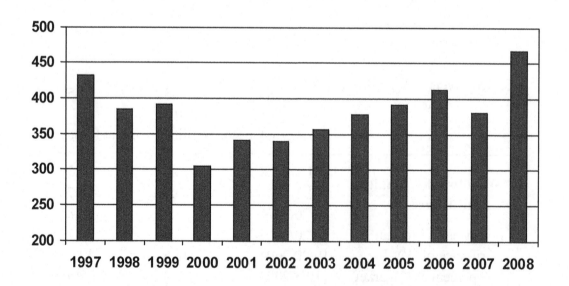

Between 1997 and 2001, West Virginia physicians experienced the full brunt of the insurance affordability and availability crisis. The West Virginia Board of Medicine reported

---

[21] West Virginia Insurance Commission 5 percent Market Share report, November 2008.
[22] Ibid.
[23] West Virginia Board of Medicine.

a significant decrease in the number of new licenses issued between 1997 and 2000 from 433 to 305, a 30 percent drop.

As mentioned earlier, much of West Virginia is designated by federal criteria as medically underserved, meaning the state can ill afford to have an environment that causes physicians to shy away from licensure. Physicians in other states recognized West Virginia's negative practice environment as well. The nation's largest physician membership organization, the American Medical Association, surveyed the medical liability environment in all 50 states and several years ago designated West Virginia as one of the few "crisis" states.

Thankfully, that perception is changing. Data show that beginning in 2001 and continuing through 2008, the trend in physicians seeking licensure in West Virginia has grown steadily. Final totals for licensure activity from the West Virginia Board of Medicine show that 2008 was the highest number of new licenses issued on record at 467.

Additional confirmation of the improved environment are many anecdotal reports from medical practice administrators and hospital-based physician recruiters who say attracting physicians into practice in West Virginia has seen significant improvement. What does this mean for the average West Virginian? Increased access to care. In 2001, almost every county had at least one recognized health care professional shortage area, according to the U.S. Department of Health and Human Services. Today, 11 West Virginia counties no longer have health care professional shortages in primary care.[24]

These objective measures demonstrate the legislative reforms in 2001 and 2003 have achieved their goals of addressing the underlying factors that jeopardized access to care in West Virginia. The number of suits filed has dropped dramatically. Insurance companies have seen a significant improvement in their financial performance and as a result cut the premiums they charge physicians for coverage by as much as 45 percent. The availability of insurance at lower rates and coupled with a more stable litigation environment has made West Virginia a more attractive place to practice medicine. Physicians are seeking licensure in the state, and that enables patients to have greater access to care.

A critical question, however, is will the positive results last? Plaintiff lawyers who fought against the passage of H.B. 601 (2001) and H.B. 2122 (2003) are working actively to have both laws undone through the judicial system. To date, their repeated efforts have succeeded in getting the West Virginia Supreme Court of Appeals to strike down several of the reforms minor provisions. No clear decisions, however, have been issued by the Court on the more substantive components of the 2001 and 2003 reforms. So the question remains on whether the Court will allow the reforms to stand or strike them down, likely putting West Virginia back in crisis and jeopardizing access to care.

JUDICIAL REVIEW OF THE MPLA

CONSTITUTIONAL ISSUES AFFECTING NONECONOMIC DAMAGE CAP

The noneconomic damage cap has generated some of the most heated arguments among the various provisions of the Medical Professional Liability Act that have come under fire in the

---

[24] U.S. Department of Health and Human Services, http://hpsafind.hrsa.gov/HPSASearch.aspx.

past two decades. Insurance and medical community representatives have said noneconomic damages are for things such as pain and suffering — damages that are impossible to calculate and therefore should be limited within reason so juries cannot use them in lieu of punitive damages. Plaintiffs' lawyers, in contrast, have said limiting jury awards goes against due process and equal protection provisions of the Constitution, because it treats patients differently than other victims of negligence.

In *Robinson v. Charleston Area Medical Center* (1991) and again in *Verba v. Ghaphery* (2000), the West Virginia Supreme Court of Appeals examined the cap on a variety of constitutional grounds: separation of powers, equal protection, due process, right to trial by jury, open court and certain remedy clauses and the special act clause.

Verba v. Ghaphery[25]

In 1996, Marjorie Verba died following complications from anti-reflux surgery performed by Dr. David Ghaphery. At trial in Ohio County Circuit Court, the jury awarded Verba's heirs $300,000 for physical pain, mental pain and loss of enjoyment of life; $21,000 for medical and funeral bills; and $2.5 million to the beneficiaries of Verba's estate under the wrongful death statute. The trial judge later reduced the total judgment to $1.02 million because of the $1 million limit on noneconomic damages imposed by the MPLA (1986).

On appeal, Verba's attorneys argued the cap was unconstitutional for many of the reasons enumerated above. But in upholding the cap, the Supreme Court said legal concerns were not the only issues to consider: "Where economic rights are concerned, we look to see whether the classification is a rational one based on social, economic, historic or geographic factors, whether it bears a reasonable relationship to a proper governmental purpose, and whether all persons within the class are treated equally. Where such classification is rational and bears the requisite reasonable relationship, the statute does not violate Section 10 of Article III of the West Virginia Constitution, which is our equal protection clause."[26] A rational basis test is the least demanding method for interpreting whether a statute is constitutional. It requires justices only to identify a nexus between the objective of a statute and the means chosen to achieve it.[27]

Addressing the separation of powers issue, the Supreme Court said the Legislature properly exercised its authority in setting the cap and, more importantly, has the authority to change the cap. The court said it cannot "sit as a superlegislature [sic] to judge the wisdom or desirability of legislative policy determinations made in areas that neither affect fundamental rights nor proceed along suspect lines."[28] The bottom line, the court said, is that the Legislature can change the common law.

The *per curiam* decision was far from unanimous, however, as former Justices Warren McGraw and Larry Starcher dissented. Justice Robin Jean Davis also dissented in part.

In her separate opinion, Davis said the "majority correctly found that the Legislature did not offend our constitution by exercising its authority to impose a one million dollar cap on noneconomic damages in medical malpractice cases. Furthermore, I adhere to the principle that it is the Legislature's 'right and public responsibility to formulate tort or liability

---

[25] *Verba v. Ghaphery* (W.Va. 2000).
[26] Ibid, syllabus point 2.
[27] Black's Law Dictionary, (6th edition, 1990).
[28] *Verba v. Ghaphery* (2000).

legislation.'" But Davis said the $1 million cap becomes invalid because in present-day dollars at the time, $1 million was worth $648,147, according to plaintiffs' arguments; therefore, Davis said it does not fulfill the legislative intent set in 1986.[29]

Justice McGraw dissented for a different reason. He said the noneconomic damage cap "denies equal protection by discriminating among tort victims in such a way as to deny recovery to the most egregiously injured."[30] McGraw said the Supreme Court should not have reviewed the noneconomic damage cap using a rational basis test, but rather via intermediate scrutiny. Using this method, courts determine whether a challenged statute is substantially related to an important state interest.[31] McGraw said an intermediate scrutiny analysis would prove the cap does not pass constitutional muster despite what the Legislature intended, because "there is no logically supportable reason why the most severely injured malpractice victims should be singled out to pay for social relief to medical tortfeasors and their insurers."[32]

In the same vein, Justice Starcher echoed McGraw's comments, stating the cap limits the ability of medical malpractice victims to collect full damages while other victims of other kinds of negligence are not limited. "Why should hospitals get more protection for their carelessness than I do as a driver or homeowner?" Starcher questioned.[33]

Whatever shaky majority the Supreme Court had in issuing its *Verba* decision, however, the justices renewed the constitutionality of the cap after granting a rehearing for the case in 2001. They decided once again to uphold the lower court's decision. This time, Davis and former Justice Elliott E. "Spike" Maynard concurred in full — no partial dissents. The majority upheld the cap based on the separation of powers doctrine and, once again applying a rational basis test, the Supreme Court said limiting noneconomic damages "bears a reasonable relationship to a proper government purpose..."[34]

With three separate majority opinions upholding legislative fiat when it comes to limiting damages that are impossible to calculate finitely, it would appear the new cap may stand up to constitutional scrutiny. The Court long has recognized that a higher standard applies when considering the constitutionality of legislation: "...(C)ourts must exercise due restraint, in recognition of the principle of the separation of powers in government... Every reasonable construction must be resorted to by the courts in order to sustain constitutionality, and any reasonable doubt must be resolved in favor of the constitutionality of the legislative enactment in question. ... In considering the constitutionality of an act of the legislature, the negation of legislative power must appear beyond reasonable doubt."[35]

Will today's Supreme Court — with only two members remaining from when the *Verba* case was decided — view the lower noneconomic damage cap in the same way? No one can predict the future, obviously, and no case has made it to the Supreme Court of Appeals that squarely takes on the constitutionality of the 2003 MPLA noneconomic damage cap. When that case finally arrives, the arguments against the cap no doubt will be asserted.

In the end, West Virginia's health care system is faring far better today than it was seven or eight years ago, as are medical liability insurance carriers in West Virginia. Without

---

[29] Ibid (Davis concurring in part, dissenting in part, filed Dec. 15, 2000).

[30] Ibid, (McGraw dissenting, filed Jan. 16, 2001).

[31] Black's Law Dictionary, 6th edition.

[32] *Verba v. Ghaphery* (McGraw dissent).

[33] *Verba v. Ghaphery* (Starcher dissenting, filed Jan. 16, 2001).

[34] *Verba v. Ghaphery.* 552 S.E.2d 406 (W.Va. 2001), syllabus point 2.

[35] Ibid.

the reforms, however, who knows what would have become of access to care by West Virginia patients.

For now, absent a new, compelling state interest to the contrary, the Supreme Court is likely to remain consistent with precedent regarding the Legislature's ability to set the noneconomic damage cap. Even with Davis' posture on how inflation erodes the value of the cap, the Supreme refrained from trying to require the Legislature to increase the $1 million cap to reflect inflationary erosion in its value from 1986 to 2000. "Just as it was within the Legislature's proper exercise of its authority in initially setting the cap, it is similarly up to the legislature to make any amendments to that legislation."[36]

It should not offend the Supreme Court's view on constitutionality if lawmakers reduce the cap to $250,000 using the same reasoning that was applied when setting the $1 million cap. The legislative findings in the 2003 incarnation of the MPLA, while similar to those stated in 1986, reflected the new reality of the current access to care crisis. Clear legislative intent remained, and lawmakers made sure to reflect some of the criticisms levied against the cap during the *Verba* case and in discussions leading up to passage of the amended MPLA in 2003. The new cap starts at $250,000 but provides for an escalation up to $500,000 depending on the severity of injury and up to 50 percent increase to account for inflation.[37]

Furthermore, to make certain doctors are insured adequately, the noneconomic damage cap disappears if the physician does not have at least $1 million in liability coverage. The Legislature made its intentions clear. They responded to the needs of physicians to improve the affordability and availability of medical liability insurance so doctors would be available to care for West Virginians. The doctors, in turn, must carry adequate insurance so injured patients will be compensated. As the Supreme Court said in *Verba*, it is up to the Legislature — not the courts — to determine whether its legislation meets the desired goal.

TREATMENT OF THE 2001 AND 2003 MPLA PROVISIONS

Several cases have made their way to the Supreme Court that involve the 2001 reforms, but few, if any, have dealt substantively with the changes made in 2003. What's more, the high court has refrained from making a constitutional analysis of many of the substantive changes made to the MPLA.

The 2001 changes to the MPLA required, among other things, that plaintiffs send a pre-suit notification to the defendant with a screening certificate of merit at least 30 days before a medical negligence lawsuit can be filed.[38] The 2001 reforms also imposed a 12-member jury requirement in which a nine-member majority constituted a verdict.[39] Those three requirements have not survived legal challenges well, although only one has been stricken on constitutional grounds.

---

[36] *Verba v. Ghaphery* (2000).
[37] 55-7B-8 (2003).
[38] W.Va. Code 55-7B-6 (2001).
[39] W.Va. Code 55-7B-6d (2001).

Boggs v. Camden-Clark

In 2004, the Supreme Court reversed a lower court dismissal of a malpractice lawsuit in *Boggs v. Camden-Clark*.[40] Hilda Boggs slipped and broke her ankle while at work in 2001. Her injury required surgery, and during anesthesia, she stopped breathing and went into cardiac arrest. She later died. Her husband filed a lawsuit that accused Camden-Clark and others of failing to adhere to the standard of care plus other non-medical allegations including an alleged cover-up and spoliation of evidence.

The first time Boggs filed suit, the summons and complaint were not served within 120 days of filing, so the court dismissed the case. The second time he filed suit, the court again dismissed the complaint, finding that Boggs failed to comply with the 30-day notice period before filing the lawsuit in accordance with the 2001 MPLA. That action forced Boggs to file his lawsuit a third time, and by this point, enough time had elapsed that the lawsuit would fall under the 2003 MPLA, which had the lower noneconomic damage cap. In the second dismissal, the lower court rejected all of Boggs' claims, even those that were not medical malpractice, and denied his motion for leave to amend his original complaint under Rule 15 of the West Virginia Rules of Civil Procedure.[41]

On appeal, the Supreme Court said it did not find it necessary to question the MPLA's constitutionality. Its standard of review, therefore, was abuse of discretion. Under this standard, an action generally is presumed to be valid and is affirmed if it is founded on a rational basis and has no clear error that indicates the decision was arbitrary, capricious or constitutes an abuse of discretion.[42]

The Court identified clear error in *Boggs*. "Though we reject the appellant's request that we consider the constitutionality of the entire MPLA scheme, we agree with his contention that the lower court was wrong to deny him leave to amend his complaint."[43] The Court said Rule 15 states a party can amend his complaint by leave of the court or by written consent of the opposing party, and "leave shall be freely given when justice so requires."[44] Even though Boggs' notice of intent to sue was sent 27 days — not 30 days — before he filed suit, the majority said the courts cannot allow a procedural device such as the pre-suit notification requirement to prevent a case from being decided on its merits. In *Boggs*, the actual medical negligence claims had yet to be litigated, and the lower court's refusal to allow the plaintiff to amend his complaint was an error, the Supreme Court said. The Court ordered the lower court to reinstate Boggs' non-medical claims and allow him to amend his complaint and proceed with the case under the 2001 MPLA, not the 2003 version of the act.

In a dissenting opinion, however, Justice Maynard said the majority had gone against the plain reading of the 2001 MPLA. Boggs' notice was served 27 days before he filed suit, not the statutorily required 30 days. Just six days before the *Boggs* decision was rendered, the Supreme Court had ruled in *Miller v. Stone* (2004) upholding a circuit court ruling that said a complaint could not be filed until 30 days after the filing of the certificate of merit.[45] Maynard said the 2001 MPLA is clear, and the Supreme Court should have upheld the dismissal of

---

[40] *Bernard Boggs, as administrator of the estate of Hilda Boggs v. Camden-Clark Memorial Hospital*. 609 S.E.2d 917 (W.Va. 2004).

[41] Ibid.

[42] Black's Law Dictionary, 6th edition.

[43] *Boggs v. Camden-Clark* (2004).

[44] West Virginia Rules of Civil Procedure, Rule 15.

[45] *State ex rel. Miller v. Stone*, 216 W. Va. 379, 607 S.E.2d 485 (2004).

Boggs' claim. Forcing him to re-file his case and have it adjudicated under the 2003 MPLA would not have been any injustice to his claims.[46] Interested parties such as the West Virginia State Medical Association said even though the plaintiff prevailed on appeal, the fact that the Supreme Court did not strike down the MPLA or even entertain a constitutional analysis was a positive step in changing West Virginia's medical liability landscape.

Louk v. Cormier

The 2001 MPLA did not fare so well in 2005, however, when the Supreme Court ruled in *Louk v. Cormier* that the 12-member jury provision was "enacted in violation of the Separation of Powers Clause, Article V, §1 of the West Virginia Constitution, insofar as the statute addresses procedural litigation matters that are regulated exclusively by this Court pursuant to the Rule-Making Clause, Article VIII, §3 of the West Virginia Constitution. Consequently, W.Va. Code §55-7B-6d, in its entirety, is unconstitutional and unenforceable."[47]

Rita Louk sued her surgeon, Dr. Serge Cormier, after a 2000 hysterectomy that resulted in perforation of Louk's cecum, which caused her assorted health problems and required an additional exploratory surgery. Louk filed a medical malpractice lawsuit against Cormier in 2002. At trial before a 12-person jury, 10 of the 12 jurors returned a verdict in favor of Cormier. Under the 2001 MPLA, only nine jurors were needed to constitute a majority. Louk then filed a post-trial motion seeking a new trial, arguing the non-unanimous verdict instruction authorized by a provision in the 2001 MPLA was unconstitutional. The circuit court denied her petition, and Louk appealed to the Supreme Court.

In a 4-1 verdict, the Supreme Court addressed Louk's separation of powers and rule-making argument.[48] The Court historically has invalidated statutes that conflicted with rules promulgated by the Supreme Court, and *Louk v. Cormier* was no different. The high court agreed with Louk that the 2001 MPLA's non-unanimous verdict provision conflicts with Rule 48 of the West Virginia Rules of Civil Procedure, which "provides only one method by which a jury may return a non-unanimous verdict, i.e., through a stipulation by the parties. … The non-unanimous verdict provision … has stripped litigants of a right granted to them by this Court under our constitutional authority. The Legislature cannot remove that which was not in its power to give."[49] The Supreme Court reversed the lower court and ordered a new trial, renewing the previous rule that medical malpractice cases were to be decided by a unanimous six-member jury.

Justice Maynard's dissent illustrated his displeasure with the majority: "By ruling that this Court, simply by its own judge-made rules, can strike down a statute passed by the entire legislature is sobering indeed!"[50] He said the majority not only had invalidated important MPLA provisions, but it also showed how the Supreme Court has the power to invalidate any part of the MPLA simply by saying the statute conflicts with an existing court rule.

---

[46] *Boggs v. Camden-Clark* (2004) (Maynard dissenting, filed Dec. 8, 2004).

[47] *Louk v. Cormier*. 622 S.E.2d 788 (W.Va. 2005), syllabus point 3.

[48] The Rule-Making Clause of Article VIII, section 3, provides, in relevant part, that the Supreme Court "shall have power to promulgate rules for all cases and proceedings, civil and criminal, for all of the courts of the state relating to writs, warrants, process practice and procedure, which shall have the force and effect of law."

[49] *Louk v. Cormier* (2005).

[50] Ibid, (Maynard dissenting, filed July 11, 2005).

Hinchman v. Gillette

Regardless of Maynard's disagreement with the majority, the trend of chipping away at the 2001 MPLA continued in 2005 when the Supreme Court ruled in *Hinchman v. Gillette* that failing to follow strictly the pre-suit filing requirements cannot prevent a person from bringing a claim. Paul Hinchman died in 2003 after sedation for a biopsy surgery, and his wife sued the nurse, doctors and hospital for wrongful death due to medical negligence. The circuit court dismissed Hinchman's claims on the grounds the pre-suit notice of claim and certificate of merit were legally defective and deficient.

In reversing the lower court, however, the Supreme Court ruled "the purposes of requiring a pre-suit notice of claim and screening certificate of merit are (1) to prevent the making and filing of frivolous medical malpractice claims and lawsuits; and (2) to promote the pre-suit resolution of non-frivolous medical malpractice claims. The requirement of a pre-suit notice of claim and screening certificate of merit is not intended to restrict or deny citizens' access to the courts."[51]

Although the Court declined the chance to take up the constitutionality of the pre-suit requirements, the majority found certain details of Hinchman's claims that gave the justices reason to find fault with a strict application of the 2001 MPLA pre-suit requirements. The defendants had the opportunity to make known what the problems with Hinchman's notice and certificate of merit were, rather than waiting to move for a dismissal of the lawsuit. "...[A] principal consideration before a court reviewing a claim of insufficiency of notice or certificate should be whether a party challenging or defending the sufficiency of a notice and certificate has demonstrated a good faith and reasonable effort to further the statutory purposes."[52]

Those statutory purposes are enumerated in the MPLA as providing a chance for the opposing parties to mediate and possibly resolve their dispute before a lawsuit is filed. Since none of the defendants made the notice and certificate defects known in a timely manner, the Supreme Court said their silence constituted a waiver of that chance to mediate, and it also prevented the plaintiff from correcting the mistakes. "Whatever technical insufficiencies the appellant's notice and certificate in the instant case arguably have had, it strains common sense to assert that the notice and certificate support any contention that the appellant's claims were frivolous."[53]

While the majority opinion did not make a constitutional argument against those provisions of the 2001 MPLA, Justice Davis' detailed concurrence made it clear where she stands on the issue. She concurred in the result, but she said the majority opinion should have reversed the case on different grounds. Davis said she believes the certificate of merit requirement violates the separation of powers/rule-making clauses and the certain remedy clauses of the West Virginia Constitution.[54]

Davis used the court's findings in *Louk* to explain the conflict between the MPLA and Rule 48 (non-unanimous jury instruction). She said a constitutionally delegated power vested in one branch of government, in this case the judiciary, cannot be infringed upon by another, the legislature. "Promulgation of rules governing litigation in the courts of this state rests

---

[51] *Hinchman v. Gillette.* 618 S.E.2d 387 (W.Va. 2005), syllabus point 2.
[52] Ibid, syllabus point 6.
[53] Ibid, footnote 6.
[54] Ibid, (Davis concurring, filed July 8, 2005).

exclusively with this Court."[55] She said the certificate of merit is a procedural law, and only the Supreme Court has the authority to set litigation procedures.

Maynard voiced his disagreement once again, this time sounding a warning bell to the medical community in the first sentence of his dissent in *Hinchman v. Gillette*: "The majority opinion may result in the complete gutting of a portion of the 2001 medical malpractice reforms."[56] Maynard said the MPLA is clear, and if a plaintiff fails to provide a certificate of merit in the manner prescribed by statute, the circuit court is correct to dismiss the case immediately. "The majority's reversal and remand indicates to me that the statute requiring pre-certificates of merit may be rendered essentially meaningless," Maynard said, adding that plaintiffs will have no motivation to be thorough with their certificates now, and the goals for requiring them may not be met.

In contrast to Davis, Maynard said he believes those requirements of the 2001 MPLA are constitutional and do not infringe on the Supreme Court's rulemaking power or the separation of powers doctrine. "Our Rules of Civil Procedure 'govern the procedure in all trial courts of record in all actions, suits, or other judicial proceedings of a civil nature.' According to Rule of Civil Procedure 3(a), '(a) civil action is commenced by filing a complaint with the court.'" Thus, Maynard said, the Supreme Court rules do not govern a pre-filing certificate of merit because the certificate is filed before the lawsuit actually is filed. "Hence (it) is a legitimate addition to the substantive law of this State."[57]

THE MPLA LANDSCAPE IN 2005 AND BEYOND

Since 2005, the Supreme Court has had the opportunity to underscore its position on pre-suit notification, certificate of merit and 12-member jury requirements from the 2001 MPLA.

In November 2005, the Supreme Court affirmed its holdings from the *Boggs* and *Hinchman* decisions in *Gray v. Mena*.[58] In March 2006, the court again affirmed *Hinchman* in *Roy v. D'Amato*, and made similar findings in *Elmore v. Triad Hospitals* and *Davis v. Mound View*.[59,60]

In June 2006 the court affirmed its findings in *Louk* in *Richmond v. Levin*.[61,62] In the *Richmond* case, in fact, the Supreme Court not only reaffirmed that the 12-member jury requirement and non-unanimous verdict were unconstitutional, it allowed that opinion to apply retroactively to any medical malpractice case that was pending when the *Louk* opinion was released and that later resulted in a non-unanimous verdict. Any case that meets that description now may be retried.

When deciding how far the MPLA reaches, the Supreme Court has defined who or what falls under the protections. In *Phillips v. Larry's Pharmacy* (2007), the Court ruled that pharmacies are not health care providers under the definition in the MPLA. In doing so, the

---

[55] Ibid.
[56] Ibid, (Maynard concurring in part and dissenting in part, filed July 11, 2005).
[57] Ibid.
[58] *Gray v. Mena*. 625 S.E.2d 326 (W.Va. 2006).
[59] *Elmore v. Triad Hospitals*. 640 S.E.2d 217 (W.Va. 2006).
[60] *Davis. v. Mound View Health Care Inc*. 640 S.E.2d 91 (W.Va. 2006).
[61] *Roy v. D'Amato*. 629 S.E.2d 751 (W.Va. 2006).
[62] *Richmond v. Levin*. 637 S.E.2d 610 (W.Va. 2006).

Court neutered the language "including, but not limited to" in the definition of health care provider and said only entities specifically listed are covered.[63]

The *Boggs* and *Gray* decisions about the pre-suit filing requirements were clarified further in 2007 in *Blankenship v. Ethicon*.[64] In this opinion, the Court said the MPLA applies to any tort or breach of contract claim based on health care services rendered, even if those claims are not initially filed under the MPLA. Intentional acts, however, are not covered by the Act. Even more recently, the *per curiam* opinion in *Westmoreland v. Vaidya* underscored the Court's posture in *Hinchman*, *Gray* and *Blankenship* regarding pre-suit filing requirements, making it clear that a required notification and certificate of merit cannot prevent a plaintiff from bringing a medical malpractice claim.[65]

CONCLUSION

West Virginia's health care delivery system always will be challenged by the state's economic condition, its topography and a host of other factors that are difficult for policymakers to address. But when the system was pushed to the breaking point several years ago because physicians could not find or afford medical liability insurance coverage, lawmakers were able to take action, and the results thus far show success.

The medical community sees improvement in how insurance carriers are performing, claims statistics, the rate of physician licensure in the state and insurance rate filings. As a result, access to health care professionals has improved in West Virginia, but all of this progress could vanish if the Supreme Court strikes down major provisions of the Medical Professional Liability Act.

The Supreme Court already has stricken one of the 2001 MPLA provisions as unconstitutional — the 12-member jury with a non-unanimous verdict. The court also has weakened substantially the pre-suit notification and screening certificate of merit requirements, favoring the plaintiff's right to bring a cause of action over the legislative intent of whittling down frivolous lawsuits.

The $250,000 noneconomic damage cap has not yet been decided in the high court, and while case law indicates the cap may have a fair chance at passing constitutional muster, the future does not look so bright for some of the other procedural requirements of the MPLA. In several cases now, the Supreme Court has said procedural details cannot take precedent over a person's right to seek a remedy in court. Whether that trend carries over into what Justice Maynard cautioned against — a gutting of the MPLA — remains to be seen. The medical liability environment is improving, but ultimately, the West Virginia Supreme Court of Appeals will write the final chapter in this ever-evolving saga.

---

[63] *Phillips v. Larry's Drive-In Pharmacy Inc.* 647 S.E.2d 920(W.Va. 2007).
[64] *Blankenship v. Ethicon*, 656 S.E.2d 451 (W.Va., 2007).
[65] *Westmoreland v. Vaidya*, 664 S.E.2d 90 (W.Va. 2008).

REFERENCES

Black's Law Dictionary, (6th edition, 1990).

Budetti, Peter P. and Teresa Waters. "Medical Malpractice Law in the States." Henry J. Kaiser Family Foundation, May 2005.

Posten, Hale J. "The Law of Medical Malpractice in West Virginia." 41 W.Va. L.Q. 35 (1935), as quoted in "Simplifying the Law in Medical Malpractice: The Use of Practice Guidelines as the Standard of Care in Medical Malpractice Litigation," by Sam McConkey IV, W.Va. L. Rev. 491 (Winter 1995).

Terry, Juliet A. "Health Care Goes to Court." *Wheeling News-Register*, May 14, 2000.

U.S. Department of Health and Human Services, http://hpsafind.hrsa.gov/HPSASearch.aspx.

West Virginia Department of Health and Human Resources. "Burden of Cardiovascular Disease in West Virginia." July 2001.

West Virginia Insurance Commission 5 percent Market Share Report, November 2004.

West Virginia Insurance Commission 5 percent Market Share Report, November 2006.

West Virginia Insurance Commission 5 percent Market Share Report, November 2008.

West Virginia Board of Medicine.

West Virginia Constitution, online at www.legis.state.wv.us/WVCODE/WV_CON.cfm

West Virginia Rules of Civil Procedure, online at www.state.wv.us/wvsca/rules/contents.htm

W.Va. Code, 55-7B.

CASES CITED

Bernard Boggs, as administrator of the estate of Hilda Boggs v. Camden-Clark Memorial Hospital. 609 S.E.2d 917 (W.Va. 2004).

Blankenship v. Ethicon, 656 S.E.2d 451 (W.Va., 2007).

Davis. v. Mound View Health Care Inc. 640 S.E.2d 91 (W.Va. 2006).

Elmore v. Triad_Hospitals. 640 S.E.2d 217 (W.Va. 2006).

Estate of Marjorie Verba v. Ghaphery, M.D. 543 S.E.2d 347 (W.Va. 2000).

Gray v. Mena. 625 S.E.2d 326 (W.Va. 2006).

Hinchman v. Gillette. 618 S.E.2d 387 (W.Va. 2005).

Louk v. Cormier. 622 S.E.2d 788 (W.Va. 2005).

Phillips v. Larry's Drive-In Pharmacy Inc. 647 S.E.2d 920(W.Va. 2007).

Richmond v. Levin. 637 S.E.2d 610 (W.Va. 2006).

Roy v. D'Amato. 629 S.E.2d 751 (W.Va. 2006).

Robinson v. Charleston Area Medical Center Inc. 186 W.Va. 720, 414 S.E.2d 877 (W.Va.1991).

State ex rel. Miller v. Stone, 216 W. Va. 379, 607 S.E.2d 485 (2004).

Verba v. Ghaphery. 552 S.E.2d 406 (W.Va. 2001).

Westmoreland v. Vaidya, 664 S.E.2d 90 (W.Va. 2008).

ABOUT THE AUTHORS

EDITOR:

Russell S. Sobel, Ph.D., is Professor of Economics and holder of the James Clark Coffman Distinguished Chair in Entrepreneurial Studies at West Virginia University. He has published over 150 books and articles, including a collegiate Principles of Economics textbook. Dr. Sobel served as the founding Director of the WVU Entrepreneurship Center from 2002-2006. His research has been featured in the *New York Times, Wall Street Journal, Washington Post, US News and World Report*, and *The Economist Magazine*, as well as appearances on CNBC, Fox News, CSPAN, and the CBS Evening News. He has received numerous awards for both his teaching and research. He serves as Senior Economist and Director of the Center for Economic Growth for the Public Policy Foundation of West Virginia. He received his Ph.D. in Economics from Florida State University in 1994. His edited book on West Virginia economic policy reform, *Unleashing Capitalism: Why Prosperity Stops at the West Virginia Border and How to Fix It*, has sold over 5,000 copies and was named winner of the 2008 Sir Anthony Fisher Award.

ASSOCIATE EDITOR:

Joshua C. Hall, Ph.D., is an Assistant Professor of Economics & Management at Beloit College in Beloit, Wisconsin. Formerly an economist for the Joint Economic Committee of the U.S. Congress, he authored or co-authored nearly two dozen refereed journal articles and numerous public policy studies for state and local organizations.

OTHER CONTRIBUTING AUTHORS:

Chris W. Bonneau, Ph.D., is an Associate Professor of Political Science at the University of Pittsburgh. He has authored or co-authored numerous articles and two books on judicial elections as well judicial behavior. His most recent book, *In Defense of Judicial Elections*, was published in Spring 2009.

Matthew R. Bowles, J.D., earned his Bachelor of Arts, magna cum laude, from Bowling Green State University and his Doctor of Jurisprudence with High Honors from the University of Tennessee. He is an associate in the Charleston, West Virginia, law firm of Lewis Glasser Casey & Rollins PLLC where he practices commercial, corporate and real property law with an emphasis in acquisitions, non-profit and tax exempt entities, health care business planning and compliance, and real property finance and development.

The Honorable Wanda G. Bryant, J.D., is an associate judge on the North Carolina Court of Appeals. A first generation college graduate, Judge Bryant received a Bachelor of Arts degree at Duke University in 1977. As an Angier B. Duke scholar, she was chosen to study for a summer at Oxford University, England. She received her Juris Doctor at North Carolina Central University in Durham. Judge Bryant made history when she was appointed the first female and first African-American prosecutor of the thirteenth prosecutorial district of North Carolina in 1983. From 1987 until 1988 she served as the first staff attorney for the Police Executive Research Forum and in 1989 she became an Assistant United States Attorney in the Office for the District of Columbia. Bryant then served as a Senior Deputy Attorney General in the Office of the North Carolina Attorney General from 1993 to 2001. She was appointed by Governor Mike Easley to the North Carolina Court of Appeals in 2001.

Ronda L. Harvey, J.D., is a partner in the Charleston office and a member of the Litigation Practice Group for Bowles, Rice, McDavid, Graff & Love LLP. Her practice primarily involves representing manufacturers, utility companies, and retailers in deliberate intent actions. Her most recent achievements include defending a West Virginia manufacturing employer in a deliberate intent trial and winning a complete defense verdict. Ronda has also represented defendants in mass tort, complex products liability civil actions, and insurance bad faith and coverage cases. She is a 1993 graduate of the West Virginia University College of Law.

Evan H. Jenkins, J.D., is a member of the West Virginia State Senate with twelve years of total legislative service in both the State Senate and House of Delegates. He received a Bachelor of Science degree in Business Administration at the University of Florida and his Juris Doctor at the Cumberland School of Law. He was a practicing attorney with the law firm Jenkins Fenstermaker, PLLC, in Huntington, West Virginia and served as General Counsel to the West Virginia State Chamber of Commerce. Currently, he is Executive Director of the West Virginia State Medical Association. Under his leadership, the organization received the 2003 Legal Reform Grassroots Organization of the Year Award from the U.S. Chamber of Commerce Institute for Legal Reform for its work on enacting comprehensive medical liability reform and he received the Medical Executive Meritorious Achievement Award from the American Medical Association, in recognition of his outstanding medical society executive leadership and accomplishments.

Kristen M. Leddy, J.D., is a graduate of the West Virginia University College of Law and has clerked for the Honorable John S. Kennedy of the York County Court of Common Pleas, York, Pennsylvania.

Edward J. López, Ph.D., is Associate Professor of Law and Economics at San Jose State University. He has written extensively in the areas of applied political economy and the law. He is editor of the forthcoming book, *Law without Romance: Public Choice and the Legal System*.

Aman McLeod, Ph.D., J.D., is an Assistant Professor of Political Science at the Rutgers University in Camden, New Jersey. He has authored or co-authored several articles and a book chapter on judicial elections as well judicial behavior. His most recent article, "Bidding for Justice: A New Look at the Effect of Campaign Contributions on Judicial Decision-Making," recently appeared in the University of Detroit *Mercy Law Review*.

The Honorable Sandra Day O'Connor, LL.B., is a retired Associate Justice of the U.S. Supreme Court. She received her B.A. and LL.B. from Stanford University. She served as Deputy County Attorney of San Mateo County, California from 1952–1953 and as a civilian attorney for Quartermaster Market Center, Frankfurt, Germany from 1954–1957. From 1958–1960, she practiced law in Maryvale, Arizona, and served as

Assistant Attorney General of Arizona from 1965–1969. She was appointed to the Arizona State Senate in 1969 and was subsequently reelected to two two-year terms. In 1975 she was elected Judge of the Maricopa County Superior Court and served until 1979, when she was appointed to the Arizona Court of Appeals. President Reagan nominated her as an Associate Justice of the Supreme Court, and she took her seat September 25, 1981. Justice O'Connor retired from the Supreme Court on January 31, 2006.

Mark A. Sadd, J.D., received his Bachelor of Arts in 1986 from the University of Virginia and his Doctor of Jurisprudence in 1992 from West Virginia University. He is a member of the Charleston, West Virginia, law firm of Lewis Glasser Casey & Rollins PLLC, where he concentrates his transaction, litigation and appellate practice on real property development, landlord-tenant relationships, title, land use, eminent domain and related areas of the law. He is listed in *Best Lawyers in America*. A former Charleston city councilman and chairman of the Charleston Human Rights Commission, he recently began a second four-year term on the Advisory Council on Historic Preservation by presidential appointment.

Alexander Tabarrok, Ph.D., is an Associate Professor of Economics at George Mason University and Research Director for the Independent Institute. His papers have appeared in the *Journal of Law and Economics*, *Public Choice*, *Economic Inquiry*, *Journal of Health Economics*, *Journal of Theoretical Politics*, *The American Law and Economics Review*, *Kyklos* and many other journals. Dr. Tabarrok is co-author (with Eric Helland) of *Judge and Jury: American Tort Law on Trial* and the editor of many books including *Entrepreneurial Economics: Bright Ideas from the Dismal Science*.

Juliet A. Terry, M.L.S., earned a Bachelor of Arts in 1998 from Allegheny College and a Master of Legal Studies from West Virginia University in 2007. She was a longtime investigative journalist in West Virginia, covering government and legal affairs topics such as workers' compensation, health care, judicial ethics, politics, civil litigation, tax reform and civil justice reform, particularly involving medical liability. She has earned top honors from state and national journalism organizations for investigative journalism, legal and government reporting, business and labor coverage, enterprise reporting and feature writing.

Matthew T. Yanni holds a Master's Degree in Economics and is in his second year of law school at West Virginia University. He is a student fellow of the American Institute for Economic Research.

424689LV00002B/78/P

LVOW03s1048280115

Printed in the USA
CPSIA information can be obtained at www.ICGtesting.com

9 780578 014500